GIRL IN A FREUDIAN SLIP
A Memoir

Frances Oliver
(Monika Sterba Schneider)

Copyright © 2005 by Frances Oliver

First published in 2005 by Perron Press
Reprinted February 2006

The right of Frances Oliver to be identified as the Author of the Work has been asserted by her in accordance with the Copyright, Designs and Patents Act 1988.

All rights reserved. No part of this publication may be reproduced, stored in a retrieval system, or transmitted in any form or by any means, electronic, mechanical, photocopying, recording or otherwise without the prior permission of the publisher, nor be otherwise circulated in any form of binding or cover other that that in which it is published and without a similar condition being imposed on the subsequent purchaser.

ISBN: 0-9550694-0-8

Printed and bound in Great Britain by
Headland Printers,
Bread Street, Penzance, Cornwall TR18 2EQ

Perron Press
19 Belle Vue
Newlyn, Penzance
TR18 5ED

To the memory of Richard and Ditha
and most of all, Enne

and as always, Dux

(In a few cases, discretion has prompted the use of false names or initials for persons or institutions appearing in this memoir)

Frances Oliver is the pen name of Monika Sterba Schneider, who was born in Vienna and grew up in the USA. Soon after graduation from college, she married and returned to Europe and since then has lived, worked, travelled and climbed mountains in a number of countries, including Switzerland, the UK, Austria and Turkey. After her husband's death she and her daughter moved to Cornwall where they live now. Frances Oliver has published five novels and a collection of short stories, and when not writing devotes most of her time to environmental campaigning for Friends of the Earth.

Also by Frances Oliver:

ALL SOULS
THE TOURIST SEASON
XARGOS
CHILDREN OF EPIPHANY
THE PEACOCK'S EYE
DANCING ON AIR

CHILDREN OF EPIPHANY
in paperback and
DANCING ON AIR (Collected Stories)
now available from Ash-Tree Press, B.C.
(www.ash-tree.bc.ca/ashtreecurrent.html)

CONTENTS

Introduction	1
Introduction II - My Parents	4
In Vienna, I Dare to Walk on the Grass	15
My Mother Packs at Midnight	23
Waiting for Visas: Aunts, Heroes and Fear	28
In Grosse Pointe, I Retreat to Ancient Greece	33
Bathrooms, Case Histories and Sex	49
The Gomper Solution: My Mother Founds a School	54
Dancing With a Patient and Other Tribulations	88
Happiness at Camp Ends With Another Flight in the Night	105
Enne	113
My Mother Goes Horse Crazy and I Acquire a Savage Beast	120
Green Mansions in Vermont	137
My Foray into Society	142
Pin-less and Letter-less in Grosse Pointe	149
Summers in Paradise	166
Rumbas and Revelations	193

GIRL IN A FREUDIAN SLIP
Introduction

On one of the last visits to my mother, I did what I should have done years before. I quizzed her about her childhood. My mother was from the petty aristocracy of Central Europe, the daughter and grand-daughter of generals in the Austrian army. She was middle-aged when I was born; she grew up before the telephone and the motor car, before the end of the last world we will ever call The Old, before the First World War. My mother's childhood was my last chance for a glimpse of a vanished age.

It was too late. My mother could only tell, over and over, with much helpless laughter, the same story. The story of a man stepping off a pier onto a sailboat, and missing the boat.

This has inspired me to record my own early memories. Before it is too late again. Before all I can tell you (with much helpless laughter) is the story of a man I saw fall on ice when I was gazing through the window of a midnight train. A lone man on a deserted street. He skidded and landed, Charlie Chaplin fashion, on his back with feet in the air. No one else saw it. The other passengers, hearing my hysterics, must have thought me mad. I did hope he was not hurt; but it remains an irresistibly hilarious memory.

I could also take my mother's story as symbolic. Not of her childhood but of mine. I grew up with two cultures and two continents. My home represented one, my new country the other, and trying to step across I usually landed, with a humiliating splash, somewhere in between.

The past becomes more spatial than temporal. Memory is a selection of pictures which hardly ever appear in chronological order. Being a child of pioneer Freudians, I find it logical as well as natural to write down memories as they occur, and then to regroup them, roughly, according to time. So this is a memoir of relatively free associations.

Which brings to mind the analyst.

An analysis can begin with the good doctor leaning forward (signalling attentiveness) or back (fatigue, resignation) - you do not see her/him, of course, as he/she is seated behind the couch, you may just notice the creak of the chair - and saying: "Just tell me anything that comes into your head."

Hearing this, you might freeze. You might say: "I can't think of a thing." You might fight desperately against a wave of obscenities from the inner demon, the one who can form compulsive chains of the unspeakable, driving everything else out of the hapless mind.

If you are unlucky and the pause is too long, you might be put off by hearing the click of knitting needles, the scratch of a doodling pen, or - horrors - the turning page of a magazine. My mother was once - just once - seen with a magazine, through a screen door. The patient didn't notice. Generally my mother knitted. She also made a large rug, and later, when more arthritic, she did petit point.

You are not supposed to turn around and look.

If this is beginning to sound like a book to feed detractors of Freud, it is not. My parents were, by most accounts, very good therapists. Moreover, they were not cruel, abusive, alcoholic, addictive, perverse, etc. They were, as parents go, pretty decent parents, plus or minus Freud, and there were no kinky clothes in the closets or strange powders on the bathroom shelves. Though like most rich Americans they did, near the end of their lives, pop an awful lot of pills. My father especially, who had an MD and could still prescribe himself things when he was nearly blind, kept enough to stock a pharmacy. But that was much later.

So anyone looking for revelations of how my parents' theories ruined my life might as well abstain. That I was/am still somewhat neurotic is partly genetic, partly the fault of history, only partly theirs. I might have been much more neurotic brought up by almost anyone else. Still, Freudian children do tend to become patients, or therapists, or both. I became a patient, and learned to live with my diminished neurosis after two years of analysis in early adulthood. My analyst was the famous Wilhelm Reich's ex-wife and she was actually a good sensible egg. (Unlike my mother she did not knit. She only did her mending.) I don't know if the analysis was really necessary. I believe it did some good, and I know it certainly did much more good than harm. I also know that, though we had our ups and downs over the years, in the early stages of my life and the late of theirs, I loved my parents and they loved me, and this is what counts.

I say loved. I don't know if this is quite the right word for how I felt about my mother. This may have been the price she paid for leaving my day-to-day care to another person. Although in her case that was probably positive. A series of nannies or day care centres might have been disastrous for a hyper-sensitive child like me, but I had a wonderful nurse who stayed from my babyhood to my adulthood, and my mother was much too overwhelming and energetic to be a mother full time, or even half.

My mother did not inspire what we conventionally call love. Unlike my witty, vivacious father, who inspired more unjudging love, especially from women, than I have ever seen lavished on anyone else. My mother was eccentric, illogical, charmless and at once over-bearing and deeply reserved. In America, she tried to disguise her inbred old-world haughtiness with a manner acceptable to her acquaintances but transparent and embarrassing to her children. She had great strength, and what she inspired was admiration, loyalty, and respect, combined paradoxically with a kind of affectionate ridicule. My mother did not belong to the twentieth century, though she did very well in it. I have never known anyone like her. I do not think there will be anyone much like her again.

My posthumous quarrel with my parents is not personal but ecological. They were rich and extravagant and wasteful. They were part of the careless top percent of humanity that has burned up the world. And still does.

My father, a very intelligent man, was perfectly aware of this. He saw no future for humanity at all. This was not only because, as a good Orthodox Freudian, he shared the pessimism of his God. He would count the number of electrical motors humming in his Grosse Pointe house, from clocks to air-conditioner - I think it came to sixty - and marvel at the waste. But it wasn't his problem. By then he was in his eighties: his motto was a cheerful, *"Aprés-moi le deluge."*

My mother, never very politically conscious, except that she was anti-Nazi and at least nominally anti-racist, was more concerned about keeping her 'top dollars' out of the clutches of the Internal Revenue than about saving the ecosystem. Except for her own patch of wilderness in Vermont. Any incursion by man or machine made her shake with rage. "Do you know that you are walking on my property?" was her greeting to the guileless trespasser in her unfenced, unposted domain.

To condemn my parents for this is only to condemn them with nearly all of their generation. And of mine. They had the humanistic but blindly anthropocentric morality of their age. Respect for the planet was not a part of it. They were born into a world that despite Malthusian warnings must still have seemed almost limitless in its riches and space. We have lost that excuse. But if I begin on that I will not write a memoir. To write a memoir you have to believe in posterity.

Introduction II
My Parents

    Memory, passed on from generation to generation, becomes sadly distorted and distilled. So that, in a hundred years, my mother's account of the man missing the boat and falling into the Traunsee may be all that is left of a once rich store. Or - another example - my great-aunts' tale of standing in the rain for fourteen hours at Kaiser Franz Joseph's funeral. It may be that the stories repeated most often - the stories of senility - are the ones that survive.

    With time, might these stories telescope and combine? So that, if humanity survives long enough, our family legend will be of seeing an Emperor drown as he tried to step into a boat after fourteen hours of rain?

    And if I myself survive to senility, having had no warning in time to reach for my pills, brandy and plastic bag, I might repeat over and over the story of the falling man I saw from the midnight train. So the story could become: An Emperor slipped on a dock at midnight, getting into a boat at the time of the Great Flood. And so perhaps a kingdom was lost.

    This may be how not only family legends, but folk myths, come to be born.

    Before there is further digression, I will formally introduce my parents. Rather, I will let my father - Richard Sterba - do it himself. The excerpt that follows is from his own book, *Reminiscences of a Viennese Psychoanalyst* (Wayne University Press, Detroit 1982), written because he was, as the blurb has it, "the last witness to some events of the Vienna Psychoanalytic Society ... and a member of the first class to receive psychoanalytic training at the Vienna Psychoanalytic Institute." The purpose of his memoir, a more exalted purpose than mine, was "to make it possible for the reader to participate in the atmosphere, the spirit and the ardent excitement that the direct or indirect contact with Freud stirred in our group."

    My father was a keen lion-hunter; but, it must be said, lions of quality. Though not generally self-effacing, he was humble and worshipful when speaking of his lions. While in their presence, thank heaven, he was less so, exercising the impish wit that was so much part of his charm. Freud, though not yet that when Daddy discovered him, was of course the ultimate lion, the one who apotheosized, sort of, into God.

I am not sneering. I do not deny that Freud was a great thinker and a great man, greater than most people now give him credit for being. Only I see the limitations as well as the greatness; I am of a time and persuasion in which the capacity for such worship no longer exists.

So here is my father, unchanged if somewhat abridged:

CHILDHOOD AND EDUCATION

"My birthplace is Vienna, the former capital of the multinational Austro-Hungarian monarchy. It was also the residence of the Habsburg emperors. In the year of my birth, 1898, Kaiser Franz Josef had ruled the Habsburg empire for fifty years.

The Austro-Hungarian empire was at that time a constitutional monarchy. The form of government was semidemocratic; approval or veto was still a powerful tool in the hand of the emperor. The former ruling class, the aristocracy, had been considerably curtailed in privileges and power, first by the revolution of 1848 and then by the ascendancy of the Liberal party in the 'sixties.

... Besides the pressures from (these) power groups, the monarchy was exposed to the forces of the different nations that wanted either independence or unification with neighbouring countries of common or related language. What held the empire together was Kaiser Franz Josef, or rather, what he represented - the Habsburg empire, a European political structure of relative stability that had lasted through eight hundred years. When Franz Josef died in 1916, the monarchy fell apart.

I was brought up amidst the struggle of the political forces which undermined the basic structure of the empire. But the waves of the stormy politics hardly reached me during my childhood. Our home was not religious, nor did my father have strong political convictions. Politics were never mentioned in my family.

The provenience of my parents was typical for many Viennese. My paternal grandparents were both Czechs born in Bohemia, at the time one of the crown countries of the monarchy. My grandfather, a tailor by trade, had settled in the province of Upper Austria in a village not far from Salzburg. He came there at the time of the construction of the Western railroad... which led from Vienna into Switzerland. Railroad building, which had to be done by manual labor, gave jobs to thousands of laborers and occupied a staff of engineers. In turn, their need for clothing did not leave my grandfather idle. Both paternal grandparents died before I was born. My father grew up as a village boy, and like so many people of Czech origin who spent their childhood in the German part of the monarchy, he identified with the Austro-German population.

My grandfather wanted his son to become a tailor also. But my father's outstanding performance in grade school motivated his teacher to urge my grandfather to let the boy enter the gymnasium (boys' secondary school) in Salzburg. In this way my father acquired a humanistic education. After finishing his gymnasium, he studied mathematics and physics at the University of Vienna and finally taught mathematics and physics in Vienna at a lyceum (girls' equivalent of gymnasium)...

Under the German nationalistic propaganda of Georg von Schoenerer, my father's ideology became mildly German nationalistic and anti-Semitic, though he was never politically active. He was narrow in his thinking and in many ways peasantlike in his outlook and habits. He was not fond of social contact; visitors in my parents' home felt unwelcome by his reserved attitude, which sometimes amounted to unfriendliness. He felt at home only when he bowled with the local peasants in the village near Salzburg where we spent our long summer vacations. As a father, he was very strict and authoritarian; physical punishment belonged to his educational arsenal. My four-years-older brother and I were mainly afraid of him and we never developed a close relationship with him in our childhood and youth. He treated his sons without any psychological understanding. Later in life, some of his former pupils became patients of mine and I heard them complain about my father's strictness and lack of empathy with his pupils. But he was respected for being very just in his grading.

It was *de rigueur* that my father's two sons - there were no other children - should acquire the same humanistic education that he had obtained. He was content and even proud when we both studied medicine and became physicians.

My mother's parents were of mixed nationality. Her father came from a family of weavers who had been forced to leave their homeland - the German-speaking northern part of Bohemia in the Sudeten mountains - when the introduction of the mechanical loom in the middle of the nineteenth century put them out of work. ...My maternal grandfather emigrated to Lodz, a Polish city that then belonged to the Russian empire. There he married a Polish woman who bore him six children. When my mother was a teenager, the family moved to Vienna, where my grandparents eked out a meagre existence by running a small restaurant. My mother learned very early the trade of seamstress; she had no opportunity for a higher education. When she married my father, she continued her trade and ran a workshop that made women's dresses. When I was a small child, she sometimes had four girls working in one of the three small rooms of our apartment. She contributed considerably to the family income, which was most welcome to my parsimonious father. Our standard of living was very restricted, which enabled my father to save a great part of his salary as a lyceum professor, only to lose it all with the downfall of the Austrian empire.

My father dominated the domestic scene and the family life was subservient to him. My mother was a very warm and loving person; she was deeply devoted to her family and anxious to do everything to my father's satisfaction. Her loving care of and concern for her two boys compensated for Father's stern and forbidding nature. It was due to her that our home life was relatively harmonious, and, with the exception of the fear of our father, I look back on a relatively peaceful childhood.

Culturally, our home life was impoverished..."

There were some interesting events in his childhood which my father's brief account did not include.

Whenever he talked about his youth, I felt very close to him; but these intense conversations were few. He was too busy with patients and papers and too devoted to the violin. Only his lions, or infatuation with a new pretty woman could drag him away from his Bach solo sonatas for more than a few minutes. He practiced them for more than half a century, with undiminishing passion. He also needed time for listening to music, and for riding, riding being the ruling passion of my mother. So there was not much time left simply to talk.

I learned most about him on the rare occasions when we travelled in Europe together. On one of his last trips to Vienna, we went to the cemetery where his mother was buried. My father had commissioned someone to tend the grave, and wanted to check that this was being done.

But where, I asked my father, was his father's grave? I knew my grandfather had been brutal to his sons. My father was once given a little cane for his birthday and then, caught saying a naughty word to the cook, beaten with the birthday present until it broke. Another choice brutality of my grandfather's was pulling tufts of his boys' hair out by the roots - he had a special word for this, *rupfen,* plucking, as one plucks a fowl. And almost worst of all, my father said, was his father's sadistic way of punishing the whole family, including his kind, meek wife, when one of the boys misbehaved. He would use the occasion to cancel some rare outing that all of them had looked forward to for weeks or months.

Even so, the dead are often forgiven. I was not prepared for the vehemence of my father's reply. He said he didn't know where the grave was. But if he did, he would go and spit on it.

Then he told me a story I had not heard before. At fourteen, his older brother Oscar failed an exam at the gymnasium. Oscar was so terrified of what his father would do that he took a gun from a desk drawer and shot himself through the head.

Hearing the shot, his mother dashed into the room, and in her panic, picked up the gun so it fired again. The bullet went through the canary's cage but missed the canary. The first bullet missed also; Oscar's brain. He survived, losing only the hearing of one ear. The canary survived as well.

After this incident my grandfather was rather less cruel to his sons.

Uncle Oscar himself, however, was a chip off the old block. He made my father's life as much hell as he could. One vicious trick was asking my father to gaze up at something and then burning him under the chin with a lighted cigarette. More dangerous was the time he told my father to look down, at something of interest he held out on his hand. When my father naively looked down at the proffered palm, Oscar blew what turned out to be iron filings into his eyes.

Uncle Oscar grew up to become a country doctor and later a Nazi. He died of a heart attack, in a snowstorm on his way to a patient. I suppose, if he'd found it, my father would have spat on that grave as well. And so might I. Though my own faint, toddler's memory is of a fat jolly man smelling of strong tobacco, who gave me "cat's tongue" chocolates, which I adored. Perhaps Oscar was especially resentful because my father was their mother's favorite. Never mind Oedipus. Women loved my father and I do not suppose his mother was immune to his charm.

On another journey, we met in Salzburg, the place my father was fondest of and might have returned to for good had my mother agreed. Salzburg or Vienna. In old age, he was heard to say, "If one of us dies, I will retire to Vienna." In the event, he didn't. But he visited his homeland as often as he could, at least once a year.

My father took me to the street where his uncle's grocery shop had been. His aunt and uncle, who were childless, had doted on him and invited him every summer. Salzburg was his paradise. He was away from his brutal father and brother and the rigors of school; he was with loving, indulgent people, in the most beautiful place he knew. He helped his uncle eagerly, a little boy hauling heavy sacks of potatoes, happy beyond words. Though my Detroit winters were never as grim as his Viennese, I had felt it too, on our summer moves to Vermont, the release, the soaring happiness. That evening in Salzburg is one of the memories I will keep as long as my memory lasts; the dimly lit lane, the small green door to the vanished grocery, the sound of my father's voice.

My father's next story was less Dickensian. With my grandmother's industrious dress-making, they could afford a maid and cook, giving the Professor a fitting bourgeois household. The cook, who was illiterate, bargained with my father to write her love letters to her boyfriend, in exchange for a feel of her probably ample bosom. My father, then age nine or so, was happy to comply. There is much to be said for the advantages of education.

This might have been damaging for some little boys. The early Freudians had various cases of patients whose psyches were damaged by over-sexed unscrupulous nannies. My father took it in his stride. I cannot bear to think what would have happened if his father or brother had caught him. But my father, as in later years, was adept at hiding his sexual peccadillos.

In those early years he also found his greatest love of all, the violin. It was partly a providential bursitis that tipped the balance between music and medicine as a profession. Probably for the best; my father was good but not superb, and my mother might not have been content with a second violin.

Which leads to introducing my mother. Again, I will leave this to my father. His biographical note on my mother's early life is even briefer than his own. But as she worked with Anna Freud, on child analysis, and not with Sigmund, this is in keeping with my father's memoir. After all, as he says in his introduction, he did not set out to write a personal book.

EDITHA

"In the winter of 1923, I met my future wife, Editha von Radanowicz-Harttmann. She was finishing her studies at the University of Vienna and working as a secretary-typist for Otto Rank, who dictated to her the manuscript of *An Analysis of a Neurosis in Dreams* and *The Trauma of*

Birth (1924). Editha's ancestry was even more multinational than mine. Her father was of Croatian stock. Among her mother's ascendants were Germans, Poles, Swiss and English; one of her eight great-grandmothers was Jewish, which her family considered a 'skeleton in the closet.'

Editha had her first education at the Sacre Coeur in Prague, where her father occupied a high command post in the Austrian army. When her father went into retirement, the family moved to Baden, a spa near Vienna. Although the humanistic gymnasium in Baden was only for boys, Editha insisted on obtaining a humanistic education. Through his connections with the top government officials, her father obtained for Editha special permission to attend this gymnasium as the only girl among more than three hundred male students; she finished it in 1918 and enrolled at the University of Vienna, where she studied psychology and musicology.[1] She began her psychoanalytic training in 1925. She and I were among the first trainees; she graduated in 1927. She had studied the piano and was an accomplished pianist when we met.[2]

Through her connection with Otto Rank, Editha obtained the position of editor at the Psychoanalytic Publishing House, which was established in 1918. She worked there from 1922 until 1932. Editha prepared, with A.J. Storfer, Otto Rank and Anna Freud, the *Gesammelte Schriften*, (the edition of the *Collected Works* published in 1926 for Freud's seventieth birthday)...

In the spring of 1924, Editha invited me to spend the holidays with her family in Gmunden on Lake Traunsee, not far from Salzburg; I had always heard people raving about the beautiful lakes of the Salzkammergut (which gets its name from its salt mines) and had read about them in Freud's case-history of "little Hans" but I had never visited this region. When Editha's maternal grandfather, who had been a four-star general in the Austrian army, retired, he bought an estate on Lake Traunsee, situated within walking distance of the town of Gmunden. On the maternal side, Editha's family was of old nobility; her father was ennobled upon his retirement. In 1914, Editha's parents moved to Gmunden and lived on the estate. The house had originally been built in the 17th century by the bishops of Passau

---

[1] *My mother never spoke of this extraordinary school career.*

[2] *But not good enough for Daddy. I remember him never playing chamber music except with professionals. My mother did not play for years and then, in her old age, began lessons again, and practiced in solitude, with fierce determination.*

as a stone hunting lodge and had been enlarged by Editha's grandfather. It was situated sixty feet above the lake, and the view over the lake, framed by the foothills and higher peaks of the Alpine range, was magnificent. The house had enough rooms for a large family and was filled with antique furniture. As long as we lived in Austria, we spent our vacations and extended holidays there. During the five to six weeks of our summer vacation, some of our foreign patients spent time in Gmunden, which was a well-known summer resort, so that they could continue their analyses. From Gmunden we often availed ourselves of the famous Salzburg music festivals during the summer months." [3]

My mother's childhood stories - of which, as *vide* the boat incident, I learned too few, too late - will appear as they occur to me. Here I only want to mention, again, a few things my father did not.

My father met Editha when she came into the room he shared with another doctor. She had planned to visit the other doctor, who had not yet arrived, and worn out with fatigue and hunger (there was hunger in Vienna then, not long after the war) lay down on my father's bed with her head on his pillow.

My father came in and said rudely, "Please get your head off my pillow."

My mother was outraged that this upstart young doctor (no doubt she knew at once from his accent that she was way out of his class) would dare to tell her where not to lay her head.

They fell madly in love.

When this romantic meeting occurred, my mother was married to someone else.

She never mentioned this marriage to her children. I heard about it from Enne, my nurse, when I was nearly grown up. My mother, for an emancipated woman, was peculiarly reticent about this relationship. She needn't have been. The early Freudians, in fact, had a great game of musical chairs. But my mother, the rebel, never shed *all* the dictates of her highly respectable upbringing.

As soon as I heard, of course, I questioned my mother about this first marriage. She said, with her usual bluntness: The marriage was already

---

[3] *I cannot help remarking that my father has devoted nearly one-half of this short sketch of my mother to her ancestral estate. But it is also true that the Gmunden villa was a major attachment in all our lives.*

doomed before she met my father; her husband was unfaithful, and a n'er-do-well, and she had to struggle to put him through medical school.

I found a few photos of this man. He was handsome, and, I believe, from the right social circle, although not a von. We do not know what became of him. My mother said she heard vaguely he had vanished in the East, an official in some Communist party.

My father added another romantic touch. Before her divorce, when my mother was in Gmunden, he would stay in a pension on the other side of the lake, and, like Hero and Leander, they would signal to each other with lights across the water.

I thought my father's memoir should have had more of this, rather than so much about my mother's noble ancestry (chiefly descended, I believe, from one of the illegitimate children of August the Strong, Elector of Poland, King of Saxony, chiefly remembered for his ability to bend a horseshoe with his bare hands and for holding the European royalty record for illegitimate children - something like 355).

It is true, however, that the very idea of nobility can confer, on those who regard themselves part of it, a persuasive confidence and style. And my father, though he made fun of it, was actually very taken with nobility. As are most Austrians, even now.

My mother's family did have its vons. But the Bishops of Passau hunting lodge tale, I heard later in Gmunden, may have been invented by the couriers on the lake steamers, who needed a seventh castle so they could call the lake circuit the Seven Castle Cruise.

Two other things my father told me: When Ditha's mother (who was called Her Excellency because of her husband's rank) heard that Ditha was to marry a poor and untitled young doctor, a tailor's grandson, a vonless nobody, she sighed and said with grim resignation, "Ah well. I suppose we shall get accustomed to it."

They must have been somewhat accustomed already to my mother's rebellious eccentricities. But there was more shock to come. My parents invited some Jewish colleagues to Gmunden for a weekend. My great-aunts, my grandmother's unmarried sisters, decamped across the lake for the duration of this visit. They would not sleep under the same roof with a Jew. And my father himself, when the local nobility came around "was hidden out in the woodshed," he said, laughing. Well, perhaps not quite. But it was their attitude.

But they did get accustomed to the marriage, and the fact of Jewish friends. And in the end, they loved my father. During the war, they asked his own mother, the little seamstress, widowed, alone and blind, for extended stays. She was with them until close to her death. There is a small portrait of her they had painted for my father, her only portrait, half-smiling, sightless eyes upraised, against the fading Imperial decor.

Digression:
My Great-Aunts

My great-aunts were lovely. I have pictures of them in their girlhood. Holding roses, holding frill-edged parasols. In snow-white dresses with tight waists and puffed double sleeves. Faces expectant and fresh as newly opened flowers. Not one, except my grandmother, married. Their father could not afford dowries fit for men of sufficient rank to marry a general's daughter. The family fortunes and hopes of inheritance sank with the loss of their only son, who died at three. My grandmother, the eldest, must have got what dowry there was. She married a man much older than herself, but he was, or became, a general.

The others did not just stay home and vegetate. They all had professions of sorts. Karoline (Lina) was a talented painter and studied art in Munich (Paris however was not allowed). Mitzi learned nursing, and was especially active during the Great War. Celina studied languages and became a nun at the "English Misses" nunnery in St Pölten, an order devoted to the education of young girls. Grete studied in Paris and Prague (languages were more respectable than painting) and taught German and French at a school for officers' daughters in Vienna.

I say: professions of sorts. Lina painted but I don't think she ever exhibited or sold. I have most of her remaining paintings. There are the conventional landscapes and flowers, not bad of their sort, but her real gift was portraits. The portraits are wonderful, done with that immediacy and strength that can make an unknown face unforgettable. And her portrait of my mother as a child has everything that was most my mother - the haughtiness, the intensity, the glowing reserve.

Tante Lina had other distinctions. She refused an offer from the Crown Prince of Romania. She also, in a surge of patriotism, it was said, refused to pour tea for Bismarck at a party. I do not know if this helped the Austrian cause.

IN VIENNA
I DARE TO WALK ON THE GRASS

In my early childhood, like my father, I worshipped heroes.
The first was Prince Eugene of Savoy, who defeated the Turks. While only a toddler, I fell in love with a big equestrian statue of the Prince. At least, that is what my parents told me later. Maybe I was really more in love with the horse, or simply the great centaur-image of bronze horse and rider towering above. My parents made much of this passion. But then they were bound to, as it fitted in so well with the Oedipus complex theory of Freud.

These are the things I really remember:
A big draught horse and wagon, parked on our block. An animated Punch and Judy window display. A Siamese cat who died young, poisoned by licking the green-painted walls of a room. A shadow play with what must have been Balinese puppets, lacy and Oriental, that led to a new, magical, exotic world, and the endless use of the shadow-image in my later unpublished poems.
Leaving my stuffed Kanga and Roo in the taxi that took my nurse and me for outings while my parents worked. Inconsolable crying till the toys were returned by Herr Sack, the obliging driver. I loved Herr Sack. He had a cap and a tweedy coat and a very Viennese smile. He looked a little like my father, and was very jolly. Or so I remember him.
Butcher's shops, with feathered ducks and geese, snowy white, hanging upside down and the fearful red gash where their throats had been cut. And the smell of fowls being plucked, singed and gutted in the kitchen. The smell of chicken guts can still make me retch.
Toddling down a flight of steps to meet my parents in a sunny garden, and falling on my face with my forehead crashing against a step's edge. Floods of tears, ardent consolation. I wasn't badly hurt; but there is no consolation for the dreadful shaming surprise, for happiness *dashed*. Perhaps I remember this because it was typical. I am the sort who, if jumping for joy, is likely to collide with a sharp piece of furniture. Some, my parents for instance, might ascribe this to innate masochism. Others

would say some unconscious sentinel, aware of hubris, warns us never to take ebullience too far.

But my most vivid memory is the incident of the trout; a trout like in the Schubert song performed at my parents' evenings of chamber music. From those evenings, I remember a shaggy pianist I called Lion and an Icelandic folk singer, Engel Lund, whom I called the Giantess because she was, unlike my parents, large and tall. I didn't care much for the music then; the loud strings frightened me.

The trout was in an aquarium in a restaurant. I watched it swimming around and begged to have one myself, at home. I loved all the animal kingdom. The new cat, the Scottie and the canary were not enough. I also wanted a fish. My wish was granted. The trout appeared a few days later, brown and fried, on my dinner plate.

Whatever mistakes my Freudian parents made, this may have been the worst. Never mind the Oedipus complex, penis envy, sibling rivalry, etc. My shriek of "Why did you kill the fish?", a question with no acceptable answer, resounds over all the decades since. There is no theory that guarantees communication; in fact most theory probably gets in the way. But even today I think: how *could* they have been so stupid? I have, of course, been just as stupid with my own child.

No. There may have been an earlier mistake still worse; though fate made it right in the end.

My mother, seeing patients most of the day, needed a nurse for me. The first one stayed only till I was six months old. My father fired her, my next and permanent nanny said, because she wore rubber gloves to wash diapers and he thought such cleanliness compulsive. A proper nanny would not mind shit on her hands.

I was shocked at this story. By the time Enne told it, I had a baby myself and knew that rubber gloves were in fact very sensible. And apparently 'Sister Lucy' was young and pretty and I was very fond of her. Enne said I cried bitterly when Lucy left, and when Enne came in, I beamed because I thought Lucy was back, then howled more than ever when I saw she was not.

I am still amazed, as with the fish, that it never occurred to anyone this change might be damaging. Maybe Anna Freud and colleagues had not yet completed studies of infant bonding. Or my mother thought that giving us lots of her own milk and rushing in and out of the nursery was bonding enough. It wasn't. There must be someone you trust and love who is always there and does not desert you.

But my father, as usual, came out on top. Enne, the next nurse employed, was the one who stayed through thick and thin, gave up her independence, her country, her separate life, who though not Jewish nor political and under no particular threat, fled with us when the Nazis came and remained until after my sister and I were grown up.

It was another example of my father's extraordinary capacity to attract loyalty and love. Perhaps he did not inspire love in Sister Lucy. There must have been something more to it than the rubber gloves. It may be of Freudian significance that I never got round to asking, and this secret, like others, has gone with my parents to the grave.

The trout episode is one of the few parental tales of my childhood that matches a memory of my own.

Another, the most embarrassing of their stories, is of my seeing a doctor because of an anal rash. This was probably the first of the minor but humiliating skin complaints that were to dog me until adulthood, along with crooked teeth, flat feet, oily hair, myopia and lousy posture.

I remember being made to kneel on a table with my small rear end raised, and delicately probed with some kind of instrument. Fortunately it only happened once. But it seems I referred to this doctor afterwards as "the shithole doctor" and my parents, with a tactlessness their Freudian training exacerbated, called him that for years, though of course not to his face. They thought it was funny. I thought it was disgusting.

The shithole, anyhow, features prominently in Central European infancy. Not just because of the traumas of toilet training. (My own belief is that these traumas can be avoided by providing a pretty chair with a pot, such as I bought for my own daughter in the Istanbul bazaar. Why do we sit on thrones and make our children squat, while the Turks, who squat as adults, produce delightful baby toilet seats?) My parents told me that as a toddler I held my movements back as long as possible; I was anal-retentive as well as oral-aggressive. I probably just didn't want to sit on a cold unsteady pot. Or I wanted to keep them waiting, since they were so interested. It must have been a great way of getting their time and attention.

There is also the adult fixation with shit itself, as an indicator of health. If your parents are so fascinated by this messy product, must you not conclude it has a value its appearance belies? In this way at least shit does, as the Freudians have it, resemble money.

Freudian or not, it is difficult for a Central European child to avoid becoming somewhat anal-fixated or anal-phobic. Central European parents, besides being so curious about your shit, are prone to shove things up your ass. There are thermometers, enemas, suppositories, and if your mother is hyper-anxious about your health, you have more than your share. Freud should have written more about the fixations of adults who administer so much in this form. Small children are perfectly capable of keeping thermometers in the armpits and swallowing pills.

Some children of course may not mind. I know I did. The eczema doctor is the only specific instance I remember. But when only a baby it seems I was given an enema when already screaming with pain, when my problem was not colic but sunburnt eyes. Ultra-violet rays were another health fetish of the time. My parents were away on a brief trip to Italy and someone left me under the sun-lamp too long, or did not notice when I pulled my goggles off. The doctor who was called when I began screaming decided it must be my stomach and used the conventional remedy. It was my nurse Enne, as usual, who finally figured out what was wrong. This story wakes no memory but I do remember hating that doctor, who was also a family friend, forever after.

My parents made this incident too a permanent part of our family saga. I do not know if this was because they felt guilty at having left me when I was so little, or because it was another convenient handle to hang my inevitable neurosis on.

My parents described me later as an appealing, confident, self-willed and stubborn child, who showed great verbal precocity and never stopped talking. Typical stories: of me, out in my push-chair, wearing a grotesque mask I'd been given, shouting at passers-by, "Don't be afraid, people, it's only me." Or, me, toddling on the forbidden grass in the park, told to get off it and demanding angrily, "Why?" It is as if we remember two different children. Mine is hyper-sensitive, nervous, easily hurt, already burdened by the mundane cruelty of the world, the hanging geese in the butcher shop, the dead trout on the plate.

I myself think that the shadows over my pampered secure existence had less to do with parental failing than with the growing tension outside. While my parents interpreted dreams and made chamber music, Left and Right fought pitched battles in the city streets, and Hitler consolidated his power in Germany and plotted his moves to the East. My own post-Freudian theory is that some children are weather vanes. They record, in their dreams, in their anxieties, not only the fears of their adults, however secret, but more distant thunders, the impending fall of a city, an era, a world.

But some of what was kept from me was personal, and perhaps not well enough kept. Before I was born, my mother lost new-born twins, a girl and a boy. My father said they might have been saved if their clinic had had an incubator; it didn't and they caught pneumonia being moved. When I was two, a baby brother was born. He too died, at birth.

My mother, that avowed rebel, career woman, emancipated bluestocking, desperately wanted a boy. When I was born - my father told me, in his old age - her first remark to him was "Will you forgive me?"

This anomaly may not have been so rare in the professional women of my mother's generation. She did not respect her own sex. She only respected the women who escaped its conventional role. This feeling was surely intensified by the ardent male-worship of *her* mother's family, left with five daughters and no dowries because the only male child, who would have inherited a title and estate, died at three. When Berti, my mother's younger brother and only sibling, was born, it was fated they all adore him. Even my mother. Her natural jealousy, my father said, was sublimated into love, though she was more clever and also more forceful than Berti.

I don't know what the third death of a child did to my mother. She never talked about it. But it seems I, the toddler, did; I asked over and over to be told about my brother's death. My parents saw in this a sibling-rivalry glee, accompanied by guilt. I had been jealous and wanted the baby to die.

I suspect something quite different - that I was looking for reassurance after hearing horror stories from the kitchen. My own analyst told me, eighteen years later - perhaps in despair as my own well-schooled free associations never yielded any major revelations - the rumor that had gone around. (I don't mean to knock my analyst, She was a sensible woman and did her best. It is hard to analyze Freudian children and you cannot be blamed for using material ready to hand.) My baby brother, the rumor went, was hydrocephalic and had to be virtually cut up in order to extract him and save my mother's life.

As Anni, my shrink, of course a member of my parents' old Vienna crowd, said this in confidence, I could never mention it to Enne or my parents. It may have been only gossip. All I know is that no one ever explained what went wrong, only that the baby died.

My mother, undaunted, tried again, though she was by then over forty and by the era's medical standards old for another pregnancy. It was a difficult birth. When I was grown up she told me about it. She lost a great deal of blood and had one of those verge-of-death experiences; she floated peacefully above the scene, looking down, unconcerned, at her body and its frantic attendants. It is typical of my mother that she was not in a tunnel heading for light or hearing angelic choirs but up on the ceiling, somewhat contemptuously looking down. She survived, and the baby was normal and healthy - but another girl. My father said that this time my mother did not ask for forgiveness. Informed of the baby's sex, she only exclaimed, *'Pfui.'* Which means, ugh.

It is to my mother's credit that she never took her disappointment out on us. But then neither my sister, Verena, nor I grew up to be conventional housewives, and we both learned to sit creditably on a horse; my sister very well. This somewhat made up for the lack of that member which Freud thought all little girls want and which my mother certainly so wanted for us.

What I remember about my little sister's arrival is a dream or fantasy in which she is being grated like a piece of cheese. There are no screams or struggle, no person, just the fleeting image of white skin against sharp steel, springing blood. The kind of hideous thing the inner demon puts into your head. My parents - later, I often confessed such things to my parents - put this too down to sibling rivalry. I think it has to do, yet again, with the gossip about my brother, and with the kitchen. In the kitchen they were always grating and mincing; maybe the cook or maid cut herself on the grater. This leads to a simple semantic explanation. Take three German words. *Abtreiben* means abort. *Abreiben* means grate. And *abreiben* is also to rub down, as one might towel a baby. I must have misunderstood something, as my parents misunderstood about the trout. From such misunderstandings obsessions and phobias can be born. I would love to tell Anni, my shrink, that I think I have at last solved the mystery of this dreadful fantasy; my analysis didn't. But Anni is now many years dead.

Out in the kitchen, language itself touched on horrors. The phrase still used then in Vienna about a screaming child was *"Das Kind hat geschrien wie am Spiess."* The child shrieked as if on the spit. Many years later I realized the phrase refers to impalement. How common must this grisly execution have been for the simile to still be current in the twentieth century? Perhaps the horrors of our own will be imortalized in a saying about "going up the chimney" which my husband told me was used by Germans when his American unit invaded during the war - the same Germans who claimed to know nothing of the concentration camp nearby.

The photos I have from my Austrian infancy show the happy, confident child my parents described. Many of them were taken in Gmunden, at the villa on the lake. One is of me riding on my father's shoulders, on a mountain path. My father is dressed in traditional shorts and jacket and looks healthy and strong and incredibly young.
There is also a photo of a dancing bear. I remember this sad gray bear and his gypsy master, perhaps from the same tribe who, when my mother was a girl, cursed her and spat. She said it was because of her long, fiery red hair.
More vividly I remember the screams of a pig being killed at the inn next door. It was then a rustic country inn, part of my mother's family's estate. There was an old farmhouse and a gravel terrace with pollarded plane trees, overlooking the lake. Old men played bowls there on weekends, and the innkeeper cut wood from our forest for the villa's tiled stoves, and in exchange, as part of his tenancy agreement, had fruit from the apple, cherry and bitter pear trees on our steep meadows for making cider and distilling S*chnapps.*
I was told the pig had a toothache and was having a tooth pulled. I think I believed it. (Had they known how much dentistry I would need, they might have used another story.) They would certainly never have told the truth. Already, my mother said later, I had an "eating disturbance" and would eat only chicken and strawberries. Enne told me this was grossly exaggerated; my mother was dramatizing, as was her wont.

There are other images but they came from my parent's stories and photo albums and flickering home movies. The images blur with real memory, become memory superimposed. The sweet smell of new-cut hay and peaceful cows chewing cud in the barn of the inn, the feel of a cow's udders, and of the tiny horns of a chamois kid in a park. And going out on the lake in a rowboat named Monika, after me. As the first-born, like my male cousin, I had named for me also a newly-planted wood, a small plantation of conifers at the edge of the mature forest on the mountainside above our orchard meadow.

But one Gmunden memory is all mine, and clear as yesterday.

I am lying in bed, during the sacrosanct "rest hour" that followed the main meal. The heavy green shutters are half-closed; sun dances on the ripples of the lake below. And I, for the first time, become aware of another dance, that of the myriad dust motes in a beam of light. It was a moment of revelation. The revelation was nothing I could put into words. Perhaps it happened before I could speak. Perhaps had my upbringing been ruled by Jung instead of Freud, I would say that what I discovered in the dancing dust motes was the astral and particle dance of the universe. I know there was an enormous feeling of mystery and discovery and happiness. And a sense of connection; of this moment to others, past and to be.

I was always to find such moments most often in mountain country. Those few early months in Gmunden began my passion for mountains, the mountains I was to be parted from before I could come down from my father's shoulders and walk up the paths alone.

MY MOTHER PACKS AT MIDNIGHT

I once asked my father why some people go through dreadful traumas in childhood and emerge cheerful and sane, while others who have led lives of apparent ease and security are nutty as hell.

My father drew a little picture, of a cup. Then he drew another. One cup is deep, he said, and can hold a lot. The other has a sloping inside. When you pour into these cups, the second one quickly runs over.

I was the kind that doesn't hold very much. And, as I have said, some of us are not cups but also sponges. We absorb what is around. In spite of all the toys, hugs, and evasions, we can absorb fear; not only feel but internalize what adults hide. Sometimes, perhaps, even the adults' own childhood fears, the fears our parents think they have outgrown.

Such fears are harder to track down than those based on personal experience; and they are not groundless. Often, no one can truthfully promise that *it*, whatever it is, will never happen. And the inner demon can tell you, even if everyone keeps it from you, how the *it* might be.

One day, I was out in the park with Herr Sack the taxi driver and Enne, when a great flurry of leaflets came down from the sky.

I toddled around, intoxicated, picking up these lovely white pieces of paper. Paper falling from the heavens, like snow!

No one told me to keep off the grass.

The streets were full of a new hectic excitement. Herr Sack lifted me up to show me, in a shop window, a photo of a blonde little girl - just like me, he said - handing a big bouquet of flowers to a man in uniform with slick dark hair and a moustache.

Herr Sack said this man was a wonderful man. Then he taught me a new way of saying hello: *Heil Hitler!* He also showed me how to draw swastikas. I practiced the swastikas at home. My father came in and saw them and for some reason I could not fathom, was not pleased.

Later, we all went to the windows and watched a big parade, with motor cars and rows and rows of stiff-legged marchers, coming down our street, the Mariahilferstrasse. There were cheering people everywhere, people waving handkerchiefs, throwing confetti, lining the streets dozens deep, leaning in clusters over the sills. Cheering and cheering. My parents did not cheer.

The next thing I remember is being woken in the middle of the night.

My Enne dressed me hurriedly, and told me not to make noise. My mother was busy stuffing things into duffel bags. My mother was a very efficient packer but there seemed an unusual haste and messiness about this one. Very quickly, we were ready to go. We took Peter the cat in a basket, and Enne carried my baby sister, and I carried, in a matchbox, a ladybird named Elizabeth I had found in the park.

I think I sensed, even then, that I would never see my bed or my home again.

My father had left earlier, with a patient. His pretext was that the patient was severely disturbed and had to be escorted home to her parents in Holland. Things had already reached a state where flight needed disguise. My parents were not Jewish and would have been suitable recruits for the new regime. They decided to travel separately, and with different pretexts, so that suspicion would not be aroused.

My father's departure must have been especially nerve-wracking. He had left all his personal documents with an application he had made for an assistant professorship in the Vienna University Department of Psychiatry. Like so many, my parents had an idea of what might come, but continued to base plans on the hope it would not. Besides the new job application, we were also just about to move to the suburbs. In the event, we did; a suburb several thousand miles away.

Going to fetch his documents, my father was greeted with *"Heil Hitler"* and the offer of an immediate, not assistant but associate, professorship. Ousting the Jews had left many vacancies. My father answered with *"Guten Tag,"* and asked for his documents. Without a word, they were given. My father's wonderful luck. We were to need it in the months that followed.

My mother had got a doctor's certificate saying my baby sister and I had had whooping cough and needed to recuperate in a warm climate.

We took a train to Milan. At one point, my mother told me later, a Gestapo officer ordered her off the train. She refused to get off. Another Gestapo said "Aha, you are fleeing from Hitler." Remembering what Herr Sack had taught me, I piped up with a sleepy *"Heil Hitler"* on hearing this name. I don't know if it was that or my mother's determination that saved us, but we reached Milan.

This is how my mother told it. I don't remember the Gestapo, except as characters in American war movies. My only memory of that trip is the strangeness of travelling at night, of being up so late, so awake, watching my tiny baby sister sound asleep in Enne's arms.

From Milan we were to go on to Switzerland, to my uncle's in-laws, and meet my father. To console me for all the upheaval, my mother treated us to a buggy ride from our hotel in Milan to the station. In my excitement, I left Elizabeth in her matchbox behind in the hotel. There was no time to go back and get her.

My mother assured me she would phone the hotel and give instructions that Elizabeth be freed and put outside. Elizabeth would be all right. I didn't quite believe it. My grief was as great as the grief for the murdered trout. If only I had let Elizabeth go, before! Elizabeth was so little and helpless, an Austrian ladybug trapped in a box and alone in a strange land.

There are things that will always remind me. Lights burning at two in the morning. Uniforms, application forms, border crossings, duffel bags.

I love motion, I love travel. I love trains. Aeroplanes, far more polluting, also disorient and desensitize. But every journey wakes an old anxiety. I sleep badly the night before. I am afraid the alarm won't ring, the taxi won't come in time. I panic about whether lights were left on or gas still burning. I have travelled more than almost anyone I know, but I still panic about my tickets, my money, whatever I might forget.

My nightmares are nearly all about losing things or missing transport. I miss the train or the plane, I forget the vital document. When my husband died, I dreamt of folding a pair of men's pyjamas, and then taking a train with my father, alone. *Pace* Papa Freud. When I was with a friend in the Himalayas, the ultimate mountains, my personal Mecca, I dreamt I was back in Vienna, with Enne (in fact long dead) and had missed my plane to Kathmandu because I'd forgotten to pack. This dream was so real that when I woke I was euphoric all day with relief that it wasn't true.

You live like a nomad, said a friend, deploring my lack of cosiness. I hate upholstered furniture, I hate knick-knacks, I resent every non-essential object that clutters my space. But I cannot part with relics of the family talents, or souvenirs of loved houses that no longer exist. Keeping them, passing them on, is a necessary tribute. I just sometimes wish there were none, that my ornaments were expendable driftwood and pebbles, things picked up on the beach. Objects bind you. And no one can ever guarantee that you will not have to pack your bags again in the middle of the night.

I am happiest living out of a suitcase or backpack, away from home. I love improvising, figuring where to hang the shirt washed in a hotel basin, finding a cheap decent restaurant, arranging a few things on an unfamiliar shelf. The reading I most enjoy is a strange book in a strange room. I feel deliciously settled on a three-night stay. I am happiest in the temporary, or en route, on the way to a somewhere else.

And happiest in expectation. Like my father as a little boy on the train from Vienna to Salzburg. In America, my favorite time of all the year was the drive from Detroit to Vermont, which in those days needed a stop overnight. A time of happiness so complete it was almost religious, too precious to dissipate in gestures and noise. The Vermont house is gone now too, burnt and rebuilt by its new owners, because it was too expensive to winterize. Not a surprise. We live in the age of blind destruction. In transit is the only place that, in its changing nature, remains unchanging, the only place no one can take away.

Digression:
My Great-Aunt Lina's Portraits

I have most of my great-aunt Lina's water-colours, drawings and oils. Among them is a sketchbook with drawings of peasant children somewhere in the Empire. Like all Lina's portraits they are wonderfully individual and alive.

I know they are peasant children from the clothes, the hair, the stance, the faces. You could get exceptions, just as you can find a peasant-type face or two in my leather and gold-embossed album of old family photos. In Lina's sketchbook there are no exceptions. The children are timid, sullen and shy. None of them look as if they wanted to pose. None of them look as if they expected fate to deal them a decent hand.

Lina wrote each one's name in her flourishing Gothic letters. Zosia Sokotowska. Marynia Swiatknowna. Siwiec Stanistawa. Marya Marienkiewig. Franciszka Kamecka. Karolina Muniak. Antonina Rukowna. Josia Beniatska. Then there is Gastwirt Hersch Przectan, the innkeeper. And one child without a name, the only one who smiles.

I often wonder what became of them. If they grew up to have children of their own, and grandchildren. How many of them and their descendants perished under the Germans and the Russians. How many, like myself, escaped.

WAITING FOR VISAS: AUNTS, HEROES AND FEAR

I was to become ever more obsessed with heroes. The invincible protectors, the holders of the last bridge, the shining swords of justice who make everything all right.

In Basel, in another old villa, where my family took refuge after their flight, I learned about Held Winkelried. I no longer know what heroic function Held Winkelried (Hero Winkelried) performed, but I remember Tante Gotte, who told me about him. Tante Gotte and her sister Tante Emmi owned the villa. Tante Emmi was a clergyman's widow, and her only daughter had married my mother's only brother. This had been promoted by my mother, who thought, on first meeting, that pretty young Emma would make a perfect wife for Berti, then given, I believe, to dalliances of a less serious character. And they too fell madly in love.

The Swiss connection had begun through my father. He was sent to the clergyman's family for a holiday on a charity program for poor students, when he was recovering from pleurisy after his service in the war. The whole family, parents, four brothers and one sister, became his life-long friends. Once again my father's charm landed him - and us - on our feet. When we fled Austria Tante Gotte and Tante Emmi housed us all, my father safely arrived from Holland, my mother and the two children, Enne, and Peter the cat.

I still find myself looking for those images of old age so vivid in my childhood. The ladies in dresses of long rustling black, with white hair in tidy buns, with sweet lined faces. Tante Emmi's and Tante Gotte's were particularly Swiss, faces that looked as if carved from fruitwood.

What you see now is blue rinse and Bermuda shorts. Old ladies in black are only found in neglected Southern and Eastern European villages, a sign of poverty and what we consider backwardness, underdevelopment. We don't need the black again. But some shred of that dignity should have remained. Dignity and magic. The old ladies of my childhood had deep, unquavering vintage voices, heirloom brooches below their high collars, boxes of little treasures and stories of princesses and heroes. I was happy with such old ladies. I do not remember that I ever missed the company of other children.

I was fondest of Tante Gotte. She was a spinster, like my great-aunts, and devoted much of her life to charity, notably something called *Les Amies de la Jeune Fille*, which protected young girls, I suppose, from the risks of travel and the white slave trade, whatever lurked in wait for them. And as I had loved Gmunden, I loved her villa, with its big garden and crunchy gravelled walks and pull-up shutters and gentle fountain that was never still. Besides her Held Winkelried stories, she had cut-outs of bright cellophane in black outlines, just like stained glass, and *"Abziehbilder,"* pictures you wetted and transferred, magically, onto a blank page. Like the hand-turned music boxes with slotted metal record discs, the wooden horses with real horsehair tails and newspaper for their inner skin, the toy train that was not electric but had to be wound, these things have vanished, like the ladies themselves, and with them an enchantment that will not come back.

My parents had an offer of work in the USA but were informed that though the rest of us, including Enne, could get visas in a few months, my mother could not. She had been born in Budapest, then Austria-Hungary, and would have to come under the Hungarian quota, which was full for thirteen years.

Meanwhile, my father received a letter from Mueller-Braunschweig, who had taken over the Viennese Psychoanalytic Society, now purged of its Jewish members and so virtually non-existent. Dr Mueller-Braunschweig urged my father to return. "We urgently need the full cooperation and assistance of the few Aryan members of the Vienna Psychoanalytic Society." The good doctor went on to say that he "would like to establish immediately a schedule of lectures for the S.S."

My father wrote back that he had no intention of returning. He tried to get visas for England. Then, discouraged by Ernest Jones, who thought that as the only Aryan member of the Freud group he should not have left, my father tried South Africa. Here too the application was refused.

In his memoir, my father writes:

"We were still stranded in Switzerland, pressured by the Swiss authorities to leave the country. Our only possibility left was to continue, or rather renew, our efforts to obtain visas for the United States.

I wrote to a former American patient of mine, whose daughter had been in treatment with Ditha, asking if she could give us an affidavit of support, which was needed for an immigration visa. My patient answered that she had already given the affidavits her financial status permitted, but she told an acquaintance of hers about our being stranded in Switzerland. This lady was Laura Z. Hobson, the well-known author of a series of widely-read novels, among them *Gentlemen's Agreement*. Hobson immediately got to work on our visas. She gave the necessary affidavits and tirelessly fought the objections of the American consul in Zurich, who threw up one roadblock after the other in order to refuse us the visas; this was in accord with the prevailing policy of the U.S. State Department, which wanted to keep the influx of refugees to a minimum.

We had to wait six months for the American visas. The Swiss authorities constantly threatened to send us back to Austria, since we were neither Jewish nor political refugees and therefore officially had no right to ask for asylum. It was an agonizing time of fighting for a series of short prolongations of our temporary permit to stay in Switzerland. In order not to overextend the hospitality of our Swiss relatives, we had rented a villa in Ascona, on Lake Maggiore ... It was here in this idyllic setting that we lived for six months ... this was financially possible because six of the foreign patients we had treated in Vienna joined us in order to continue their treatment ... the villa was large enough that we could house a series of Viennese friends who, after they had obtained exit permits, were on their way to England or America ..."

Here, in this idyllic setting.

I remember the meadows, overwhelmingly fragrant, lush and wild, crickets singing in a warm dusk. As Gmunden began my passion for mountains, so Ascona began my Northerner's passion for the south. But there was also foreboding, under the beauty, a tinge of death. As if something, someone, lay buried under that sweet high grass.

I remember lunch at a sister-in-law's of my aunt, where I refused a vanilla pudding because of the skin. Milk-skin was something I really did hate. While my hostess scolded me, her Swiss thrift outraged, I stared at a painting on the wall, a painting of a white horse with black ravens pecking at its body and its eyes.

I remember another picture, in a book, a tiger that gave me nightmares. I remember, for the first time, being afraid in the night.

I remember a walk up a Calvary hill: The iron-barred chapels, each with its gory Passion scene, the life-size, vividly coloured statues so beloved in the Catholic south. The thorn-crowned Christ, stumbling under his cross. The crucified Christ with his drooping head and bright streams of blood on the pale wooden flesh. The adults must have tried to hide their fears. But these are the things I remember.

There are two other memories. The first is one my Freudian parents would hold highly significant.

In Switzerland I played my first - and only - game of "doctor" with little boys. Their own father, my aunt's brother Andres, was a real doctor, but their medical inspiration was fortunately limited. I think all they did was put wads of cotton between my legs. I was willing enough at the time but felt odd about it later. So when, soon after, I saw the boys in their bath, having their hair washed and crying with pain from soap in their eyes, I was secretly, sadistically, pleased.

There was also a horseback ride. As once in Gmunden, I was put on a big horse. The horse was led by a woman equestrienne friend. I must have sat awkwardly, and began to slip sideways. But I did not - would not - could not cry out. Some perverse courage, an overdose of Held Winkelried, or that embarrassment is sometimes stronger than fear. I went down, still voiceless, and my foot caught in the stirrup. Before anyone realized what was happening, the horse stepped on my other leg.

There was a great fuss. Uncle Andres, who was there, cut away my trouser leg to inspect the damage. This impressed me much more than the pain. I was even then a parsimonious child, and I thought for them to ruin my pants I must be really badly hurt. I wasn't. The horse had only stepped on my calf, and no bones were broken. After a week bandaged and in bed, I was up again and no less fond of horses.

My father continues:
"When our U.S. visas were finally granted, in late January 1939, the American consulate demanded that we obtain valid passports. This meant that I had to apply for them at the German consulate in Lugano. When I appeared before the consul, he was very inquisitive and seemed reluctant to issue them. He asked my why I needed the passports and why I was leaving the German Reich now that it was coming to glory. Then I used a trick. I told him that I was sure the authorities in Berlin would not approve of the hesitation to issue a German passport for me and my family. I did not directly answer his question but I made him assume that I was on a secret mission. We got our passports the next day."

The next memory is of running on the deck of a ship.

The deck tilts at a fantastic angle. I am excited and proud because I am on my feet while everyone else is desperately seasick and shoved full of suppositories.

At night the furniture slides in the dark, and my little sister's cot ricochets from one wall to another. The ship is the *Normandie* and it is one of the roughest crossings she ever made. I revel in it.

I would like to fill this with period detail of the great steamers, with their dramatic crossings, banquets and balls. My uncle was fond of telling how he once danced with the then Wallis Simpson on such a crossing. But a small child does not register much period detail. Human legs and low furniture are what you see best. Most of the period goes over your head. So this is all I have of that momentous journey, the tilting deck, the sliding cot, the moans of the seasick. And I, I am running. With a great sense of being free.

And then we land in America.

IN GROSSE POINTE,
I RETREAT TO ANCIENT GREECE

When we arrived in New York, my father, with my mother and then again with Enne, went to see the World's Fair.

I only remember seeing dark hallways filled with suitcases and duffel bags, and that Enne was nervous and unhappy. She could speak not one word of English and must have been devastated by the strangeness of everything. She had never been out of Austria before we left there. Unlike us, she had blood relatives in the States; she was one of seventeen children - seventeen, thirteen living - some of whom had emigrated. But I don't think they had ever been close.

The dark hallways did not last long. My father had a practice waiting for him in Detroit. This was to be shared with a Catholic analyst who lived in Grosse Pointe, and was probably overjoyed to find someone from the Viennese society with a Catholic background. Grosse Pointe, at that time, unbeknown to my parents, was off limits to Jews.

My parents bought a house in Grosse Pointe Park, near the lake. Soon after that, they bought a bigger house, nearer the lake. This house my parents were to live in until they died. As for me, I left Grosse Pointe at sixteen, vowing never to live in a suburb again.

Our first street, with the smaller houses, was the friendlier street. Across from us lived a family with two red-headed daughters who tried to make friends. I was too shy to respond much to their overtures. I was a very verbal child; words were my staff of life. I had coped with Swiss-German, which an Austrian joke defines as not a language but a disease of the throat. But this land, this language, were too new, too far away. I became, altogether, desperately shy; I know I went to a birthday party and turned at the door to run back home, my carefully wrapped present in my hands. Anyway, there was not much socializing between our parents, and after we moved I did not see Shirley and Sherry again.

The new house, a dark red and black brick pseudo-Tudor, was much more pretentious as well as big. It had mullioned windows, an oak-panelled library, a large laundry chute (wonderful for games), a basement with boiler room, rec-room and bar, a big balcony on top of the screened porch, a two-level garden with a sunken lawn, and all the accoutrements of suburban elegance. Grosse Pointe is like that: pseudo-Tudor, pseudo-Colonial, pseudo-Spanish, etc. Later, the ranch house came into vogue, rambling one-storey buildings with big picture windows facing big picture windows across the street.

As nearly everywhere in the States, the front gardens were unfenced. Children and dogs ran freely across their friends' front lawns. My sister Verena did this when she was old enough, with a little girl from next door. I hardly ever played with anyone on the street. I mostly stayed in the back garden, sitting on the swing or in the Japanese cherry tree which even a child as timid as I could climb. I would perch there among the spring blossoms, feeling I was in Fairyland. There wasn't much fairyland, otherwise, in Grosse Pointe

Except, in a way, the yearly fish-fly invasion.

This invasion is one of my first and happiest Grosse Pointe memories. The fish-flies were small, shaped more like dragon-flies than flies, with delicate, transparent wings. The trees, the screens, the gardens were covered with them. Streams of dying fish-flies, two feet wide and inches deep, blown against the curbs by passing cars, flowed down the street like storm water. I made a fish-fly village of paper houses on the garden table under the oak. I studded the house with captured fish-flies, which sat there obediently. I was enchanted.

The adults were not. The fish-flies ate nothing, bit nothing, simply lived three days and died. But their billions of corpses made an enormous mess. To me their sudden appearance was something miraculous and wild; and there were such billions that even I, who would rescue trapped moths or beetles, could not get upset about the rivers of fish-fly dead.

And I loved my new swing. But not at first.

I am, to coin a word, a dysmechsic. I lack affinity not only with the mechanical but almost any object with a motor function. It is not unfitness, though that can come into it. I learned very quickly to ride a horse, I was a good runner, and later on I climbed mountains - as a weak second, but I climbed. It is just what I call it; dysmechia.

Dyslexia is now generally recognized. Dysmechia is not. Dysmechsics are laughed at, dismissed as lazy malingerers. If female, they are regarded as male-dominated weak sisters, if male, as lacking virility. In our mechanistic age dyslexia is pitied but dysmechsia is a sin. No one insists that dyslexics spend their time in the library, but if you are dysmechsic people wear themselves out trying to talk you into a word processor, a car, a washing machine (I have an ancient one that turns by hand). They cannot realize that not only may these things go against your grain - as well as, in my case, your environmental convictions - but that life can actually be just as happy without them. And dysmechsics who drive cars often end up in cemeteries. Or worse, put someone else there.

I admit, however, to being an extreme case. I am perhaps the only child who grew up in the suburbs of Mo-town and never learned to drive, and the only child anywhere who took a whole afternoon to learn how to swing.

I had wanted a swing. I got one. I ran out happily to the swing, held the ropes, and sat. Then I began with great energy to bend and stretch my legs.

I had watched other children but somehow not registered what they did. I went on and on, convinced that the swing must sooner or later move. I remember the frustration, the bitter tears. Finally, when my hysterical sobs must have reached the sacred precincts of the couch (my parents had an office but often saw patients at home) someone came out and explained to me that you also have to lean back and forth.

There was, of course, also the lake.
Not that we really used the lake. My mother had sailed in Austria but never sailed in the States. Nor did we swim much. In the early days, when my parents had more time, we did often walk the three blocks to the lake, whose waves and ships broke the monotony of manicured flat suburbia, and my father skipped stones. He was wonderful at skipping stones, as he was at other such things. Flying kites. Playing lion, getting on all fours and roaring and letting you ride on his back. My father, agile and fun, was a natural with children.

My mother was not. Enne said that when I was little and my mother popped into the nursery between patients, I would dismiss her with a rude, "Go away. I want to play with Enne." But it was my mother who treated mainly children and adolescents, while my father treated only adults.

My mother doted on us but never knew what to *do* with us. Until I was older, and we rode together, and sometimes played board games with our extended household in Vermont, I don't remember anything my mother could manage as entertainment. Except be the butt of our teasing. This included one rather sadistic game, where she pretended to be not a healthy lion like my father but a timid inarticulate creature who whimpered and cowered while I shouted commands. She must have thought, in her Freudian way, this was good for my shrunken ego.

And we would make fun of her English and her mannerisms. My mother never seemed to mind. She was above it, or simply withdrawn, or had some Freudian knowledge that it was the family's compensation for her being, however much we teased, the strongest and a cut above.

In our early years in America, my father, so he wrote, and told me later, was often deeply depressed.

He was Viennese through and through. And nothing could have been much farther from Vienna than Detroit. For my father, *culture* and its *ambience* were everything. He was lost without opera, cafés, frequent concerts, friends to play chamber music with, beautiful old buildings, parks and old churches and European art.

My mother was not so lost. Being more reserved, she did not lack so for company. Outside of office hours, my mother talked as happily to animals as to people. Sometimes more happily. And my mother, the aristocrat, entered the brave new, supposedly egalitarian world, with self-assurance and boldness; though unlike a number of immigrants who acquired one at the border, she kept her von to herself. Over my father's hesitations, it was she who decided almost at once to embark on the house-buying, leaving him amazed by her confidence, her absolute certainty that they would do well. My mother was right. And the brave new world soon gave her two things her impoverished family lost in the old; horses and land. Two things my mother really loved having. Which may be why, though she too remained stolidly Austrian, she felt more at home in America than my father, and never - until she was getting too old to ride - thought seriously of going back.

It was not only my father who felt depressed. Whether because of the flight trauma, or the dullness of our new life - no bronze heroes, no Herr Sack, no Punch and Judy or horse and cart across the street, no Tante Gotte with books of stained glass - I was not happy, and I did not want to learn the new tongue. Spending all day with Enne, who never did learn it well, was of course not a help.

The carrot my parents devised to make me speak English was a pair of baby alligators.

They lived in an aquarium in the house of Mrs Cowe, an ageing lady with curly white hair and glasses, who was my English teacher. They crawled over each other and hissed.[4] I don't think my English progressed. During this lonely period, however, my German progressed by leaps and bounds. Not only did I read, having been taught very early by a Viennese Montessori friend in Ascona, but I read Schwab's *Gods and Heroes*, the classic German version of the Greek myths, a beautiful illustrated book bound in gold-tooled red. The Greek myths fascinated me, and I had no problem with the Gothic print. Not tempted by the alligators - they were unresponsive, and I didn't like Mrs Cowe - I withdrew into a private Classical world where I rode Pegasus the winged horse and helped Hector to reverse the defeats of the Trojan war. I had not yet learned that in history the success of the underdog, however desirable, is very rare.

In spite of my poor English, when I was six and it could be postponed no longer, I was taken away from *Gods and Heroes* and sent to public school. Since I already read so well and my parents thought me unusually intelligent, I was put not in first but second grade.

The teachers made much of me; their only little refugee, and clever, and polite. The other children teased or ignored me. I remember no real brutality, but in one incident my brand new coat was yanked away from me in the playground. I was a good bourgeois European child; I could hardly believe they were stealing my coat. But with their nasty gloating,

---

[4] *Baby alligators reappeared in my life later, when I came home from college to find two in the tub. "The Boys," my mother said happily. "The Boys" were a gift from the great pianist Rudolph Serkin and hence of enormous sentimental, as well as exotic value. Serkin himself had been presented with this dubious gift on a concert tour and passed it on to my animal-crazy parents, along with an infra-red bulb to keep the pair warm. I asked my mother how I was to have a bath. Just take them out, she said, and put them in a basin. I did not relish touching The Boys, they hissed and smelled awful, though they were fed on nothing but the best minced raw beef. I bathed in another of the tubs in our fortunately multi-bathroomed house. Katya, my mother's best friend, who shared that bathroom, muttered that she contemplated flushing The Boys down the toilet. She didn't of course, but they soon got too big and were passed on to a zoo. I hope they lived as happily as with my indulgent mother. The only creatures my mother did mind using her tub were the giant centipedes which occasionally crept up through the drain.*

I could not believe either they would give it back. They didn't, until a teacher intervened. I was crying pitifully, and the other children were made to apologize. They must have hated me the more. I was both a teacher's pet and a tattle-tale, two things anathema in an American school. But I wasn't American, I didn't know the rules. I didn't know children's rules anywhere. I had never been with children except for short times and mostly under watchful eyes, and never with so many. I had been nearly always with doting adults.

Psychoanalysts or not, my parents didn't seem to know the rules either, and were no help.

One or two fellow misfits made overtures to me. A girl with thick spectacles and mousy hair and a bad complexion, and a little boy with a hoarse voice who wished to come over and play with my train. I didn't really like him and was glad when he went home. Most of the time, I cowered at my desk and in corners of the playground, simply hoping I would not be seen.

The girls who teased me most were called Mary and Nina. Mary was big and ugly, Nina just big. They were both very Grosse Pointe, definitely from the right side of the city limits. They and others asked me if I liked Hitler. Confused and frightened, I said I didn't know him. I knew it was bad to draw swastikas, but no one had yet made clear to me the disgrace of my beloved Herr Sack. It was the wrong answer. At Hallowe'en, when one of the 'tricks' was soaping windows, someone decorated ours with swastikas. I remember the adults, upset and angry, wiping them off.

Those first two years of school were perhaps the worst of ten; but school was to be mostly misery.

I was outcast material on several counts. My age, my size, my accent, my poor performance at sports (my instinct if a ball comes towards me is to duck and run. It seems to me a sensible instinct but it does not endear you to your Team.)

Then, sissified warm dressing (American girls will all have bladder trouble, my mother used to say, because they don't wear their snowsuit pants to school) and being driven when everyone else goes on foot, bike or roller skates. And besides being a teacher's pet, I must, at six, have been rather a pain. Serious, earnest, awkward, with the febrile egotism of the very shy, a small head crammed with feelings of inferiority fed by school, and illusions of genius, fed by my mother.

School being misery, I developed defenses. The first and best was being ill. I never caught any children's diseases except for chicken pox. My anxious mother had us inoculated, and was very careful about crowds, chills, swimming pools and germs in general, especially in the polio season. But at that time, thank heaven, there were no flu shots. Since the slightest fever or sore throat made my mother keep me home in bed, I got every cold, flu and stomach bug available, and succeeded in missing a good part of the school year. I never faked, but by the time I reached high school, my body was so fine-tuned I managed a feverish cold just before a dreaded 'hag party' the whole class was supposed to attend, asking boys, if they knew any (I did not).

Then there was withdrawal. This is a talent that runs in my mother's family. I think it helped my uncle survive fifteen years as a prisoner in the USSR. You withdraw into your own world of memories and fantasies, or, as my mother did, you converse with the four-footed, who do not generally answer back. People who greet acquaintances they have passed a minute before, hum to themselves tunelessly, and interrupt you in the middle of a sentence to address the cat, or read the shopping list out loud, often have this gift. They can be profoundly irritating, but they sometimes stave off damage where others do not. However, withdrawal is a habit difficult to break. You may find yourself somewhere else when you really want to be where you are. You may find yourself chronically unable to live in the present. And needless to say, when faced with real violence, withdrawal is no use.

In my case, this was supplemented by something more active but equally schizoid, which I called play-reading. This meant; running around house or garden with an open book in your hands, telling yourself a story, as if you were reading aloud.

This story is of course about yourself. You do the things you cannot do in real life, or you enter, as hero, into actual books you have read. You ride the big black hunter no one will let you mount and win a ribbon going over six-foot fences. The most beautiful and popular girls you admire from a distance choose you as their best friend. You bloody the nose of the bigger girl/boy who has just beaten you up. You help Hector and Priam win the Trojan War.

I don't know if this activity worried my parents, or if they wrote a paper about it. They did sometimes use their children's quirks or fears as case material. My mother may have hoped it was just part of budding verbal genius. Besides, with a now full schedule of patients, she didn't have much time to observe me trotting around the dining room table, clutching my book like Hector's shield.

I wonder now if play-reading was unique. If not, whether there are play-readers who did it seated; for me the restless motion was an essential part. And I wonder if they sometimes still feel the world is too much, and long for their old stories, for the books with the dirty thumb-prints, the books that were their barrier to the world.

Play-reading too has serious dangers. Dreams couched as stories are doubly real and so an even more seductive escape. Adulthood, I decided years later, is ceasing to think of yourself in the third person. Sadly, even in the first person, adulthood turns out to me mostly another mirage.

After I grew out of play-reading, the only person who ever mentioned it was the wife of our butler Gibson, Mamie, who also worked for us for a time. "I remember Monika running around the garden, reading her book and reading her book," she would say when she came to visit. And shake her head, that way you do about people who are slightly nuts. I could only answer with embarrassed smiles.

Gibson and Mamie.

My parents soon had a part-time secretary, a chauffeur cum houseman cum butler, and extra laundry and cleaning help. There was always Enne who cooked and supervised, and either a second live-in person or someone who came several days a week.

These employees were sometimes black and sometimes white. When white, they were usually fellow immigrants. When black, they were often part of butler Gibson's family or entourage.

Gibson was of indeterminate age (he subsequently lived to a hundred), very bald, very black, tall and distinguished looking. My brother-in-law used to say of Gibson, who was still around when my sister was married, that Gibson had never heard of the Emancipation Proclamation. This was not quite true. Gibson was simply a perfect butler type, a syndrome independent of colour. He had once worked at the Country Club, where things were done in what he considered a proper manner, and he was frustrated in our household, which lacked the show and formality he obviously loved. On the very rare occasions when he could put on a white jacket and serve drinks and canapés Gibson was in his element. But even then, the guests were mostly psychiatrists and mostly from the wrong side of town. None of the great Grosse Pointe names, the doyens of automobile and chemical industries, entered our doors except, possibly, as patients. I think Gibson held us all in contempt. Me most of all because, even in high school, I never went out. Except with other wallflowers.

The only one who met his approval was my sister, who eventually did go out a great deal, with friends whose parents' names appeared in the society columns. "There's our social butterfly,' Gibson would say to me, somewhat nastily, following it with his perpetual small, meaningless laugh. This laugh was I suppose a tic left over from true Jim Crow days, the kind of laugh that made plantation owners claim their slaves were really happy because, look, they laugh and smile all the time.

As my mother knew nothing about housework or cooking, Enne ran the house. She referred to the black domestics as *"die Schwarzen,"* the blacks, then a term of opprobrium. Convinced they were lazy and prone to steal, she kept an eagle eye out and ordered them around in her broken English. "Gibson you go it now to the store." It was her general gruff manner and I think they took it in their stride. And of course with my parents she always prefaced her speeches, rough or otherwise, with the obligatory *"Herr Doktor"* and *"Frau Doktor."* The Austrians hold their titles sacrosanct, even today, and have them inscribed on their tombs.

My parents were duly appalled by the history of slavery and by segregation, and treated their black domestics with generosity, kid gloves, and oblivion. This oblivion became quite expensive when Enne was no longer there but on the whole did not work out badly, except for Ernest the Grosse Pointe Cat Burglar, a scholarly-looking man who worked for them briefly and then came back to rob the house.

Like all such households, ours had its etiquette. Enne ate with us, slept upstairs, and used our bathrooms. The daytime help ate in the kitchen and used the bathroom in the basement. At lunch, when all the staff was there, the swinging doors between dining room, breakfast room and kitchen were left open. When older and given to fits of adolescent longing for privacy, I complained about this. I did not want everything we said at lunch overheard. My parents said closing the doors would be looked on as colour prejudice. I said I did not see why as I also wanted them closed when the people in the kitchen were white. My parents were adamant. Sometimes, in irritation, I simply got up and closed the doors. I do not know if this created a racial incident.[5]

In Grosse Pointe I grew up in a time warp. Outside was the suburb of open front gardens, country clubs and yacht clubs, Junior League and Best's and 'open houses' and cocktail parties and bridge. The money that kept all this was made in Detroit and except for one school tour of a Ford assembly plant, I saw nothing of the workaday world. It might as well have been on the moon. This is the schizophrenia of suburbs. Mine was double. For inside our house was Austria, frozen in 1938 and itself harking back (as Austria still does) in much of its decor and sentiment to the still earlier, imperial Austria, the one that ended with the First World War.

My parents spent their spare time with music and books and later, horses. Until we had a live-in musician friend with music contacts, their socializing was mostly business and mostly grudging. My parents hated drunkenness and drinking, except for a glass or two of quality wine with a meal and a small brandy just before bed. Drinking was very big in Grosse Pointe. And "culture" in the Viennese sense was in short supply.[6]

The Austria inside. My parents had been much luckier than expected. They managed to have quite a lot of their possessions shipped to Grosse Pointe before the war, including some things from Gmunden. There were carpets and kilims from my grandfather's Bosnian military occupation

---

[5] *Many years later, when my father was in his eighties, a black family moved into our street. This could not have happened in my childhood. Grosse Pointe had a "point" system for real estate buyers. Black and Jews were not admitted. Several grand houses, however, were bought by families reputed to be Mafia.*

My father declared his intention of visiting the black family to bid them welcome. My sister and I, visiting at the time, pointed out that as he had never called on a single neighbour in over forty years, he might make the black family's lives harder by choosing them alone for his favors. Also that they themselves were probably much more anxious to fraternize with their normal, bigoted, right-wing, solid Grosse Pointe neighbours. And that he could hardly welcome them to a street where he had remained a stranger. My father saw the truth of this and did not go.

[6] *Though my mother, in her last months, was sedated by the last housekeeper with Black Russians, a drug which certainly made her happier than the cocktail of pills her doctor prescribed.*

days. There were antique cupboards of inlaid wood. And from his Vienna office, my father's behind-the-couch armchair. This had a wonderful secret box in its side, where he kept his pipe, pipe cleaners and tobacco. Like his hero, my father was partial to pipes and cigars.

There was also my father's embryo art collection. Though an apostate, he collected, all his life, chiefly religious art. There were a few Gothic carvings, a few paintings. The biggest statue, two feet high and ending at the hip, was a crudely-fashioned worm-eaten martyr, encased in curly flames to just below his navel. His hands were clasped in prayer and his face stretched in an ecstatic smile. I called him Ichthyosaurus after a dinosaur; it seemed somehow right. The flames were unobtrusive and for years I didn't register that this was a statue of a man burning alive.

Nor did I understand another of my father's treasures, an Egon Schiele drawing of a woman masturbating. This hung in our living room, where my father sometimes saw patients. As it showed only the back of a bent head and part of legs and arms, all at a curious angle, I didn't realize, until I was grown up and my father told me, that it was a human figure. My father said most of his patients didn't notice it either. Perhaps he considered it a kind of Rorschach test.

My father bought Schieles when Schiele was inexpensive and unknown. His greatest treasure then was one of Schiele's rare large oils, 'The Plum Tree'. I loved this painting, as I loved the big chair. And again, I didn't know, till years later, that the tree was a tree. But I always knew (as one knows about St Exupery's elephant in a boa constrictor, which ignorant adults think is a hat) that the box-like object in one corner was a coffin. 'The Plum Tree' (he had promised it to me, but forgotten) was later sold by my father, to buy a new, high quality bow for his violin.

I myself was always to be haunted by a bittersweet nostalgia for a world I had never known, that of the old ladies in the black rustling dresses. Nostalgia for a time kept by slow-ticking pendulum clocks, for music heard through shuttered windows in a formal garden, for sleigh rides on a frozen lake, hoofbeats on an unpaved road, avenues of chestnuts and lindens, fountains, candlelight... for somewhere beautiful and doomed and maybe never real at all in the way I imagined it.

Later came another regret just as intense, for the great opportunity missed at the century's turning. Could we not *then* have foreseen that we might exhaust the earth that keeps us? A nostalgia for all that lost space and green countryside, for that then still vast, untainted realm now so ravaged, with what brutality, with what amazing speed. But in my childhood what I felt was mostly the exile's nostalgia, which becomes in the end nostalgia for nostalgia itself, like the facing mirrors reflecting infinity. Exile is a land of its own. I was never to feel at home in America, until I found the Vermont wilderness, or until I moved to that part of New York that other New Yorkers called the Fourth Reich.

Meanwhile, my parents, having so little to distract them from work, started to earn more and more money.

Like many children who live in two worlds, I was somewhat two people. At school, the cringing, timid child with a thick German accent. At home, still a shadow of the child who refused to let policemen order her off the grass. I was loved and indulged and got almost everything I asked for. It never occurred to me, though, that I might use my parents' indulgence, rather than illness, to get out of school. I accepted without question, until adulthood, my parents' bourgeois ethic. Not to go to school was unthinkable. It did not even occur to me that alternatives might exist.

The bridge between two worlds is often love.

I fell in love, sort of, with Miss Martin and Miss Sylvester, the teachers of 2B and 3A. I suppose it was love born of despair. Miss M and Miss S were the one part of America I found distinctly kind; and they were permed, dressed up, made up, unlike my mother with her severe suits and 'twenties flapper crop. I was beginning to realize that in Grosse Pointe my parents were somewhat freakish, to be embarrassed by their presence; though the only school function I remember them coming to was a short play about the planets. I was Pluto, the smallest, and had to declaim that "I vass disscoverrd only rressently.'

This love was not displayed at school, where I sensed it could lead to still worse teasing. I think the teachers did paste gold stars on my forehead when I did well, as they did others, and sometimes cuddled me; maybe I just couldn't stop them.

At home I expressed my love freely. At night I bounced on my bed and chanted the teachers' names over and over again. Perhaps this mantra put me in a kind of ecstasy. It must have been a pain to hear, and may have worried my Freudian parents. Though not necessarily presaging the love that dares not tell its name, as teacher crushes were, in Europe, part of normal development, it may have seemed a bit obsessive, a bit extreme. And Anna Freud was in England, too far away to consult.

Soon, however, I discovered more interesting objects of passion.

Of all my parents' Viennese medical, musical, artistic circle, not one had emigrated to Detroit. (If they had, being Jewish, they would have lived on the other side of town.) My parents sometimes spent a few days in NY or Chicago to visit old friends. One trip to Chicago, I was along, and was taken to the Natural History Museum.

The only image I have from this milestone trip is a long long jawbone filled with enormous teeth. This hardly seems a fit object for love; there were surely giant skeletons and models to inspire my fantasies. *They* would come back and I would be their friend. I would ride them in triumph through trembling cities. On their backs, I would win the Trojan War. I would raise the just and put down the unjust. (I was always a highly moral child.) And I had always been on the side of dragons, even when I saw in Gmunden my great-aunt Lina's tapestry-like reproduction of Mantegna's St George. I had not wanted the dragon dead; I felt in my bones that the Georges are the true villains. Whenever armed human fought beast, I wanted the beast to win. And oh, the glory of that fantasy - tiny Monika, rider of dinosaurs.

I learned their names: Ichthyosaurus, Stegosaurus, Tyrannosaurus Rex. I bounced on my bed and chanted their names too, like an incantation to bring them back. I wanted desperately to believe in dinosaurs, more than I ever wanted to believe in God. As I had asked about my baby brother's death, I asked again and again if there might not be, somewhere, at least one dinosaur alive. The adults, scientific, told me no.

Besides teachers and dinosaurs, I fell in love with long blonde hair.

My own was blonde but cut short like my mother's, and oily and straight. I wanted the hair of the fairy tale girls, like the one with a lilting young voice on my American Disney-musical record, singing at her spinning wheel, dreaming of her prince. I didn't give a damn about the prince; regarding princes, I was definitely in the latency period. All I wanted was to *be* the girl I pictured with long, wavy, pale silvery blonde hair crowned by a network pearl fairy cap, as I'd seen on a child down the street.

The long blonde hair was all desirable things at once, a symbol of beauty and power, adulthood and youth. The hair of Amazons and bold young witches. Persephone, who comes back from the underworld. Rapunzel, who lets it down from the tower. The Sleeping Beauty, who wakes to eternal happiness. Helen of Troy, and Aphrodite rising from the sea. The hair of the Snow Queen, and the wild mermaid, and the virgin warriors who ride great horses into battle and win everything, cutting their armoured enemies down as neatly and bloodlessly as flowers. And the most popular girls in school, those who wield their hockey sticks like Joan of Arc her sword, who carry a stack of schoolbooks on a tartan-skirted hip with the ageless grace of an ancient Greek dancer etched on an amphora.

I remember at Trombley School an older girl I never dared speak to. She had exactly the hair I craved, pale silver-gold hair softly curling over a sweater of fuzzy cherry-coloured angora wool. I never found out her name, I probably saw her not more than four or five times. She sits somewhere in 5A or 5B or maybe even 6, somewhere in the back of my mind, along with the Amazons, Miranda the Mermaid, Sheena the Comics Queen of the Jungle, Helen of Troy. Had she spoken to me, I could only have stammered and turned scarlet as Aphrodite's apple; but only to see her profile put a moment of fairy magic into my miserable day. At that age, the keenest passions have nothing to do with sex. They centre on what you wish to *be*, and if you desire a word or a touch, it is for the gift it might convey, the starry dust of courage, confidence, beauty.

It was the beginning, in me, of Thomas Mann's Tonio Kröger syndrome, the artist's obsession with beautiful people, the outsider's with insiders, the observers with those who act. I have no real recollection of her face, but I know she was very pretty. And I remember the feeling. It was not like my embarrassed, embarrassing, faute-de-mieux crush on Misses S and M. The feeling was pure exalted obsession.

There were to be other girls who obsessed me. But not as much. And not at my next school, Gomper's. Because Gomper's was a collection of misfits like myself.

I sometimes dreaded going to bed as much as school.

It was fine to fall asleep while the house was still full of light and noise - but dreadful to wake in the dark, to be defenseless against the mysterious noises of the night, against the horrors that visited your mind.

As well as often ill, I became morbidly sensitive. Some children can watch horror movies and remain unmoved, though a large diet of such stuff surely has an effect. Some are inspired to imitate. Others have nightmares. I was the nightmare type. There were no horror videos yet, but in my parents' extensive library, which I explored, were Wilhelm Busch and Heinrich Kley.

Wilhelm Busch was supposedly a comic genius. To me his sadistic cartoons are one of those weathervane signals for the coming of the Third

Reich. Overweight pet dogs slaughtered by butchers, severed noses spouting blood, an exploded Frenchman with nothing left but his legs still standing in their boots. Heinrich Kley was worse. Two smiling men sawing another in half. (Do these things really happen, I wanted to know, *And why are they smiling?)* It is better not to see such pictures until you are old enough for some acceptance of what the world is like.

Kley also drew the *Hauskobold*, the House Goblin. Half-believing in fairies as I did, I had to half-believe in goblins. Kley's *Hauskobold* is like a giant fungus that starts under an armchair downstairs and grows and grows, a grotesque head on a giraffe's neck, up and up the stairs, till his giant arm can reach inside a bedroom, where it disappears.

After seeing these pictures, I couldn't sleep for nights. My parents gave me a night-light in the bathroom, and doors were left open so I could hear Enne snore. The simple expedient of keeping the blinds up, like many simple expedients, I was not to find until I myself was grown up.

Digression:
My Great-Aunts' Devotion to the Monarchy

My great-aunts were devout monarchists. The two surviving I saw again when I was adult told not only the story of standing in the rain for eight - or was it fourteen - hours to attend the Kaiser's funeral. They told another, even less exciting, but it shows how far devotion to monarchy can go. Or, for that matter, devotion to Madonna or Elvis Presley. Any devotion. My great-grandfather, whose genes in this respect I do not inherit, was the tallest General in the Austrian Army. He once had an audience with the Kaiser Franz Joseph. The Kaiser looked him up and down and said, *"Herr General, ich glaube ich habe Sie in Ischl letztes Jahr gesehen."* (I believe I saw you in Ischl last year.)

This mark of divine condescension, being remembered being seen, was enshrined as a family legend, the other story my aunts repeated in their senility. It may have shown more royal favor than appears, for the Emperor, ageing, himself became legendary for his forgetfulness. My father told a less reverent story. The Kaiser goes to open an art exhibition, stops in front of each painting, and murmurs, "It looks a little pale, but it will be better tomorrow." His entourage is puzzled until someone realizes he thinks this is the day he was to visit the children's hospital. My father did not tell this story in front of the aunts.

BATHROOMS, CASE HISTORIES AND SEX

The books, paintings, music my parents loved remained constant throughout their lives. At one stage, they might prefer Haydn to Mozart or Mozart to Haydn, or my father might even sell a Gothic carving to buy a sleek bronze Archipenko torso or a Picasso drawing. But it was always *Hohe Kultur.*

I remember only a few ancient items of the Popular - thick solid 78 records with a dog-cocking-his-head-to-the-trumpet-speaker label of *His Master's Voice*. There were two German songs, *Fräulein Pardon* and *Wenn Du einmal dein Herz verschenkst*. And three English; *You're the Cream in my Coffee, Marie,* and pioneer crooner Rudy Vallee's *Lost in a Fog.*

Already in my childhood, these records seemed ghostly and nostalgic, calling up a world of ballrooms, flappers, travel first class, the world of the faded labels of the great hotels, Sacher, Dolder, Baur au Lac, that covered the old trunks stacked in our Grosse Pointe boiler room, labels with stylized sailboats and mountains and grinning bellboys uniformed in red. The thin reedy tenor voices, voices like echoes of themselves, were echoes of the youth of my elders, which only becomes imaginable as you yourself grow up.

And as befitting that generation, my mother, for all her rebelliousness, had acquired the skills that were meant to keep busy a lady's hands.

During her analytic hours, she produced, over the years: A large hooked rug in two shades of blue, for the floor of my room. Countless knitted garments for my sister and myself. When I was in my twenties, and her hands were becoming arthritic, she turned to crochet, still making us waistcoats and cardigans. And in old age, when she did petit-point, she made us beautiful tapestry bags.

When I was five or six, she knitted me a birthday present, a dress of soft blue wool. The first time I wore the dress, I fell into the toilet. It was the downstairs toilet, the patients', which I didn't normally use. Anyway, there I was, sitting *in* the toilet, horrified, disgusted, ashamed, in my brand new dress.

The dress was washed, of course, but my day was ruined, and I don't think I wore the dress again. Like the fall down the garden steps, this is a vivid early memory. Happiness dashed by pain or humiliation, as by the cold, dirty water of the toilet bowl.

The patients' bathroom. It was always immaculate. It had a separate 'powder room' with a counter, a large mirror, an art deco ebony stool with a green and beige woven seat, a brush and comb that were never used, a Kleenex box and coloured powder puffs in a round celluloid container. Beyond that there was a smaller room with a toilet and sink and metal towel rail holding small pastel guest towels (I will always think of such towels as 'patient towels'), also immaculate and beautifully pressed. The patients' bathroom was the only room in our house that was solidly American.

The patients' bathroom also contained infinity. When you opened the toilet door, you had two facing mirrors. "Two mirrors that reflected endlessly reflection's end,' said a poem I have lost. Anyone who has stood between two mirrors will understand how a child arrives at the infinity concept.

I could stand between the two mirrors and lose myself.

More mundanely, the patients' bathroom, great for games out of patient hours, was also, a bit later, the scene of my only venture into perversion.[7] I once asked an older friend when we were playing mother and child, and I, the child, was due for a spanking, to wield the hairbrush, gently of course, on my bare bottom. This mild outbreak of anal-erotic masochism was probably inspired by the fact that physical punishment, anathema in my family but suffered by most of my peers, including the girl playing mother, must have seemed very exciting because my parents so disapproved. What your parents forbid themselves can be as seductive as what they forbid you. Especially if you are timid and small and cannot think of many forbidden things that you really want to do.

Also forbidden in our household was disturbing my parents' sacrosanct rest hour, the thirty or sixty minutes, in this case no Freudian fifty, they slept after their main meal at noon. My parents were always at home for

---

[7] *One may expect more from a Freudian memoir but I am trying to tell only the truth.*

lunch, and kept to their Viennese schedules all their working lives. To compensate for the afternoon break, later extended till four or five on Tuesdays and Thursdays for horse-back riding, they saw some patients on week-ends, and in evenings up to half past ten.

In our early Grosse Pointe days, my father worked mostly at the office in Detroit. My mother saw some patients there, but quite a few at home, generally children. The world of the patients, too, was forbidden and secret, though you were occasionally allowed to open the door for them. And there was a little fraternization with a select one or two; later there was to be more.

My mother had an interesting array of patient toys. The best was what I called the *Kleine Welt* (Little World) - miniature wooden animals, persons, houses, gates, trees, benches, fences, vehicles, in bright Bauhaus colours. You could assemble farms, zoos or villages, whatever you chose. These Austrian toys were sold in a jumble in little net bags, and part of their delight was the unexpected. In such a bag you might find, among the upright people, a single seated figure with a tiny bench to fit, or a giraffe in the middle of a flock of sheep. And when you were ill you could raise your knees under the blankets and make mountains and valleys for your world, like the boy in Stevenson's poem *The Land of Counterpane.*

The Little World, long superseded by Lego, Video Games, Ninja Turtles, etc. is still to my mind the most delightful toy ever invented. To my mother it was the perfect therapeutic tool. Obviously, you cannot put children on the analytic couch, but by letting them set up *their* Little Worlds and asking leading questions, you can get all sorts of information.

I had a Little World of my own but the patients' set was better and I was envious. It seemed to me so complete a set was wasted on problem children and should be kept in the family. Perhaps it was my resentment which made me start trying to decipher the sounds that came up through our heating system from the analytic hours below (I never succeeded) and search through the cupboard in my mother's bedroom where, I discovered, she kept her typed case histories, and little stories the child patients dictated. Typing their stories seemed to me quite natural, as my mother also typed mine.

One patient, a large dark-haired girl reputedly afflicted with a lightning phobia, broke the rules the other way. She escaped into our premises, dragging the cat Peter to my mother's bathroom where the scales were. Peter by then was fat as a Byzantine eunuch and she was evidently seized by a compulsion to weigh him. My mother got the situation back under control and there was no more weighing. But I, in my sneaky research, did find material on someone I met.

Fraternization, for me, began with what my mother considered a highly suitable little girl to have her lonely eldest meet. My sister, unlike me, made friends on her own.

This girl came from a rich suburb on the other side of town, then one of Detroit's two social poles. She was older, and had all that I envied; glossy thick hair, athletic prowess, that snub-nosed, peppermint-smelling, brown-legged American high society prettiness as impressive to me as absolute beauty. She was also really nice; the casual noblesse oblige of people at the top.

Tongue-tied and trembling with shyness, I went to a costume party at her family mansion in Bloomfield Hills - now the district of Detroit's Jewish rich, then strictly WASP. I was dressed in a child's kimono a Japanese patient had given my father back in Vienna. I still have the kimono, never worn again. I don't remember the party, but I do remember the excitement of going through my mother's case history cupboard and finding the wonderful girl's name.

I hadn't known that she was a patient, and I read the few pages with feverish eagerness. There was something about bed-wetting and fear of storms; and an awkward story about a pony. My poems and stories, I thought, were better and more grown-up. The revelations were meager and disappointing, but they gave me a small secret feeling of triumph - and made me even more shy when I saw the girl again. Which was not often; there were no more parties in Bloomfield Hills. In this case, as others, my mother's attempts to propel me into American social life were doomed to fail.

This being a Freudian memoir, I must mention sex.

At some point in my early American years my mother handed me an enormous medical book, almost too big for me to hold. Perhaps I had asked some leading question. Or my mother just felt it was the right time, going by some calendar of hers or Anna Freud's.

The book was opened to two large as life pictures of the human reproductive organs, male and female, with every duct, vein, gland etc, exposed in glorious technicolour. My mother must have explained what functions these organs were supposed to perform. I was probably too horrified to listen. I was afraid of doctors. I didn't want to look at medical books. I didn't want to know what was inside grown-ups. Nor in me. I still don't. Any interest I might ever have had in human biology was squashed by that superbly mistimed moment. I don't think, however, that it gave me nightmares. Nor, fortunately for my mother - for that would have been a true Freudian defeat - did it affect a later interest in sex. Anyway, my mother had done what she thought her duty; and I cannot recollect, for the next ten years, asking for anatomical information again.

THE GOMPER SOLUTION: MY MOTHER FOUNDS A SCHOOL

With the dinosaurs, the illnesses, the bogey-man fears, my parents must have concluded that something was wrong - and not just the masochistic (or was it anal-retentive?) character formation (probably presumed the fault of my nannies) that Anna Freud had commented on in Vienna, after my mother's reports.

It was dawning on everyone that I was very unhappy at school.

My mother devised a solution. There being no schools in Detroit she thought suitable for a sensitive plant like me, no Steiner or Montessori, my mother, typically, founded one herself.

It happened like this. My mother heard of a German couple, the Wunders, new refugees like us, who had run a celebrated progressive school in Bavaria and were now setting up a similar school and summer camp in Vermont - or they heard of her. My mother became the camp's resident psychologist. She recommended the camp to the parents of her young patients, and some patients went there and continued treatment in their holidays. This gave us a very long summer vacation in Vermont. With mountains, and riding, and a whole new set of fellow refugees, some quite famous, who were to be my parents' chosen circle from then on.

The Wunders' daughter and son-in-law, the Gompers, who were also teachers, were urged by my mother to start a small school in Detroit, which I believe she helped to fund. The major enterprise was a nursery school run by Mrs Gomper and named after my mother. Appended to it was an initially tiny upper school, run by her husband.

Mr Gomper's school began with three pupils. My sister, myself, and a patient of my mother's, Dickie, a handsome little Grosse Pointe boy, one of the secret phobics or bed-wetters whose details I tried to ferret out of the cupboard case-histories. There was certainly nothing visibly wrong with him. He was bright, gentle and polite, and I think remained so throughout the vicissitudes which followed.

The school was in a private house, on an unfashionable street near the heart of downtown Detroit. Downstairs was the kitchen, and the nursery school. Upstairs were the Gomper living quarters, one room of which, in daytime, housed the upper school. Our playground was the yard, which backed onto an alley. When it expanded a little the school moved, to a similar house but with a little more room for the staff.

In this area, houses were much closer together than on our street. Instead of screened porches at the side, they had large open ones in front, with squat rectangular pillars. The houses seemed lost behind their cumbersome porches. These were streets where families would spend a lot of the hot humid summer fanning themselves on the porch swing, drinking beer or coke, while the kids played baseball in the street or turned the hose on each other in the yard. They were not built for those who would be sailing from the Yacht Club or riding in Vermont. Curiously, that drab and ugly street has survived the fires and mayhem of post-war downtown Detroit and become an outdoor museum, a Detroit heritage landmark. I went to visit it not long ago with a fellow ex-pupil and was unable to recognize a thing. It looked small, artificial and vulnerable in the surrounding inner city despair. A strip of green ran down the street's middle; this was surely new. I remember a yard of packed dirt, only redeemable by snow, and an alley with garbage pails, somehow inviting and mysterious because our neighbourhood had no alleys and something may have reminded me of European lanes,

I was, of course, too timid to explore that alley far, And it was nice, every day, after a long slow journey, to get home to lawns and luxury and big trees. I became aware how differently the rest of the city lived. I still did not realize that we were rich. [8]

At first Dickie, Verena and I were driven to school by Gibson. The drive took an hour. On the way home, Gibson indulged himself in his favorite soap opera, *The Light of the World, the Day to Day Story of the Bible,* brought to you by Pilsbury Flour. The book then dramatized was the story of Ruth. The dialogue was much like other soap dialogue, with a lot of breathless, tearful exclamation (Oh Naomi! Oh Ruth! Etc.) but I listened with interest. The story was dramatic, and Gibson seemed so moved by it. Anyhow, I was soon to enter my religious phase.

---

[8] *In a later conversation with my father, he indignantly denied this. He said rich people are ones who do not have to work for their money.*

Very soon, the school acquired its own car and driver, and we were joined by a few nursery school children. Later, some of the rough older ones were also squashed in, and near the end of the trip you had to sit on a lap or be sat on, and these rides became another ordeal of humiliation and fear. But at the beginning it was fine.

Fine, that is, except for Adi.

Adi was the first school driver, a fellow refugee, a young man with black hair and very white hands and face. From the first, I felt Adi was creepy. Our relationship soon blossomed into open hostility. While shy with American children and awed by glamour or beauty, with nondescript adults of my own background I could still be impudent and stubborn, as I'd been in Vienna under my household's protective wings. And Adi teased. Adi was a bit sadistic. Hearing I was to be immunized against smallpox, he gleefully told me this involved an incision with a knife.

I must have gone in hysterics to my parents or Enne and been reassured. And in fact the smallpox vaccination was not nearly as bad as a DPT shot. Perhaps in my rage at Adi for scaring me so I was especially rude; and one day Adi announced that if I went on being rude he was going to put me out of the car and make me take the bus home.

I had never been on a bus in my life. I had never walked alone for more than a block or two. I didn't think he meant it, until he suddenly stopped the car at the next bus stop, bundled me out and pressed a nickel into my hand. And drove off.

I waited, shaking, got on the bus, dropped my nickel into the box and sat down, looking through a blur of tears at the strange old black and white faces around me, wondering if I would ever get home, if Adi was not cruel enough to have left me to the wrong bus. Being very small and myopic, I was also in a panic about missing my stop. But it was the right bus, and I didn't. I got out, still shaking, and walked down the block to home. It hadn't been so bad after all. It is a sign of the times that now even Adi would probably not leave a green terrified eight-year-old alone on Detroit's Jefferson Avenue.

Shortly after that Adi vanished, perhaps at the request of my mother. And that, until I was fourteen, was my first and last experience of public transport in Detroit.

Otherwise, in those first months at Gomper's, I had no fears. The work was easy, the atmosphere cosy and cheerful. But it didn't feel like going to school. Being a Gomper pupil made me even more special, more odd.

I wanted by now not to be so special, to belong to America, and I felt, in some way, I had already failed.

America then was the Great Melting Pot. There was huge pressure to belong truly, to Americanize, to love your new country heart and soul. I longed to be more American. It may have begun with the daily Pledge of Allegiance to the Flag at Trombley School. My family were not church-goers, grace-sayers, or otherwise given to ritual except for Christmas trees and Easter eggs. The Pledge impressed me. It was my first solemnity of the kind; and the teachers I had crushes on obviously paid it enormous respect.

I began to steep myself in American pop culture; songs, comics, movies (the few not too upsetting for my delicate nerves), children's magazines, movie magazines (depicting the Stars as full of homey virtue), slang and clothes. None of it worked. My accent lessened but the All-American image eluded me.

My parents bore this with patience. They let me have as many comics and almost as much radio as I wished. They were curiously oblivious to what I read or heard, as long as it did not set off a bout of neurotic fears. In those days of censorship, there was anyhow not much drastic material around. My parents were not the sort who carefully chose hand-crafted toys, literary classics and educational games. They had the classics and I found my way to them, but otherwise they simply got me what I asked for or what anyone they approved of suggested for me. I grew up in, and out of, this cultural hodge-podge without much harm.

My parents themselves remained immune to American fads and social habits. Unconsciously, however, they adopted bit by bit American wastefulness, American greed. So by now has all the rest of the world that can afford it. With a whole new continent to despoil, American greed, anyhow, was never more than basic human greed, writ large.

And like me, my parents began to feel at home in places where they didn't live; New York and Vermont.

The pull of Vermont for European refugees is now part of its history. Rudolf Serkin, Adolf Busch, Karl Zuckmayer, the Trapps, later Solzhenitsyn, were some of the famous who came under the spell of the rounded, wooded hills, the blue lakes, the stone-walled pastures, the Colonial towns with marble sidewalks, the covered bridges, the streams of pure sweet water. Vermont then - before skiing became big in the American East, before hotels filled up on 'Foliage Weekends,' before the new parkway made Vermont an easy weekend drive from NYC - was, to European eyes, largely almost virgin wilderness. And yet the old cemeteries, the sober Georgian houses, the old English names, gave a tang of history to the mountain air. Vermont has ghosts. And its rough green slopes are as close as New England will get you to the Alps.

The most spellbound was myself. What is left of that first camp summer or two is mainly a haze of happiness. As my father loved Salzburg, I loved Vermont immediately and forever after.

The Wunder Camp was not, like many summer camps, a cluster of rustic lodges, but an old mansion in tended grounds. My mother, sister and I had our own little flat in it. But I didn't stay under my mother's wing. I had no major problems with the other children. They were mixed in background and age, and many were refugees too. So were most of the staff, and their eccentricities and even stronger accents made my mother and me seem quite normal.

In keeping with a disastrous tendency that has dogged me through life - when I fall in love with a place I often fall for someone in it, as if the setting needs a figure, however unsuitable, to be complete - I switched my adoration from the Trombley teachers to Marlene Gomper, daughter of the camp directors and wife of Franz, who was to run my school.

It wasn't really Marlene, it was her role - Titania in *Midsummer Night's Dream,* the camp's summer play. Marlene in an ivory satin dress (her wedding dress) with a wreath of flowers in her curly brown hair, a Queen of Fairies in that sylvan setting. And I, an attendant fairy in white net, with my own daisy crown - how could I not fall in love? But as often with such passions, I disgraced myself. I got a nosebleed just before our entrance and dripped blood on Titania's ivory satin. The dress was rapidly sponged, and the entrance was almost on cue. My sense of disgrace remained, and the production became a family legend - not for my nosebleed, but for Franz Gomper as Oberon, declaiming in an accent worthy of me in A2, "Brrring me zat flower." The magic, however, stayed as well; forest and fairies and Shakespeare. We had a home movie to make it immortal.

My passion for the mountains grew, while that for Marlene rapidly waned. It wasn't just my ignominy. Marlene became pregnant and less attractive. Worse still, faced with the more delinquent charges of camp and then her nursery school, she manifested a saintly patience that seemed to me downright perverse. My image of Marlene, superimposed on the satin Titania, is a harassed woman with mussed clothes and tangled hair clutching a screaming brat who is trying to kick her in the stomach. It was not an image to keep love alive. And soon after that, following American custom at the time, where crushes on the same sex were never mentioned and seemed not to exist, I developed crushes on men.

My male crushes were an extension of my passion for horses; they began with riding teachers. Horses by then had ousted dinosaurs, and I had loved horses since the cart-horse of Vienna, the bronze statue of Prince Eugene, and my toy riding horse on wheels.

The first riding teacher at camp, however, inspired more fear than love. German Thomas's method was to start you off on a pony, bareback and helpless; no saddle, no reins. You just had to learn to sit and stay on. The pony was so fat my little legs could hardly grip; but when we took a path through the woods, Thomas leading Dimples by the slung-forward reins, he assured me, in the confident manner of grown-ups, that he was in full control. No sooner had he said this than the pony bolted, tearing the reins out of his hands, and threw me. I wasn't much hurt; only my faith in adults was shaken a bit more. From then on, we did have bridles and saddles, and it didn't take me long to get my nerve back. I was a natural, if never daring, rider, and in the horsey decade that followed I was not thrown again.

The next horseman I met was a freckled redhead named Leonard, at the riding stable on Belle Isle. I don't think Leonard was a teacher, more just a stable hand. Never mind; I wasn't class conscious. Leonard was American and nice, and though I didn't feel the ardour I had felt for Marlene, I did ask Leonard to marry me when I grew up. I'm not sure what he answered, but I think he said it was a bit early to decide.

Leonard's function on our outings was to ride beside my tiny sister, leading her horse. Verena rode from age three or four, strapped into a Western saddle. This is a dangerous way for children to learn, but my mother wanted us all together on horseback, and in the way of anxious mothers was not always logical about her anxieties.

The horse my sister rode was anyhow incapable of bolting. She was a tall, leggy bay mare with a clipped mane and scrawny tail, who might once have been a good hunter or even a racehorse but had come down in old age to a stable hack. She was so ancient her lower lip wobbled pathetically and so overworked and dulled that the greenest rider could safely take her out. Carrying my featherweight sister, at a walk or gentle trot, must have been the nearest she got to a holiday.

The stable on Belle Isle was called a riding academy and lessons were available, but anyone could hire a horse and ride alone. I felt pity for

Margaret, who was my own first Belle Isle ride as well, because she looked so old and helpless and sad. But though I had read *Black Beauty*, one of my favorites, I did not realize, until I saw her out with a rough rider, what Margaret must have suffered. She would come back and stand patiently in her tie stall - box stalls were luxuries, for the boarders - tacked up for the next customer, apathetic and resigned, sometimes lifting one leg to rest it, her pendulous lip trembling, her eyes dim. To this pass they come, the beautiful proud steeds of your dreams, this and then the knacker's. I loved riding; but now, when I think of Margaret, I wonder if it is not another human self-indulgence imposed far too thoughtlessly on another kind.

Belle Isle is an island in the Detroit River, connected to Detroit by bridge. In my childhood, it was a park with woods and walks (did people walk?) and bridle trails, a marina and Boat Club (no blacks, no Jews, etc.) with a big swimming pool. It also had playgrounds and picnic grounds, and Shetland pony rides, and wandering free in the woods, brown and albino deer. The white deer were a Belle Isle speciality. In fact they were mostly gray with city dirt; the big tyre factory was just across the river, and on the drive along Jefferson you held your nose for several blocks. The deer wandered tamely and boringly among the trees.

Belle Isle was best in the fall, when coloured leaves drifted along the canals (I wrote an affected poem about this, which was printed in *The Grosse Pointe News*) and you might sometimes see a possum in a tree or a muskrat darting into its canal-bank hole. Belle Isle was Detroit's family park, but I have not met anyone who has been there in years, and it made international news a few years ago when a British tourist was murdered at a Belle Isle fountain. For me, once I'd seen Vermont, Belle Isle even then was shabby and sad.

In those early days we also sometimes walked for an hour, but not on Belle Isle. At the edge of Grosse Pointe, where now there is endless suburban and commercial sprawl, were accessible woods with paths. They too did nothing for me. All the country around Detroit was wrong, wrong and dull, because it was flat.

My contempt for flatlands was bolstered by literature. With the summer in Vermont came another revelation; I read *Heidi*. My identification was instant and complete. I knew what was wrong with me. It wasn't only school (soon a trial again), and loneliness, and whatever traumas had been caused by our emigration. It was lack of mountains. Life in the lowlands made me, like Heidi, sicken and pine away.

My parents were not impressed. They loved Vermont too. But they would not move from Detroit. Detroit, it was explained to me later, was where you made the money to spend summer in Vermont.

It was usually Enne and not *"die Schwarzen"* who opened the door for patients. My father would ask her how they were. She never failed, he said, to spot the bad cases. I sometimes opened the door myself when older, for those who interested me.

One of the interesting ones, either patient or trainee, who turned up in my early school years was a thin handsome young man in a purple suit. My sister and I were out on our tricycles, and saw him come up the walk. We had no idea then, and perhaps neither did he, that he was to become my teacher and later my parents' secretary; but what I felt at that first sight was so striking I never forgot it. Something about him, his face, his thinness, made me think of the gory Christ crucified statues I had seen as a very small child, on the Calvary hills of the Ticino. Afterwards, when I knew him, much of that aura of sacrifice and doom was effaced - but never its memory. Had I been a Sybil, I would have urged WR to turn and run. But whatever happened, I think his story might well have ended as it did.

I think of WR in connection with Belle Isle because it was from the Belle Isle bridge that he jumped to his death some twenty years later.

My English reading actually began not with Heidi but with the rather uninspired adventures of two sets of twins, the *Bobbsey Twins*. I read the whole series, and for a while spent my whole dollar-a-week allowance on buying two at fifty cents each. I read them because other children did, and they were so American.

I went on to classics; Beatrix Potter, A.A. Milne, Stevenson, Kipling, Lewis Carroll. And Grimm and Andersen, and any fairy tales with my still beloved dragons. I read *Tito die Wölfin* in German, and *Bambi* in English. These two books made me anti-hunting for life, though now I think hunting for food a virtue compared to farming animals as if they were cauliflowers.

My library was especially strong in horses and dogs. I read *Lassie Come Home* and the Albert Payson Terhune collie books, and all the books by C.W. Anderson, the superb painter of horses, books with titles like *High Courage* and *Deep Through the Heart*. He wrote short biographies of the famous racers, and also fiction, with heroines such as Patsy, who had a devoted black groom, Holly, and a jumper, Bobcat, being schooled for a steeplechase. Holly was very deferential and always called her Miss Patsy, but gave the best advice on how to handle her huge wild steed. "I whipped him once - Oh Lordy!" I remember Patsy saying to the soothing groom after an especially trying bout with Bobcat, who did not take kindly to being whipped. And the groom's sage remonstrances, "Whoa there, Miss Patsy - never trot downhill 'less you're lookin' for a fall," etc. were warnings I took forever to heart. Bobcat, needless to say, calmed down and won his big race.

My favorite American-West author was Dr Thomas C. Hinkle, who did a whole series of horse books rather on the lines of *Black Beauty*, with many distressing adventures but happiness in the end. Children do not want unhappy endings. I read one German dog book with a sad end, the story of a puppy named Herr Brown who sickens and dies, a sort of canine *Death of Ivan Ilyich*. It put me in a deep depression for days.

My reading was voracious, and I made no distinction between Stevenson and Milne, Kipling and Dr Thomas C. Hinkle. I was moved and enchanted by them all.

There were also comics, of course, and soon movie magazines, and I began to look at *Life* and later *The New Yorker*. One 'educational' comic my mother got me on someone's recommendation was *True Comics*, about heroic figures in politics, sports, science and war. "Truth is stranger and a thousand times more thrilling than fiction" was its motto. I dutifully read this boring comic, and believed the *True*. For decades after I had trouble getting the idiotically simplified, whitewashed figures of *True Comics* out of my head. I would have been better left with Sheena, Queen of the Jungle, Superman and Brenda Starr.

With equal inattention, when we began to own dogs my mother subscribed me to *Dog World*. This was actually a magazine for breeders, but I was unaware of it. Compulsive and conscientious, I leafed every month through endless pages of kennel ads, worm medicine ads, show schedules, suggestions for training and feeding, de-fleaing and improving the coat. I have forgotten my American history dates and my Latin conjugations but I could still identify a Mexican hairless, a Skye Terrier, a Russian Wolfhound and a Papillon.

Our own first dog, nothing so exotic, was a Springer Spaniel puppy. He was not with us for long. He escaped, followed our laundress up to Jefferson Avenue, and was at once killed by a car. Before my mourning was over - my parents believed in rapid replacement - came another Springer puppy. This one proved impossible to housebreak and had to be sent back.

I was then allowed to choose a Cocker puppy from a litter at someone's house. I chose a black female, and named her Ticki, perhaps after Viennese Tickitainya, the only baby doll I ever played with. Though she was not very bright and incessant retrieving of balls or stones her only accomplishment, we all doted on Ticki, a sweet-tempered, jovial little dog, and she was spoiled and pampered and medicated like another child. She was allowed on beds, given lots of toys, shots and pills, and veal for her delicate stomach, even during the war. I loved Ticki, but she wasn't really *my* dog. What I wanted, like my mother, like Patsy with her Bobcat, was something big and fierce, and I was to get it in spades.

The reason or excuse for a big dog was Ernest the cat burglar.

Ernest was a butler-chauffeur who left us after some altercation, and was followed by another short-lived chauffeur who said to Enne before he quit, "This is a crazy house." Most employees stayed with the crazy house for years.

Soon after Ernest's departure, on one of my parents' rare nights out, he broke in through a living room window and made off with the strongbox he knew was in my father's desk. My sister slept through it all. Ticki barked dutifully from the stairs, and woke Enne and me. We went bravely down, and Enne in her broken English called the police. The police came and shone flashlights around, and my parents came home, and everyone talked a lot, and that was the end of the matter.

The strongbox held mostly bonds and Ernest didn't profit much. But he went on to more daring exploits, climbing through upstairs windows, sneaking into full houses and taking wallets from trousers hanging on chairs, without waking the sleepers in their beds. Having served them once, he knew his victims had probably drunk enough to stay asleep. He continued to work as a domestic and used his employers' cars to do his jobs on his nights off. I somewhat admire Ernest. He was never known to hurt anyone and he was daring, skilful and neat - a very old-fashioned sort of crook, or maybe just lucky. When he became unlucky, choosing a house next door to a cop's, the cop caught him and he did attack the cop and was shot. He spent some time in hospital and then went to prison, admitting many burglaries, including ours. At least, that is the Cat Burglar story. It may also be that Ernest just agreed to be the peg for a number of unsolved crimes.

After the burglary, though I was calm enough at the time, my fears of the dark multiplied. My parents got bars for the downstairs windows, and phosphorescent stars for my walls. Burglaries were still rare then and almost no one thought of alarms, lawn spotlights, etc., all the things that are standard Grosse Pointe equipment now. I was not reassured by the bars and stars. The burglary remained unsolved, as Ernest wasn't caught till years later, and I was afraid the burglar might come back. Illogically, I was most afraid he might lurk in the attic, which could be reached through a trap-door in my walk-in closet. The large closets of American houses feed bogey-man fears, as do the basements, with their big boilers, laundry chutes, cedar closets, and appliances behind which a body might be concealed. Wonderful for hide and seek. Wonderful for terror. Adults are not immune. A later housekeeper swore our basement was haunted.

I took to locking my closet door at night, a habit I kept almost till I left home. And my sleep was still more disturbed. There *was*, after all, something to fear in the dark. I remember terrible nights of waking in the silent house, darkness pressing on my chest like a weight, ashamed to call out, afraid to move, listening breathlessly for the sound of a door softly opening, a step on the stairs.

Until my parents bought me the dog I named Wolf - of whom more later.

Gomper's, which was later to specialize in 'gifted' children, was in my time open to both gifted and under-gifted, those with what we now call learning disabilities. Also, to my eventual grief, those with behaviour problems. The nursery school, it seemed to me, was almost exclusively for behaviour problems. But at the beginning we had little contact with the nursery school. There was one dreadful moment when a hefty three-year-old brandishing a big wooden mallet burst into our classroom and advanced towards us with murder in his eyes. A harassed teacher rushed in after, scooped him up and carried him off. To my immense relief, he didn't escape upstairs again.

Soon, the upper school acquired pupil number four. She was a large overweight fourteen-year-old with lank brown hair and thick glasses. I discovered later, probably from my mother's cupboard, that her IQ test (Gomper's liked IQ tests) gave her, at that stage, a mental age of six. It was poor Shereen's misfortune to enter the school just when I was in my Jesus phase.

The Jesus phase, odd in our deeply irreligious household, began innocently enough with my reading Hendrick Willem van Loon's *Stories from the Bible*, another educational book someone suggested to my mother. For no clear reason I suddenly switched from wanting to be an Amazon fighting for the Trojans to wanting to be a disciple of Jesus Christ.

I put myself to sleep - or kept myself awake - with ardent fantasies of going round the world at Jesus's side, preaching and washing feet (or having my own washed? It is hard to remember but I think washing feet came into it somewhere.) My Jesus dressed in long brown robes and was young and handsome, with rich shiny shoulder-length hair. He smelled of incense and radiated warmth and light. Walking beside him, holding his hand, I was ready for any danger and adventure; but the actual fantasy never got much beyond the great moment when Jesus told me I was Chosen. I didn't think of the crucifixion. I would try to prevent it, as I would have reversed the defeat of Troy. Or maybe my Jesus was already resurrected, the Messiah returned. I who always wanted to resurrect the victims of myth or history had at last found one whose resurrection was generally agreed.

Looking back, I see these fantasies, with their emphasis on touch and physical warmth, had a hidden sexual charge, latency period notwithstanding. However, there was never any connection between my Jesus and the young man in the purple suit, who also came into my fantasies, later, and who had briefly reminded me of the pale dead Christ of the Ticino Calvaries. My Jesus was hale and hearty and eternally alive.

My parents were a bit alarmed. My father, the devout Freudian - though Gothic remained what he loved best in architecture and art - looked on orthodox religious faith in an educated person as a failure of intelligence and nerve, as neurosis and regression. This was not only Freud but revulsion from the childhood Catholicism of his own schooling. He told me once that the priest who taught him Catechism declared that when a chicken lifted its head after a sip of water, it was gazing piously up to thank the Almighty. As for my mother, she probably regarded God as something for the kitchen staff. Believing in free expression, my parents could not very well deny me my Jesus. But they were a little disparaging.

While they worried, I went on dreaming and praying. I burned to express my new-found zeal. Dickie and Verena were too young to preach to. I decided to try Shereen.

Shereen was Orthodox Jewish. My persistent questions about her faith and urging that she believe in Jesus brought anguished refusals and finally tears. I look back on this episode with shame, wondering if I was inspired only by Jesus, or also that there was someone twice my size whom even I could browbeat, in a supposed good cause. At any rate, Shereen complained, or someone overheard, and Mr Gomper explained to me, sternly for once, that Shereen had her own faith and I was to leave her alone.

I don't know if this dulled my religious ardour; but to my parent's relief the Jesus crush, like most childish crushes, ended soon after, as suddenly as it began. It has left little trace, just the image of the chestnut-haired holy man, the brightness of his halo, the warmth of his handclasp and his smile. He was always quite distinct from God, whom I prayed to when the Springer was run over and prayed to again later, in desperation, when the Cocker was dying, and who neither helped or said a word. When God did not save the Cocker, it was the end of what remained of my scanty faith.[9]

The connection with Wunders and Gompers had made many changes in our lives.

At the end of our first summer at the camp, its piano teacher, a young German refugee, came back to Grosse Pointe with us for a visit. The Wunders had not even paid her, and she lost her New York apartment. The planned visit of two weeks turned into twelve years.

---

[9] *When my father, at ninety, was paralyzed by a stroke and lay bedridden for two years before he died, he had twinges of reversion to that primitive Catholicism. What had he done that God was punishing him so, etc. Alarmed in my turn - my father's scorn for religion had been such an article of his Freudian faith - I told him that God was surely not in it and it made much more sense to imagine the ghost of my mother was seeking revenge for his infidelities. He saw the logic of this and was calmed.*

Later, Barbara, the companion of his last years, brought around a nephew who was a Jesuit priest. He spent half an hour alone with my father, while I hovered outside, fearing a deathbed conversion which would be an ignominious end to everything my father had believed and lived by. When the priest emerged, he announced in oily tones that my father wished to take communion. The priest then drove frantically around Grosse Pointe from church to church to find holy wine and host. When the ceremony was finally accomplished, the Jesuit left, fortunately to catch a plane back out West. I could not resist asking my father what Freud would say, and why, after preaching atheism to me all his life, he had taken communion. My father sighed. "It made the priest so happy," he said. Which is certainly more than I could have said about poor Shereen.

Katya was a neat, attractive, very small person, with tiny hands she had once been told would never reach an octave. They did. Unlike my careless mother, she was always well-dressed, however poor, had well-coiffed hair, wore fashionable shoes, and never appeared without her makeup on. She had pure silk lingerie and nightgowns of silk and crêpe de chine; some of these glorious things were passed on to me. Katya brought an aura of that sophisticated femininity my mother so lacked.

And with Katya, another past, memories of other distant cities, Paris and Berlin, came into our Viennese oasis. Katya had lost far more than my parents had. In Germany, she had been on the threshold of a great career, a star pupil of the renowned Edwin Fischer; she had toured as soloist with Fisher's orchestra. All this had ended with the Nazis. After her flight and a hand-to-mouth existence in Paris - her mother and brother escaped to England - Katya had got an American visa and tried to start again in New York. Her career never took off in the U.S. A hatred for writing letters, which made keeping up contacts difficult, and a predilection for Bach, Mozart and Schubert and not the big show pieces then loved by American audiences, were possible reasons. But I have wondered ever since if my parents' hospitality and devotion were not fatal to Katya's ambitions. By the time she left Detroit, it was too late, and she was already plagued by the back trouble that soon confined her to teaching. In this at least, at the two universities where she taught, she gained some of the acclaim she deserved.

Katya's room in our house had only a few personal objects, all of them evocative, mysterious, charged, like objects at a shrine. I would not have dared to touch anything in Katya's room. There was a tiny toy koala bear, a photograph of Edwin Fischer, two photos of handsome young men, two photos of very beautiful women. One was the actress Eleonora Mendelssohn, a descendant of the composer, the other a Czech actress who was, I believe, to die in a concentration camp. They had been Katya's best friends. She never talked about the men. I heard later that one had become a Nazi but never found out if this was true and never dared ask what role these men played in Katya's life. Katya was a very private person. Her photos and her koala, her perfumes and lipsticks and powders and pomades, her silk lingerie, were to me relics of a mysterious, romantic Bohemian past, even more divorced than my parents' past from the Middle Western world outside.

There was also a photo of Katya's father, a fat jovial man who had owned a factory in Germany. He died, mercifully, before the Nazis took over. Katya's father was dear to me forever because of a story she told. He had gone stag-hunting with business colleagues, much against his inclination, and when a stag appeared as the hunters lurked in their hide, he deliberately farted so loudly the animal took fright and fled.

Katya had non-musical talents too. She was very funny, a superb mimic who would do Wunders, Gompers and other characters to perfection. She could also wiggle one buttock at a time. She was often depressed and touchy, but these gifts endeared her to my sister and me. Nothing, however, endeared her to Enne, who saw Katya as an interloper and a drain on my parents' generosity and time.

My parents also befriended Katya's cousin Karl in New Jersey and his sister Meta in New York, and through Meta and Katya met lions of the pre-Nazi German cultural scene. The publisher W.K. and the historian K.E. became, like Meta and Karl, lifelong friends. This meant a great deal to my father. Next to music and pretty women, my father loved brains, wit and cultural success.

My parents began to make regular trips to New York, where my father also took violin lessons again, with another famous new friend, the violinist Adolf Busch. My father practiced more than ever, mostly the Bach solo sonatas he was to work on all his life, and he played sonatas with Katya whenever they were both free and Katya was in the mood. Sometimes she wasn't; Katya, like my father, did not find the New World as easy as my mother did.

Katya gave piano lessons, and through these, a few more congenial Detroiters were discovered and my parents' social life picked up, though never to an extent that might have satisfied Gibson. Katya also met some of the Detroit Symphony and once in a while there were evenings of chamber music again.

Even my social life improved. I met Nina, an older girl, one of Katya's pupils. It was she with whom I played mother and child in the patients' bathroom and Commandos and French Resistance, later, during the war. Nina's family had lost their money in the depression and now lived in a small apartment in Detroit. I was rather in awe of Nina. She was sophisticated and fun but also capricious, patronizing and a snob, very conscious of having come down in the world. It was not an ideal friendship but I steeped myself eagerly in Nina's America, her favorite funnies and movie stars.

My little sister was now old enough to be company too. She was lively and cheerful and an even better mimic than Katya. After Katya moved in, Verena and I shared a room, and at night Verena regaled me with her 'acts' of Gomper pupils and staff. We fought, but not seriously, and when she made a friend of her own age next door and began to play with other children on our block I felt betrayed and devastated, more alone than before.

Nina too became a Gomper pupil. The school continued to expand, and was soon divided into two classes. My sister, Dicky, Shereen and a few others were in the lower. The upper consisted of Nina, a pretty dark girl named Eleanor, jovial, witty Bernard whose father ran a bar downtown, and me. I suppose we were all in the 'gifted' category; only I was an obvious misfit, as well. And we had a new teacher; the young man in the purple suit.

This was my best Gomper's year. I was by far the smallest and youngest, but in that little group, it didn't matter. Bernard was nice, Eleanor polite and quiet, Nina domineering - she sometimes helped herself to the best of my packed lunch - but imaginative and entertaining. WR, our new teacher, lectured me, privately, about allowing myself to be exploited by her. He himself could be hard on Nina, who tended to be flippant and lazy. When she claimed not to grasp the difference between the Latin active and passive voice, WR asked her to hit him. She did, gingerly. "Now you're active." Then he slapped her so hard a whole red print of his hand was left on her thigh. "Now you're passive." This learning experience, my first sight of WR's violent streak, passed without comment. Nina, impressed, did not cry or complain.

WR taught us English and Latin, Hans Gomper maths and geography. Our time with WR was nearly all wonderful. We developed, gleefully, our own Montessori coloured card system for learning Latin conjugations and declensions. We read Shakespeare out loud, unabridged and unexpurgated, and loved it, though I was sometimes embarrassed by the sexy bits. We learned about poetic metre and figures of speech, how to parse a sentence, how to scan a line. We read Alfred Noyes and Browning and Brooke and Keats, Inspired by Browning, I wrote a whole Pied Piper of my own, in iambic pentameter, which was duly performed by the school, the nursery kids acting the children and myself the Piper. It was my brief moment of theatrical glory.

Almost everything we did was interesting and fun. Even when Hans Gomper taught, we derived entertainment from his mannerisms and accent and some of his teaching was good as well. The Gompers were scatty, disorganized, too lax about discipline, but also lucky - at the beginning, nothing dreadful resulted from their laissez-faire, and they did make education happy. But soon the school expanded again and the honeymoon came to its end.

Once or twice a year, I was allowed to join my parents or my mother and Katya on their trips to New York.

We took the sleeper from Detroit to Grand Central. I lay awake till late with my shade up, happy and excited, watching the mysterious stations and towns, the factory chimneys spouting dragon-breath of smoke and flame, the crowded tenements, the solitary houses in desolate fields, the lighted windows of people whose faces you would never see, slide by in the night.

We stayed with Katya's cousin Meta's family on Central Park West, or at the Barbizon Plaza Hotel. We went to theatre, concerts, department stores, ate at a French restaurant, the Canari d'Or, or at the Russian Tea Room, where I devoured blintzes and blini and kasha with mushrooms and pink Russian Cream for dessert. We walked in Central Park and had coffee in the Barbizon café, listening to ageing Central Europeans not as well off as we play lugubrious waltzes on piano and violin. Our hotel room was always high up, and I would look through the closed windows holding my breath (the inner demon loves skyscrapers, loves urging you to jump). But at night I fell blissfully asleep in the bed next to my mother's, hearing the car horns far below, lulled by some dim memory of the Mariahilferstrasse.

I knew almost at once that this city of exiles, this glittering bridge between two worlds, with all the excitement of the new and the nostalgia of the old, was *my* city, and one day I would live there. In fact, I imagined, except for Vermont, I would not want to live anywhere else. This made it even harder to live in Detroit.

During my years at Gomper's America went to war.

I "remember Pearl Harbor" as the song says. In our house, I was the first to know. I was listening to a broadcast of two pipe-voiced singing sisters - that period abounded in performing children - which was interrupted by the announcement of the Japanese attack. The adults took this news very seriously, and during the early defeats that followed, I, the ever-anxious, needed to be repeatedly reassured that the Allies would win. America, my parents explained, was big and strong, not like Austria. America couldn't be invaded, America wouldn't lose.

I saw the patriotic movies suitable for a hypersensitive child, Sonia Henie dancing and romancing on her skates being replaced by Betty Grable and Betty Hutton entertaining the troops, joining the WAACs, and Rita Hayworth performing in London during the Blitz. I also read the appropriate precocious book, by two English evacuee children about their new lives in America. They seemed to have adjusted much better than I.

For civilians, Over Here, the war seemed a matter of just being brave and bright and getting on with the assembly line and waiting faithfully for the sweetheart who was Over There. Of more toothy smiles than ever (though sometimes Through Your Tears, like Rita Hayworth going on with the show even though David Niven, RAF, had just been shot down over Germany). Even the evacuee children grinned broadly on their book cover, showing the boy's unfortunate buck teeth.

I was eager to do my bit. I planted a little Victory Garden of radishes and strawberries, most of which did not come up. I learned all the patriotic songs, *The White Cliffs of Dover*, made famous in America by Kate Smith. *Over There* (we won't be back till it's over over there), *Johnny Zero, Coming in on a Wing and a Prayer.* Even the slushiest (The same old sweethearts, the same old place, the boy in khaki and the girl in lace). My indulgent parents had to hear them over and over on the drive to Belle Isle. I saved tin-foil, I saved postage stamps, until someone pointed out that 'saving stamps' meant the stamps you bought to exchange for a War Bond when your stamp book was full. Embarrassed at yet another gaffe, I put away the postage stamps and dutifully used my allowance to buy the proper thing.

There were a few air raid drills, and our attic was covered with some fire-proof stuff that looked like rabbit food. No air raids came. We had a bit of worry about whether my father would be drafted. He was over forty but a qualified M.D., though he had not practiced medicine in years. In the event, he wasn't drafted. Perhaps, as a refugee, he should have made the grand gesture of enlisting. According to my husband, who was at Normandy and in the Battle of the Bulge, psychiatrists were needed and in short supply. But my father was not a hero; voluntary self-sacrifice was not in his line. One war, he declared, was enough. We were all very relieved when he stayed home, the only man in that overwhelmingly feminine houschold. Only I, always the conscience-stricken, felt a little uncomfortable when I heard of fathers or brothers in the Services. My father explained to me he was doing important work training younger psychiatrists who did go to war.

As another patriotic act we entertained, on their leaves, a couple of lone soldiers of German origin. I think their parents were still in Germany, which must have put them under terrible strain. One was the boyfriend of a student nurse, also a refugee, who had a room in our house for a while in exchange for some help to Enne. Other staff, including Gibson who later came back, had gone to more important and lucrative work in the booming arms factories of Detroit.

I fell briefly in love with these - to me - hero figures, especially Manfred, Eva's friend. I loved his clipped red hair, his Army cap perched at an angle, his smell of soap and after-shave, the sight of his clean strong hands. His memory is vivid and curiously sensuous. The soldiers were shy and polite, probably overwhelmed by the extravagance of our Christmas. I wrote to them, and they obligingly wrote back, and sent photos which I displayed proudly in my room. Topper, the second, I think survived; I know for certain Manfred did, but Eva eventually married someone else, which seemed to me a betrayal.

I also wrote to Jack, a purely American camp counsellor who enlisted in the Merchant Marine. He was the most literate of the three, wrote the best letters and seemed to really like getting mine. I treasured his letters for years, and forgave him his gravest sin, putting a snapping turtle I'd found into the camp swimming pool, under the tragic illusion that all turtles can swim.

The *Anschluss,* the German annexation of Austria, changed our lives completely and forever. The American side of the war hardly touched us. Gasoline was rationed, and we couldn't drive as much. We had to take a boat from Detroit to Buffalo to get to Vermont, instead of driving all the way, across Canada. This was only a plus. I loved the overnight boat trip, in a comfortable cabin, over the great lake. Some food was rationed as well, but supplies were generous and we seemed to eat as we always did. Enne melted down butter before rationing began (she had seen bad times before), so the rich Austrian cakes and cookies and *Knoedel* my father loved appeared as usual on the table. Enne's *Butterschmalz,* which keeps indefinitely, lasted us till the end of the war.

We did have some little excitement when a member of the Austrian-American Friendship Society that Enne (with complaints) frequented on her days off turned out to be a spy, and was subsequently executed. And more excitement when another refugee my parents knew slightly was questioned by the FBI. She was not a spy at all, but she had been writing denigrating letters about American products to relatives in Germany, pleading for proper needles and thread or whatever she missed. The FBI intercepted these letters and decided, in their wisdom, that the letters might be a code and the old lady an enemy agent. After her interrogation, she panicked and hanged herself. She was as near as we personally came in Detroit to a casualty of the war.

This was my father's First World War.

"When I had to join the army in May 1916, shortly before my 18th birthday, I, along with most of the draftees, was more concerned with survival than with sacrificing my life for 'God, Kaiser and fatherland.' I expected my intellectual and artistic interests to be buried under the commonness and vulgarity of military life and the misery and deadly danger in combat. However, the two and a half years that I spent in the army were not lost for my cultural and artistic development." [10]

Indeed they were not. It was in the "military wasteland of the barracks and exercising grounds I discovered psychoanalysis." For among Daddy's fellow recruits were some older men, intellectuals, drafted to replace the many losses of combat, whose conversation stimulated him to begin reading some of Freud's work.

It was also due to the manpower lack that my father, only eighteen and hardly the right material, was made an officer and put in charge of a group of newly recruited peasants who were to defend a stretch of barren land somewhere on the front. They were terrified and unable to grasp the point of fighting for such useless terrain. When the firing began they took out their rosaries and began to pray. My father, in despair, ran about hitting them with his rifle butt and exhorting them to shoot before they were all slaughtered. For this act of bravery he was given a medal.

Enough has been written about the horrors of trench warfare, and my father had not much to add; but two things he mentioned have stayed with me. One was a story of being soaked in the pouring rain while out on patrol, but having left a pair of dry underwear - his last - in the trench to come back to. When he found his underwear floating in a flooded trench, he burst into tears like a child.

The other was the wounded horses, screaming and struggling in the mud. For him, he said, this was almost worse than the dying men, because

---

[10] R. Sterba, *'Reminiscences of a Viennese Psychoanalyst'*.

the horses could understand nothing of why they were dying in agony. "The horses," he said, "were totally innocent."

What saved my father was his luck and his music.

He was hospitalized with a minor wound. Then someone in the field hospital got typhoid and the whole ward was quarantined and sent back to Vienna. There, a priest who wanted the Sunday mass at the hospital chapel celebrated with music discovered my father could play the violin, and contrived to keep him "hospitalized" for seven months. At the end of this time, my father somehow wangled another four months leave in his beloved Salzburg before going back to his regiment. By then it was obvious the war was lost. "More and more cadres of the army disintegrated until, in early November 1918, I saw no reason to stay at my command post any longer. I was fortunate enough to catch the last train to Vienna, where I arrived just a week before Armistice was declared." [11]

This story, more complete than what appears in his autobiography, is what he told, in bits and pieces, to me.

I was to find it hard later to explain to Europeans how little the war affected us in Middle America, affected anyone there who didn't have a relative or close friend in the draft. For Detroit it was mainly positive. It meant the end of the Depression, it meant jobs. But in our bourgeois oasis I wasn't aware of economics. At school the war coloured our insults and jeers. "Shereen, Shereen, the big fat submarine, guess who she kissed, the Jap marine," the nastier boys would sing until poor Shereen was in tears. The ack-ack and nyaaaaa noises of the littler ones as they zoomed round the yard were now aeroplanes zapping the Japs. And our comic books sported villains with jackboots and swastikas, or evil grins and yellow skin.

Hans Gomper, now a father, was not drafted. Nor was WR, who said he had a strangulated hernia. I wondered if this had something to do with his very prominent Adam's apple. My parents explained. In fact the reason may well have been psychiatric. But no one was to be told.

My parents could not reassure me about everything. Two of the boys got hold of a small grubby paperback called *Bushido*, which detailed Japanese atrocities. The concentration camps were not yet common knowledge; for most Americans, the biggest villains were the Japanese who had so treacherously attacked Pearl Harbor. Everyone at school read the book. I

---

[11] R. Sterba, 'Reminiscences of a Viennese Psychoanalyst'.

did too and was obsessed and miserable for days. But that was the inner demon; any horror could set it off. Curiously, my friend Alice, who was very devout, was the most indignant and vengeful about Japanese crimes. "The Japs should have boiling water poured in their ears," she wrote later in an essay. "They should have done to them the things they did to our boys."

Except for the soldiers, our Christmases were always private affairs. And pure magic. My sister and I got just about everything we wished for. Guilt-ridden as always (*think of the starving children in Europe* was by then the stock phrase to make you clean your plate), I was quite modest in my demands. But the best thing was not the presents. Not even Enne's wonderful Christmas cookies, some of which were hung from the tree, not Katya playing *Silent Night*, which we all sang solemnly in mixed German and English before gifts were opened, nor the porcelain Nativity figures which I was allowed to set up. Nor even the clumsy making and wrapping of my own cards and gifts for the family, a task I adored. The magic was the tree. The tree was a link to the old vanished Europe and for me a link to fairyland. The tree had everything - gingerbread rings, candies wrapped in fringed crêpe paper, bright red, green and blue (my mother joined in their preparation), strange antique ornaments, an angel head in a silver circle, a small stuffed giraffe, which went back to my mother's own childhood, walnuts dipped in gold and silver paint, chains of tinsel and coloured paper, shiny foil icicles, tiny wool dolls my mother taught even me to make, baubles and sparklers and at first, real candles. Sometimes, at night, I would sit all alone in the dark dining room under the tree, watching the glitter, breathing the smell of pine, and feel there was fairyland after all.

Along with our own tree, as befitted the family pet mania, we had a smaller tree for the dogs and cat, with a tin winged and haloed Dachshund on top. The animals' delight in their new sterilized bones, squeaky rubber toys and catnip mice was almost the most fun of the evening.

Our *"Bescherung,"* present giving, also took place Austrian fashion, on Christmas eve. This did not tally with Anglo-Saxon custom, where presents came in the morning and Christmas eve was for drinking with your friends. Sometimes a couple of my parents' colleagues dropped in, expecting an eggnog or two. On such occasions my father's impatience was painfully obvious; especially if, rendered convivial by Christmas spirits, they dared to call him Dick. In due course they gave up - though not without resentment - and we had our family ceremony in peace.

There was one local Christmas tradition which was also magical; trees flanking front doors were festooned with fairy lights. You cruised slowly along the best streets to see what Christmas wonders your neighbours had produced. In the most elegant gardens, instead of the usual multi-colours there might be tiny bulbs of icy blue, or some simple and delicate combination of two or three hues. The best ones were spectacular. During the war of course, to save energy, most of the front door conifers were left dark.

After the war, things got more brash. Smaller houses, without trees, began to sport Christmas greetings in lights on the façade; one had a big plastic Santa and reindeer on the roof. There was even neon cynicism; large light-bulb letters that said simply SAME TO YOU.

The war also changed my games with Nina. Nina was more sophisticated than the other Gomper girls. Her parents had travelled in Europe, and she knew about France and the Resistance. So we played French Underground. We rode our bikes along the street fleeing the Gestapo. I had only just learned to ride mine, and never acquired advanced skills, like riding with no hands. All other kids could, but the only time I tried, I fell. I would never have escaped the Gestapo on my bike. Nor ice skates, nor roller skates, which then were all metal and had no brakes. My memory of skates is chiefly the impact of concrete or ice on the base of my spine.

Everyone else could ice-skate tolerably, including my mother. They enjoyed occasional hours on the frozen lake, after the sacrosanct weekend horseback rides. My father quite prided himself on his skating. In later years, they turned the sunken garden into a winter rink, and between patients my father would pop out to do a few elegant turns on the ice.

In the hope that *something* would suit me, I even tried stilts. Only on the grass, where I couldn't fall too hard. Stilts were another failure. Then inspiration struck. I asked my parents to buy me Kangaroo Spring Shoes.

Kangaroo Spring Shoes were advertised on the back of my comic books. They were two metal sole-shaped plates with springs like bed-springs between. They strapped onto your feet like roller skates. The hero of the ad, another comic like many comic-book ads, was called Johnny. He was a flashy little boy with a shock of dark hair and what the artist meant as an engaging grin. Johnny did rescues and punched crooks in the jaw, propelled to astounding heights by his Kangaroo Spring Shoes.

My indulgent parents, oblivious as usual to the real efficacy, or danger, of American gadgets, ordered the Spring Shoes. I waited for them in high excitement. No one on the block, no one in school, had Kangaroo Spring Shoes. The mastery of Kangaroo Spring Shoes, described as truly simple, might give me my chance to shine at a physical feat, even to set a trend. I saw myself running and leaping, in pioneering glory, past the uninspired on their bikes and skates.

The Spring Shoes arrived, I put them on. I managed to walk once around the garden. They tilted precariously at each slow hesitant step. To jump in them, even six inches, I knew at once would be disaster. The Spring Shoes were put away for good. I never saw them on any other child, and now I knew why. My great consolation was that I hadn't told anyone, that no one was there to witness my latest disgrace.

The sunken garden. In spring, when the snow melted and the heavy rains came, the sunken garden, rather lawn, flooded to the depth of a foot. Giant earthworms appeared in the black, brackish water, twisting and struggling and dying.

In spite of my dysmechsia I decided to build a raft to pole across this interesting sinister pond. I got as far as collecting a few boards. The water was really not deep enough to float a raft, even if I could have made one. I didn't know yet about rubber dinghies. If I had, my parents would have got me one, as they did the Spring Shoes. As they did everything. Countless Storybook Dolls. Miniature glass animals, another favorite child collector's item. A life-size spotted stuffed hound I saw in a toy shop and coveted; when he arrived for Christmas I felt guilty because I really did not know what to do with him, and racked my brains to make up some games in which this droopy faced, floppy toy could be used. The hound cost five dollars, which seemed to me an enormous sum.

They bought me, too, any book I wanted. Including, in my early teens, when I was as usual, ill in bed and getting bored, the forbidden edition of *Memoirs of Hecate County,* Edmund Wilson's then scandalous novel. Nor did they stint me on goldfish, canaries, white mice (who ate their babies) and tortoises.

In those days, tiny tortoises could be bought at the five and ten, along with the usual domestic items and wonders like artificial fingernails (we tried them once) and Bobbsey Twins books.

The tortoises mostly had painted shells, bright red or blue or yellow, sometimes with a printed name. I kept mine in an enamel basin with water and coloured flakes of stone. I fed them the dime-store tortoise food, and carefully scratched and peeled all the paint off their shells. I had read somewhere that the paint would kill them, since the shell was meant to breathe.

At one point I had eleven. Each had a name, Dimples, Dabbles, etc., sometimes the printed name, sometimes my own. Their cleaned shells had beautiful individual patterns, as did the markings on their heads and feet, and I could tell most of them apart. They didn't do much. They crawled around aimlessly, stepping on each other's heads, and snapped up their tortoise food, But I loved them.

The smelly basin stood in a corner of my room and I checked it as soon as I awoke. Still, in spite of my paint-stripping and devoted care, after a few months the little creatures died, one by one. They were buried in matchboxes in the garden, and like the occasional dead or dying bird I found, were seriously mourned.

I had no heart to start another reptile collection. I did covet one boy's chameleon, which he wore to school like a brooch on his lapel; it had a tiny collar and chain attached to a pin. This chameleon didn't last long either, probably exhausted by the colour changes it was made to perform, living on fabrics and human skin instead of in trees. I sometimes wonder how much rare wildlife vanished in the forties and fifties, not only on women's heads, backs and feet, but in children's rooms or on children's lapels. Not one of my adults ever gave it a thought.

Except for the five and ten, shopping with my mother was another ordeal.

My mother would drive us to Grosse Pointe's Kercheval Avenue for shoes or clothes; hardly ever did we shop downtown. We were marched into the hushed, plush, carpeted precincts of Jacobson's or Best & Co., into an atmosphere of gently rustling tissue paper and the smell of polish, crisp new cloth and perfume, the smell of money. Graying saleslades waited with rigid smiles. "So, Monika," my mother would urge in stentorian tones, "Say what you want!" I usually didn't really want anything. Or if I did I was too shy to say it. I would stay tongue-tied and flushed with shame while we went through the racks. Eventually something was tried on and chosen. It was always too big, so then came the fitting. I stood meekly in yet worse embarrassment, hoping my nervous sweat didn't smell and my stomach wouldn't growl while the fitter, mouth full of pins, knelt beside me and pinned up the hem. I hated the fitting most of all, a stranger's head and hands so close to me, my mother impatiently watching, doing piano exercises with her fingers. I didn't belong there. Nothing was right. My mother, bless her, soured me early for the consumer society.

It was almost as bad when my mother, with me along, went to buy herself a new hat. Her head was big and her short stepped flapper haircut made it seem bigger. All the hats, I thought, looked grotesque. I would try to persuade her to get what I considered the least of the evils. Sometimes I succeeded, Then we went home, both of us pleased, she with the purchase, I that it was over.

But one thing that my sister and I did enjoy was the shoe-store x-ray machine. No one seemed to twig till much later that these machines, then ubiquitous, might not really be very good for you. While parent and saleslady smiled indulgently, we stood in the x-ray machine a minute at a time, gazing in fascination at our wriggling skeleton toes.

Like most shy children, I was also nervous of using a toilet in a strange place.

This basic human function is not freed from shame simply by Freudian upbringing. Perhaps certain shames are inherent, based on ancient dangers (a squatting *homo-erectus* is easy sabre-tooth prey) and excessive openness makes them worse. My parents, thank heaven, did not perform such functions in front of their children. No - my mother did. But later.

Besides the initial embarrassment of asking where the place was (Enne would have said: I must go where even the Kaiser goes on foot) there was a triple fear. That someone would hear your toilet noises. That someone would burst in. That, having locked the door to prevent this, you would not be able to get out. I was clumsy with locks and bolts, as with everything else.

At Gomper's the fear had foundations. The nastier boys did try to get in; did bang on the door, and giggle, and threaten. And WR and Hans Gomper themselves, with an incredible lack of sensitivity and common politeness, traumatized me by marching in when I was sitting on the john, greeting me, and washing their hands slowly before they left, without even a word of excuse.

In the end not only I, but my less inhibited little sister, gave up using Gomper toilets at all, except in unbearable need. I had probably never peed at Trombley either, but Trombley days were shorter and the school only five minutes drive away. At Gomper's, our continence had to last from a quarter past eight in the morning till half past four in the afternoon. When we got home, we galloped to the nearest toilets and peed like Niagara. Fortunately we both had strong bladders. But they have been prone to ache ever since.

We did not of course tell our parents. When I developed chronic constipation, I was taken to Chicago to see an internist, the second husband of an old Vienna friend whose first husband had married the ex-wife of Bruno Bettelheim. Anyway, he was part of the Central Europe network to which other CE exiles turned for help and advice.

My parents had long classified me as anal-retentive, and probably expected I would need psychological as well as physical cure. The internist, a sensible man, pronounced there was certainly nothing wrong with my insides. He put me on a strict breakfast diet; a glass of warm water, half a grapefruit, a piece of black bread, a jar of sour cream. I was freed from constipation for life. And soon I was able to have a great emptying of bowels right after breakfast, before the school car arrived. So at least one of two painful pressures was removed.

The toilet troubles were the beginning of the end.

Gomper's soon had some twenty children in the grade school, still divided into two classes, according to age and/or supposed ability. The upper class, besides Nina, Bernard and me (Eleanor left that year) took on three girls and four boys in their teens. One boy, the nice one, was Dickie's brother Jack. Another boy, Henry, was the son of a German refugee psychiatrist. This might have created a link, and Henry apparently felt one, but he was huge and rough and his sometimes marked attention terrified me. The other boys were slightly retarded and/or disturbed. I suppose that's why they were there. Students with special needs. One of their needs was bullying and by far the youngest, smallest weakest person in the class was myself.

When the teachers were around it wasn't too bad. And I had some protection when with the other, bigger girls. But during our unsupervised lunches, or any time we were left to our own devices, I quaked with fear. More was threatened than ever actually happened. There was the odd squeeze or grab, tickling (which drove me wild) and Indian sunburn, when you put your two hands round someone's arm and twist in opposite directions. There was the birthday spanking, one blow for every year; at least they didn't pull up my skirt. Henry spanked especially hard and also broke my first ever watch, the birthday present from my parents. I didn't wear a watch again for years. But mostly it was just the constant fear itself, the threat of something worse yet. I was afraid of pain. I didn't know how to fight. I had no experience of physical violence; my parents never hit, hardly ever raised their voices. I had never engaged in the rough and tumble of kids on a block. The teachers said things about fighting back, but I did not see how you could fight someone twice your size without being hurt much more, made to cry uncle, plunged into final humiliation, maybe really injured. But among children cowardice has no excuse.

Sometimes, during lunch, one of the boys locked me in the closet at the back of our classroom. The closet was big, only mildly claustrophobic, so this was not too bad. As long as I was alone in the closet, no one could hurt me. In a cluster of damp coats, in the dark, with a nervous ear on the turmoil outside, I munched Enne's carefully prepared sandwich of the day; egg salad, or cream cheese and jelly, peanut butter and jam, baloney with mustard, Austrian Liptauer, or her own special chopped pickle and mayonnaise spread. I remember it well, the taste of those sandwiches in the dark. After a while, someone would let me out, because the next class was about to begin.

Often I did retaliate; I used my sharp tongue. Sarcasm is a weapon that does not stop bullies, only infuriates them. But it was the only weapon I had. Sometimes I clowned, playing up my oddities, snarling with closed lips so my projecting new eye-tooth (rectified later by seven years of orthodontia) stuck out like a Dracula fang. Rat-face, the boys called me. I didn't mind. When I showed them my rat-face they laughed but didn't hit.

Even WR, who had a temper himself, let me down. Once, he hurled a book at a pupil; another time, when I was impudent - I was not afraid of the teachers, and the kids admired impudence - he put me on top of a high rickety book-case, just before leaving the room. I sat precariously, sweating and trembling, trying to put a good face on it. I knew if the jeering boys below, threatening to grab my legs, shook the book-case, it would fall, perhaps with me under it. Somehow I managed to balance till WR came back and lifted me down.

I don't know if I'd been rude again, but WR, another time, took it into his head to join the teasing. In fact, to initiate a new game. It involved Shereen's brother, the truly backward Teddy. Teddy was actually quite sweet and pathetic. His proud announcement of "Me no jerk. Me go bathroom," a new accomplishment, became a byword at the Wunder camp, which he also attended. Teddy developed a crush on me, and WR decided to make me dance with Teddy in the playground. I do not know what inner demon of *his* took over WR on that occasion, though I was to see more of it. While Teddy waited, tittering, smiling his sad, buck-toothed Down's Syndrome smile, WR dragged me toward him to join our hands, in spite of my near-tearful shrieks of outrage and disbelief.

On this occasion, Hans Gomper, who happened to look out, decided enough was enough. At least as regarded the founder's daughter. (Though this fact must have riled him. He confessed to my husband, when we met the Gompers decades later, that he himself had given me a hard time. "Monika Sterba, don't disturba," was his own particular invention for my discomfort, a jingle the kids gleefully echoed for weeks. He also, with German chauvinism, informed them that the Austrians were known for their over-large heads.)

Hans took me upstairs to his private quarters, and offered me a picture book to soothe my jangled nerves. The pictures were all of classical statues, nearly all naked. I saw things I had never seen pictured before (in my mother's educative medical tome they were in cross-section interior view). I wondered miserably why *this* book, whether it was meant as yet more malicious teasing. It may have been that Hans knew I was fond of Greek myths, or simply handed me the first picture book he found. Though this is not what Freud would say. Anyway, it was hardly what I needed. I turned the pages rapidly, hiding my disgust and shame.

I did not tell my parents how bad it was at school, and I never actually asked the teachers for protection. I had learned at Trombley that it was disgraceful to tattle-tale. Tattle-tale, ginger ale, stick your head in the garbage pail, the kids would chant. Besides, my mother had founded the school, for me. I could hardly ask to go elsewhere; and there did not seem to be anywhere else to go.

Now, whenever I hear about school phobics, about counselling and cures, I am enraged. If a child is afraid of school, chances are the child has good reason and reason for not saying so. You do not restrain school bullies by counselling the victim.

If there were laws about the number who can be squashed into an ordinary six-seater car, Gomper's must have broken them daily. Our school car now took not only Dickie and Jack, my sister and me, but one or two nursery school children and two girls who, though from the lower class, were older and much bigger than I.

Sylvia lived in a posh apartment house on the Detroit River, near the Belle Isle Bridge and the skeleton of another, unfinished, high-rise, that gaped against the sky like some avant-garde monument to The Depression. Ruby lived on a distinctly lower-middle-class street near the outskirts of Grosse Pointe.

I had been quite friendly with animated, humorous Ruby, and indifferent to Sylvia. Sylvia was overgrown and gawky, with large grim features, lank hair, and big hands like a boy's. I didn't like her looks - I had my father's snobbish aversion to ugliness - but I had nothing more against her. Somehow, out of a playground game, or one of my ill-timed sarcasms, a quarrel developed. Ruby pulled me across the classroom by my hair, and in the car on the way home, where I couldn't escape, Sylvia beat me up. She was in front and I in back, but she reached out a long arm, like the *Hauskobold's*, and hit me smartly in the face until my tears poured down. She also threw my schoolbooks out of the car window. I managed not to sob aloud, but to my eternal shame, I did not hit back. I only said, trying to smile through my tears, that now at least I would have no homework to do. Craven to the end.

The school driver then was a young Grosse Pointer from a wealthy socialite family, who had probably taken the job for charitable or therapeutic reasons. While blows rained and books flew, she stared straight ahead and kept on driving. Perhaps she had been instructed that even in vehicles moving at forty miles an hour Gomper children were to be allowed maximum free expression.

I got out of the car that evening more desperate and humiliated than I have ever felt in my life. Again, I didn't know the rules - that to cry when you're beaten up is *not* final defeat, especially for girls, that calling for help in pain and distress does not make you an eternal pariah. I had concentrated on not sobbing, when the real disgrace was not to hit back. Now I hated myself so much for my cowardice I wanted to die. And I knew I would have to face Ruby and Sylvia the next day.

I did not develop one of my handy fevers. Somehow, in a nightmare daze, I managed to get to school next day, expecting something terrible but determined this time to defend myself. The socialite must have spoken to the Gompers, for Sylvia came up to me at school; neither she nor Ruby had been in the car. Sylvia said flatly, "Do you want to make up and be friends?" I did not want to be friends. I wanted to see Sylvia dead. But taken aback and hardly tough enough to throw out a new challenge, I said okay.

After that, Ruby and I did become friendly again and Sylvia left me alone. Half a year later, I stood by with the rest, including teachers, and watched Sylvia defeated by a boy her own size. No one moved to break up this fight. They seemed evenly matched; and Gomper's, in its chaos, upheld the principle of female equality. I saw Sylvia on the ground, striking, struggling, gasping, growing beet red, finally bursting into tears. It was nice but hollow, a coward's victory. I should have done it myself, though given my size and hers, there wasn't a chance. I should have been like the heroes of myths and comic strips and Charles Atlas body building ads' turning worm. I was a refugee child, obsessed with courage in battle, with stories of the Resistance, the Underground. I had been obsessed with courage ever since Schwab's *Gods and Heroes*, since Prinz Eugen and Held Winkelried, and courage was what I conspicuously lacked. Why had I not hit Sylvia back, even just once? And why was this incident, out of all my childhood, the hardest to live, as it is the hardest to tell? This question may be Adlerian rather than Freudian. Or is it always the *failures* to act that haunt us to our graves?

My mother, so anxious for the safety of her two surviving offspring, seemed quite unaware of the hazards of our daily transport to school. Cars moved more slowly then, but with undisciplined children packed in like sardines, it seems miraculous that no accidents happened, except one minor bump.

The Gompers were always lucky. Even when they did lose a pupil. In their later much bigger and famous school, one child was missed and found drowned in the school lake. The parents, I heard, far from instituting lawsuits, donated a scholarship in the child's name.

My transport terrors did not end with Sylvia. There was another addition to the crowded car, a noisy, manic boy also from the lower grade, who was sometimes dropped at our house to take the car with us. It was the time of the spring flood. He charged around the garden making the usual airplane noises and gleefully pocketing worms. In the car, he tore them into small pieces and tried to put them down our collars. "Diced worms," he chortled. "I'm gonna put diced worms down your back." I think I did report this one. Cruelty to animals, even worms, was one case where my tattle-tale rule did not apply.

With Gomper's now such a trial, I took more refuge in illness again.

Gomper's being so small, I escaped the typical children's diseases, except for chicken pox. I got my usual colds, sore throats, flu and stomach flu. I have a diary from that school year; there was only one week when I did not miss at least a day of school.

My mother and Enne battled the germs. Antibiotics were not yet in general use, Vitamin C not yet in fashion. Aspirins, chest rubs, compresses, cod liver oil, cough syrups, inhalations, infusions were the order of the day.

I lay swaddled like a mummy in compresses now hot, now cold (*heisser Wickel* and *kalter Wickel*) with layers of towels and blankets around me to keep out chills. I inhaled great quantities of steam. I drank chamomile tea, beef broth, orange juice, hot lemonade, cold lemonade, hot milk and honey for coughs. For diarrhoea there was *Zwieback*, black "Russian" tea, grated apple, and gritty charcoal pills to chew. It was fun to look in the mirror and stick out my black tongue. I had hot baths to make me sweat, alcohol rubs to keep me clean and stimulate circulation, fresh slices of cucumber skin on my forehead to soothe the fevered brow. There was sulfa for the rare, more serious looking cases. And of course there were always visits from our paediatrician Dr Strapp, with his black bag, cheek-pinching and terrible needles. That was the risky bit of being sick. Fortunately, for what ailed me, there wasn't much that he could inject.

Enne did and undid various wrappings and prepared the drinks and steam, and my mother popped in between patients to instruct and assist, look worried, feel the heat of my neck and study the thermometer. My father, the qualified doctor, was summoned to produce tongue depressors and gaze at my throat. Unlike my mother, my father was not anxious. He would order me to say Ah, declare that the throat was in fact red, make a joke and go back to patient or violin,

Being sick was wonderful. Unless it was stomach flu, Enne cooked me my favorite foods. When not being ministered to, I would do a little homework, draw and read. I had the company of Peter, the fat Viennese cat, who would linger on your bed if you were really sick. He was as good as a thermometer; he must have enjoyed the extra body heat, And I listened all day to the droning soaps, heralded by their themes of bombastic organ music.

During the war, the soaps became a little more dramatic. Husbands and boyfriends were away at the front. The heroines waited bravely for news, and were sometimes approached by Nazi spies. This was at least a change from the crippling car accidents, amnesia, and difficult mothers-in-law that dominated their peacetime lives. My favorite was *Portia Faces Life,* in which Portia, a glamorous female lawyer, was courted by a Gestapo agent pretending to be her fiancé Walter, imprisoned by the Nazis in Germany. Meanwhile, Walter was threatened with torture by the Gestapo. "The use of a dentist's drill - without cocaine!" the Gestapo interrogator snarled at helpless Walter, strapped in the chair. Walter did not blanch. I don't remember how he got out of the chair, but he came home with all his teeth, the villain was unmasked and the lovers were reunited in the end.

All these characters were exotically normal to me. Their lives, even with amnesia, enemy agents, accidents etc. seemed of quite a different order to ours - inconspicuous, uneccentric, American. Sometimes my English was still not quite up to them. It was only years afterward that *Our Gal Sunday*, "the story that asks the question - can a little Ivor girl be happy as the wife of England's richest, most handsome Lord?" revealed the answer that eluded *me*. What *was* a "Little Ivor Girl?" Was Ivor some kind of handicap? Or was it a chorus, like Ziegfeld? Had it something to do with having posed for Ivory Soap? Fortunately, I was too shy to ask at school, having already been laughed at for pronouncing Wisconsin with the accent on the Wis. What I heard as Ivor was, of course, Iowa.

Abetted by sickness, my reading list grew.

It was Nina who introduced me to my first really adult novel - Romain Rolland's *Jean-Christophe*. My parents explained that the central character was inspired by Beethoven. I devoured *Jean-Christophe*, staying awake late with my eyes aching and my orthodontic bit chafing my mouth. My head swam with ideas of genius and greatness. It was after *Jean-Christophe* that I asked my father if it was true that one had to suffer to be great. My father, caught in the usual five minutes between patients or siesta and violin, said yes. I pondered this sadly. I wanted to be a great poet. But I didn't want to suffer more than I thought I was suffering already. Though it didn't seem quite the right kind of suffering. And you needed not only suffering but genius. "Genius" was my parents' form of canonization, admission to the brethren of cultural sainthood. So I vacillated between secret hope and fear. Both inspiration and suffering seemed to lie, dangerously, in the hands of fate.

Digression:
Tante Grete's Romance

My Tante Grete, the youngest and the last to die, also wrote. Her stories were published in gentlewomen's magazines. When we lived for a while in the old villa in Gmunden, after Tante Grete's death, Frau Endlinger, her last housekeeper and nurse, gave me one of the stories. It was about an officer and a girl who are deeply in love but cannot marry because there is not enough money and their families are opposed. Each thinks of braving it out and, I suppose, eloping. In the end, neither has the courage, neither speaks; and they go their separate ways.

It was the story of Tante Grete's life. There was a brief romance with a young Polish nobleman. Her father could not afford a dowry adequate for such an alliance; perhaps his rank was also not high enough for the Polish family's ambitions. At any rate, when surely nothing had gone beyond waltzes or walks in the garden, his father wrote hers, and citing the financial grounds, demanded an end. (I found the letters.) The young nobleman went home to Poland and died of cholera. Even Frau Endlinger, a toady to aristocracy if ever there was, waxed indignant at what happened next. After their son's death, his parents sent Tante Grete an invitation to visit them. Tante Grete, needless to say, did not go.

DANCING WITH A PATIENT AND OTHER TRIBULATIONS

My father took a few notes on his patients in "Marble Notebooks," pocket-size notebooks with black, white-flecked covers. There was always one in the secret compartment of his big armchair, with the tobacco and pipe.

My father's notes were, alas, illegible; I had to be content studying his doodles. One he did for his children was three mice, back view, sitting on a wall. A line (wall), three circles (mice) with half circles on top (ears) and fish-hook lines at bottom (tails). This remains the only thing I myself can draw.

I did try to draw other things. Some were inspired by Nina's and my favorite comic, the very romantic *Mary Worth's Family*. Mary Worth was a sweet white-haired old lady who involved herself, as confidante and advisor, in the troubled romances of various beautiful girls, who fell for tall, square-jawed men all of whom looked like Cary Grant. After some alarms and excursions, decently sexless except for the occasional kiss when the characters were drawn locked mouth to mouth, all worked out happily. Mary Worth still exists but now wears make-up and looks twenty years younger. I also loved Brenda Starr, the gorgeous red-haired reporter, who faced various quite unjournalistic problems, such as the schemes of two ugly sisters who wanted her cut up so her head could be grafted on one and her body the other. Such horrors, of course, are now becoming reality.

Nina and I drew profiles of these glamorous heroines, though ours looked more like Dagwood's Blondie. And of course I drew horses, though I never got the bodies right. Nor were my glamour girls at all like Hedy Lamarr or Maria Montez, the stars I admired. Still, fortified by my parents' praise for everything I did, I tried whole comic strips. I started, but never finished, stories of beautiful slave girls with veils, bare midriffs, harem pants. I also did strips about my family, making up funny situations with famous people turning up as patients. And I did a family newsletter in the style of our society paper, *The Grosse Pointe News*. When I was home ill, these were favorite activities.

My total inability to draw and the derivativeness or forced humor of my plots must have been evident even to my parents. I was obviously not destined to be another Al Capp. But my mother lauded these puerile efforts, and kept them all in her bedroom cupboard, along with the case reports on bed-wetters, thumb-suckers etc. and the woolly lamb glued cotton picture I had made at Trombley and been hurt not to see hung, with Schiele, on our walls.

Sick or well, at half-past five every day I turned my radio dial to the Canadian system for Cohn's Conga-Rumba Time.

I listened to songs in English, Spanish and Portuguese, lilting female voices and warm husky male, quick erotic drumbeats, shouts of "Olé." A music that spoke to me of palm trees and leopards and another favorite comic book heroine, Sheena, The Queen of the Jungle, who dove into crocodile-crowded swamps to rescue her mate, Bob. Of places I had only seen in movies or the *National Geographic*. Tropical forests with crimson birds. White beaches, white villas, turquoise sea. I knew rich Americans (I still did not think of us as rich) took holidays in that other America. I also pictured them. Slim, elegant, tall. A girl in a white sharkskin suit (what *was* sharkskin?), then the height of Hollywood chic, a dark-haired man in a tuxedo, dancing through a warm perfumed night. Images at once exotic and canned, like the music itself.

In between the songs, another sort of male voice would speak. A dry hard voice eulogized the clothes of Cohn, the coats and suits which could be bought right off the rack. No display, said the voice. Nothing fancy. Just the honest bargain that can't be beat. Racks, said the voice. Racks with thousands on them. You just can't help finding the suit of your personal choice. Come to Cohn's and see for yourself. And now let's hear Chiquita del Mondo singing *O Tico Tico.* Olé!

Much of that music, with its trite American translation lyrics, its edgy, compulsive rhythms, grated on my nerves. But I couldn't stop listening to it, I couldn't get it out of my head. When I was feverish the coats and the tropical sounds combined, the big bleak warehouse with its racks and racks of suits, the drummers with ruffled sleeves, the gypsy dancers in tight toreador pants and swinging skirts. Gaudy flowers opening to the sun. And gabardine, the voice said. Real gabardine. I knew nothing of urban poverty, nothing of South America, really nothing of Detroit. But through that voice a kind of despair, an acrid breath of those who would never see a tropical paradise or Heidi's shining mountains came into my clean, bright Grosse Pointe room. And in the music itself, under the colour, the sensual excitement, something still more disturbing, a faint, hot blood scent of death. It was arousing and obsessive and, underneath, terribly sad, and I listened obsessively every day, as the dry toneless voice of the announcer heralded fiestas, sunshine and love, while he stood (so I pictured him) alone in the warehouse among the thousands of empty garments, like so many ghosts, like so many shrouds.

What first inspired me to listen to Cohn's may have been one of my rare visits to the theatre.

There wasn't much in Detroit my parents thought worth going to. But once a year the dancer-anthropologist Katherine Dunham came with her troupe, and performed to South American music and native jazz.

My father liked the sensuousness, the beautiful women, the most beautiful of whom was Dunham herself. Her face was perfect, as was her body; her skin that wonderful colour the French call *café au lait*, which seemed to me the best colour a human being could have. I was enchanted by everything, the dancing, the costumes, the music, not debased and Americanized like most of the stuff played on Cohn's, and not least by the handsome Spanish singer with whom I fell in love.

Though I was a very puritanical child, my adoration of Dunham was so great it was not dimmed by the shocking moment when, at the end of one dance duo, her strapless white dress slipped down, just before the curtain fell. In the forties breasts were taboo, and my father shocked me still more by remarking he thought it was done on purpose. He added, admiringly, his favorite euphemism, "She has beautiful eyes."

I too did some dancing, in a way. My sister and I had private ballet lessons with a Miss Heather Basilisk.

We never got as far as dancing on our toes. We worked at the bar, doing points and pliés, while Miss Basilisk's pianist thumped on the piano and Miss Basilisk counted and exhorted. Miss Basilisk had curly brown hair, much lipstick and perfume, but wore glasses, which seemed to me, for a dancer, wrong. "One tyou, one tyou," Miss Basilisk sang. We also learned to flap our arms about with third finger and thumb lowered and the other fingers raised. "Pretty fingers," Miss Basilisk trilled. "Pretty fingers."

The best thing about Miss Basilisk's (I had no illusions of becoming a great ballerina) was getting out of Gomper's for an afternoon, and going home in our own car. The worst thing was the studio, which was the basement of the house in downtown Detroit where Miss Basilisk lived with her mother. Miss Basilisk's fiancé, we learned, was away in the Army. When we arrived, we were sometimes let in by the mother or someone and then kept waiting. The studio, before Miss B. turned on the big lights, was dark and spooky. We sat tensely on a couch, listening to mysterious sounds from upstairs or the ominous rumbles and hisses of the basement boiler works.

Miss Basilisk's life was altogether mysterious and dramatic. One day we were kept waiting a very long time while a woman cried upstairs, terrible heartbroken crying. We had never heard anyone cry like that. We sat shivering in the cold gloomy studio until we were so frightened we thought we must act, call, go for help - but then at last Miss Basilisk came down, with red eyes, and said our lesson could begin. Burning with irrepressible curiosity - the one thing that always over-rode my shyness - I asked Miss Basilisk what was wrong upstairs. She made it clear, politely, that I was never going to find out.

Another time, Miss Basilisk did tell us of a tragedy - though if it was what inspired the crying we were never to know. She had had a "lodger" who smoked in bed and had burned himself to death. We were so overcome with horrified awe we could hardly do our pliés. Curiously, the basement had no trace or smell of fire, and the dead lodger was not mentioned again.

In spite of these alarms, we made enough progress to be included in Miss Basilisk's pupil recital. We had frilly pink costumes and were supposed to be two little girls fighting over a hatbox. We got through the performance all right, and looked forward to getting up on our "points" next term.

Miss Basilisk also taught me, the dysmechsic, how to tie my shoes - as my husband was to teach me much later how to properly light a match. Watching me put my street shoes on, "Weren't you ever taught how to do up your shoelaces?" she asked indignantly. And showed me how to put one lace over the other and loop it under instead of making two loops and tying them together. But the most interesting thing we learned from Miss Basilisk, more exciting even than the story of the poor burnt lodger, was the story of how her soul left her body in the middle of a ballet.

She did not tell this to us. Carried away, she told it to her quiet, unobtrusive accompanist, during a break in our lesson. Her soul had soared up into the wings while her body went on with the performance below and then, quite simply, re-entered her body again. She had asked the rest of the troupe if they had noticed anything strange; they said her performance was fine. It was evident way from the glowing way she described it that this episode had been the greatest thrill of Miss Basilisk's life.

That evening, Verena and I decided we would emulate Miss Basilisk. We picked up garden sticks, like magic rods, and marched around on the grass, chanting and singing and gazing at the moon, trying to put ourselves in a trance, waiting for our souls to take off into the trees. We marched and marched, in vain but still hopeful. We were still marching and chanting, feeling we were getting closer, when my father came home. He asked what we were up to. We explained. My father had one of his rare displays of anger. Not at us. At Miss Basilisk. He told us it was all nonsense and shooed us inside.

The next day Miss Basilisk got an irate phone call. She did not mention her soul again, and the ballet lessons did not go on much longer. I felt sad and guilty about this, as I knew the story of Miss Basilisk's soul was one only for adults, one of those forbidden stories children are not meant to hear.

There was not only ballet. At the suggestion of a socialite riding companion of my parents, I went with two of her children to dancing school, one of the two that most Grosse Pointe society attended. Later, my sister went to the other. Mine was run by a graying gentleman and his younger lady partner. They taught the two-step, fox trot, waltz, polka, rumba, conga, samba and even the jitterbug. I went there not only because ballroom dancing was thought an essential accomplishment in Grosse Pointe but because the other Gomper's pupil at this dancing school was Jack Bingham, with whom I'd fallen in love.

While the teachers showed us the step, we stood in segregated halves, boys on one side, girls on the other. The boys had to wear jackets, the girls came in pretty pastel dresses, white bobby socks, black patent leather dancing shoes with flat grosgrain bows; I was allowed out of my orthopaedic shoes for the occasion. After the teachers' demonstration, the boys asked the girls to dance.

I was a lousy dancer, clumsy, tense and anxious, hating the feel of my sweaty palm against a strange hand. I was usually one of the last to be asked, and once or twice the odd one out who had to dance with the teacher, whose belt-buckle was on a level with my chin. Dancing school was one more miserable humiliation. But the pain was worth it if - as did rarely happen - Jack asked me to dance.

At the end of the year came a dreaded occasion; an evening dance for which you had to wear "formals," long dresses, and go with a date. I didn't have a date. Jack didn't ask me, and I didn't know anyone else. I could only pray for another flu. But my mother, in her usual resourceful if unorthodox fashion, produced a solution. One day, after his fifty-minute hour was over, she called me into the library and introduced me to her patient, a boy named Johnny. Johnny was "cute" in a juvenile, impish sort of way, except for strange, staring blue eyes which made me uncomfortable. My mother waited somewhat sternly while Johnny asked me to the dance.

I couldn't remember ever dancing with Johnny in the classes, and asked my mother if he really wanted to take me. She assured me he did. I felt it was somehow all wrong, but to refuse was worse than to go.

When the fateful evening arrived, I put on the pink taffeta dress I had got my mother to order after seeing it on the cover of *Calling All Girls* magazine. It wasn't off-shoulder or strapless, or low-cut with bouffant sleeves, like most formals. It had a high neck, a Peter Pan collar with two beaded flowers, little cap sleeves and a light blue grosgrain sash. On the magazine cover, it looked pretty and very original. On me, with my skinny arms, bowed head and flat chest, it looked the sort of dress in which no Grosse Pointe girl would be seen dead. *Calling All Girls*, I realized later, was anyhow a bit plebeian. Grosse Pointe wore the sort of dresses you saw in *Seventeen* and *Mademoiselle*.

Johnny and I were driven to the dance by his, or our, chauffeur. I don't even remember whose; I was paralysed by embarrassment. We had nothing much to say to each other, but he did dutifully present me with a corsage. I didn't ask if my mother had bought it.

We danced a few dances, me still speechless and sweaty-palmed; but Johnny was good and I did manage not to step too often on his feet. Then Johnny disappeared. And to my amazement, for the last dance, when it was announced that you should ask your best girl, Jack, who'd brought someone else, asked me. I didn't know if it meant anything. I hardly dared hope. In any case there was never a sequel.

Johnny reappeared for the ride home. His was the first stop. "Goodbye, Big Eyes," he said cheerfully - an odd farewell since *his* were the noticeable eyes - and got out of the car. I never saw Johnny again. I don't know how long he went on seeing my mother, or for what. She maintained professional discretion and never told me. He had seemed relaxed, a bit brash, and except for that staring gaze, quite normal, taking the odd date in his stride. It was hard to imagine him running in terror from small dogs or wetting his bed. I looked through the case histories, of course, but never found him.

Jack, whom I loved, was tall and solidly built, with crew-cut blond hair and glasses and big, capable-looking, well-shaped hands. He was certainly the handsomest boy in our class, the best at sports, except for Bernard the most intelligent, and definitely the most civilized. By that I mean he never bullied, he always played fair, he never made an unwanted pass. Once, during a recess, Jack on some impulse flung his arms round me and hugged me. I found myself suddenly squashed against his warm flannel-shirted chest, and I think he shouted my name. Then he let me go. That was all. I lived on this hug for most of the year.

We were all in love with Jack; Alice, Ruby and I. Or maybe Ruby wasn't - she never said. But he was certainly, again except Bernard, the only catch in the school. The other boys were impossible, or too young.

Ruby and I had the luck of going back in the same school car with Jack. We often contrived to sit on either side of him. When the car was very full, one or the other of us had to sit on his lap, which I did with embarrassment and Ruby with ease.

I could not imagine that mature, clever, attractive Jack would fall for Ruby. I thought all loves of Jack were equally unrequited. Then one day, in the car, I saw something that was like a shot of ice in my stomach. I looked again, thinking it couldn't be. But it was. Ruby and Jack were holding hands.

They did not smile or gaze at each other. They did not talk much. They only held hands, for half an hour, all the way to Ruby's house. For me, the half hour was eternal. I tried to chat, to pretend I didn't see, not to blush or let my voice show my anguish, I prayed it was just that once. It wasn't. Ruby was in the junior class, and their contact at school did not increase; Jack seemed as indifferent as before. But the hand-holding went on for the rest of their time at Gomper's.

Surreptitiously, on those miserable rides, I studied the hands. They weren't squeezing or moving, certainly not making that awful obscene motion (someone explained it) one of the cruder boys had once made with a finger on my palm. They just rested in each other, Jack's nice long strong hand with slightly dirty fingernails and Ruby's pale thin one with bitten nails flecked with white, which I had been told was a sign of calcium deficiency. How could Jack want to hold Ruby's hand? How could Jack like Ruby? If at least it had been Alice, who was beautiful and bright and my friend. (Ruby was now supposed to be my friend too but I had never trusted her since the Sylvia episode.) Ruby, who was pasty and freckled and unhealthy-looking and sometimes nasty, Ruby who was (to use my father's word) vulgar, who was not for a moment worthy of Jack.

The pain of those rides home was almost as great as the fear of being hurt or teased at school. I had only a few dances, and my one hug. Ruby had Jack's hand. Every day. Every day. And every day, I sneaked looks, hoping against hope that the hands would not be joined. Nearly always they were.

Alice and I stayed in love with Jack until we had all left Gomper's. When she and I met again, months later, we decided to write a book about Alice's year at Gomper's and our passion for Jack. We began it one afternoon when Alice was at my house. "One year," we began, "one grain upon the sands of time." We got as far as a page or two. We also embarked on a poem. "My love for you is like a storm-tossed sea," was the poem's first line. We had to interrupt our writing to go to a concert with Katya and my parents, to hear Katya's friend Bredshall and one of his pupils. The pupil was to play the first movement of the Tchaikovsky concerto, with Bredshall playing orchestra on piano two.

We walked into the Detroit Art Institute auditorium still glowing with the thought of our memoir and our love for Jack. The Bredshall pupil, who was then about eighteen, slight, a bit Oriental looking, came out and bowed, sat down at the piano, tossed back a shock of coal-black hair and struck, with tremendous panache, the opening chords.

Alice and I instantly fell out of love with Jack. We fell in love with the young pianist instead.

It was so sudden, unexpected, simultaneous, overwhelming, we marvelled at it. We continued to marvel at it during the further years of unrequited love that followed.

I met Jack again when I was in high school. He went to the "brother school" of my all-girl one. We saw each other at joint school functions, but we never spoke. He was always with the same two friends and seemed to be quiet and rather out of things, not at all the leading light he'd been at Gomper's. I never saw him with a girl, or saw his name linked with one in the society columns I avidly read to learn where I had not been invited. Before we graduated, I heard he had leukaemia; and soon after that, I heard he was dead. Ruby I never saw again. In my mind, their hands remain, vivid as yesterday, but now somehow very innocent, fixed in their ghostly clasp.

Some of the supervised Gomper periods also became nightmares.

Outdoor games at Gomper's were not segregated. This didn't matter too much as long as we had only the back yard and there were no sports to speak of, just trotting around or playing tag; except in winter, when you'd be hit by hard expert snowballs.

But then Gomper's rented another school's playing field for a period each day. We were taken there by car, even more packed than on the school run. I had to sit on hated laps, pinched and tickled and teased. I remember a candy store near the field where we bought Oh Henrys and Baby Ruths and Wrigley's Spearmint gum, and bubble-gum with tiny comic strips on the wrapping. The rest is all gray sky, wind, packed desolate earth, cold and fear.

What we usually played was Endball, a German favorite and the most sadistic of ball games. You have two teams, who try to get each other "out" by hitting with the ball. You must either dodge the ball or catch it. If you catch, you get a turn to throw at the enemy. If you're hit you go as a prisoner to the back of the other team. When prisoners get the ball, they aim at the enemy in turn. This continues till one side wins by getting all the other team out.

Gomper's upheld sexual equality in sports as in fights. Never mind if you were a girl and the youngest and half the size of the several louts trying to smash into you a ball bigger than your head, aiming gleefully at your knees, your rear, even your face. I had not liked ball games before; I learned to hate them passionately and for life. I hardly ever caught; the throws were too hard. But I was an artful dodger, so often I was the last one left, hopping about on the ugly field, trying to ignore the jeers and threats, hopelessly putting off the painful denouement - "Come on, Sterba! Catch it, Sterba, you sissy!"- the blow on the ear or nauseating whack in the stomach that marked my defeat and the end of the game. Which then, if it was not too late, would begin again.

Once, almost on reflex, perhaps after WR had cavalierly exhorted me to fight back, I kicked out at a boy tormenting me on the playground ride, and inadvertently hit his chin with my snow-covered boot. Leering, he swore that now he was *"really* gonna get" me. I was in terror, but managed to avoid him the rest of that day. Next day, mercifully, he had forgotten.

There was also the problem of big Henry, the one with the German psychiatrist father. Henry developed a crush on me, and decided he would cement this passion with a kiss. I was pulled along the yard, screaming and protesting, the other louts cheering Henry on. On this occasion, in the nick of time, Henry was ordered to let me go.

That night, I had a visit from the inner demon. I was plagued by a hideous impulse; to get a pair of scissors and cut off all my tortoises' heads. I did not really want to do anything at all like this but I could not get the idea out of my mind. It was so bad I told my parents.

My parents asked if anything special had happened that day. Reluctantly I told them about Henry. My parents, delighted with this apparent vindication of Freud, explained that what I really wanted to do was cut off Henry's prick.

This did not seem very logical. I hadn't thought about Henry's prick. Even about the fact that he had one. And I could not quite see the connection to my tortoises. But I accepted my parents' superior wisdom. Maybe in this case they were right, or just telling someone made the obsession go. The demon left me, and I fell asleep.

Having mentioned it again, I must describe the inner demon.

When you stand at the edge of a precipice, the inner demon is what urges you to jump. When you are on your best behaviour, making polite conversation, the inner demon may put a string of obscenities into your head. Or, when something disgusts or frightens you, run the image through your mind for hours, maybe days, until you almost scream to get away. Or simply make you hum the songs that you hate the most.

I used another, typical demonic urge in a long-ago published story. You sit in the balcony first row of a crowded theatre, and suddenly think of dropping your opera glasses on a defenceless bald head below. And this impulse becomes so frightening you have to put the glasses away. (In my story, the girl does drop them in the end.)

Unfortunately, a lot of these promptings do not succumb to pat Freudian explanations; nor Jungian, Adlerian or whatever. Most of what the demon urges are the kind of things done or said by those judged, in previous ages, possessed. Possession is what it feels like; thoughts or impulses *from someone else;* unmotivated, irrational, and often directed against what you actually love and want to protect - urges from an alien being whose purpose is to destroy *you.*

The demon was not always there. It might leave me alone for days on end; then something, anything, set it off. My eventual two years of analysis mollified but never completely erased or unravelled it. I simply stopped being afraid that I might obey it or that it would drive me mad. And after that I had other things, real practical problems on my mind. The inner demon thrives on idleness, loneliness, surfeit and ennui. Hard work, especially physical, risk and adventure drive it out. At least it was so with mine.

My shrink and I sifted in vain through my store of early memories and her store of pre-war Viennese gossip to find an explanation. I was too focused on myself to ask her how many patients have such demons; if they are a source of real criminality or 'Possession' phenomena or if they stick to shy neurotics and desert saints, existing only to torment the psyche in which they reside.

My own interpretations are tentative and eclectic. The demon may be just bottled-up rage at the world you are too weak to fight, and rage at yourself for your weakness. Or that same process of osmosis that made me incorporate my parents' unexpressed fear at the time of our flight. And also, as so much is now deemed to be, a flaw in the chemistry of the brain. I will never know; but I know what it looks like. It does not look like a psychiatrist's diagram, a tangle of neurons or a genetic code. It has claws and an evil snout and a barbed tail, and big sharp ears and pupil-less eyes, now red, now bilious green, depending on the light in the cave inside your head. It is not a beast, because beasts are guiltless. It is a demon, which means, a little more, a little less than human. And writing about it, I still knock on wood.

Besides the inner demon, I had to contend with more of the outer.

Gomper's, like most progressive schools, believed in hands-on education. Only there was not much to get your hands on. There were no labs, no studios, no place to keep little creatures to torture in the name of science. All of that was to come later, when Gomper's expanded and moved. For the moment, there was only clay and finger paints, soap carving and Christmas cards printed with linoleum blocks and potatoes, things like in *Children's Activities* magazine. There was however one golden opportunity for learning by doing: the nursery school.

This program, like the school itself, was started by my mother. My mother began to visit Gomper's to give talks on psychology. I sat at the back of the class, red-faced and silent, too nervous to take in a word, cringing with embarrassment while my mother held forth at the front oblivious of her accent, her awful haircut, her foreignness. Her small plump figure exuded confidence, but I dreaded the rudeness she would get and the teasing I would get when she left. My fears were not realized. The children listened and asked polite questions. Even the great louts behaved with decorum. Perhaps Hans Gomper had warned them they had better shut up or for once really face detention. Perhaps my mother cowed them. (She did cow people, including, after I'd left home, a neighbour with a psychotic breakdown who marched into our house waving a gun and demanded she get him exemption from the draft. My mother persuaded him to put the gun down and then called the police to have him removed. Nut cases were after all her business.)

The other girls in my class, fourteen or fifteen to my eleven, had done baby-sitting or helped look after younger siblings. They were quite responsive to the lecture, and eager to learn more. In conference with Marlene Gomper, it was decided we would have a new subject: Child Care. Each senior girl would spend a period per week supervising nursery school children at meals or play. I was asked if being so much younger I wanted to participate. Ashamed of being left out, I said yes.

The child care period was unrelieved terror. The nursery school kids were totally wild and almost as big as I was. I have a vivid image of sitting on stairs while my little group spat in my face and hit me on the head with a toy locomotive. I knew I was not supposed to hit them back and as always I was too embarrassed to call for help. I don't know how I got through that hour.

Another session included their noontime pee. Again, no segregation, girls and boys together. They lined up before the one toilet, aimed with more or less accuracy, scrambled on, scrambled off. This time there was a teacher, exhorting them to wipe bottoms and wash hands. I only watched, horrified. Not dear Freud at the little penises, probably the first I'd seen since I was too small to remember, but because the whole scene was so sordid, unhygienic, and unfair to any child who might have been shy like myself and want privacy.

The other sessions are mostly blank. I remember only spilled food on knee-high tables and a darkened room where the little monsters squirmed on cots. Maybe someone twigged that the founder's child was in danger and saw to it that I had an adult around. Maybe I managed to be ill on most of my remaining Child Care days. Next fall there was no Child Care. The upper school was in another building, and there was no remaining student even Gomper's could put in charge of a child.

This is not to say that Gomper's had only bad moments. There were many good ones, mostly due to the inspired teaching of WR. We continued to read Shakespeare, unsimplified, unexpurgated, and something got through to even the thickest and most disturbed. The warm response of that mixed and bizarre class showed me how great Shakespeare is. If you do not have to dissect him too much and kill all the fun.

We also read an abridged *Don Quixote,* which I loved. We performed Molière - more embarrassment because I, tiny and flat-chested, had to play the wet nurse opposite Bernard's lecherous *Doctor in Spite of Himself* - but except for that it was good. We scanned poems and wrote essays and struggled with algebra and enjoyed Hans Gomper's party piece, the tale of how he went to his own funeral in Hamburg, everyone having supposed him drowned. For punishment we learned sonnets and elegies; for recreation WR read us exciting stories, *Dr Heidegger's Experiment, The Monkey's Paw,* and we listened spellbound and I forgot I was lonely and afraid. In fact, I wasn't completely lonely. I saw less of snobbish, impatient Nina who was now in her teens and getting back to Society. But the two other 'intelligent' older girls had become my friends.

Alice, my best friend, was very bright, musical, very pretty and one quarter (or eighth) Iroquois (or Seminole) which I found immeasurably romantic. Alice's family were devout Baptists. When she left Gomper's she went to a well-known Baptist boarding school and college. Later she married a missionary and became a very active pillar of her church.

Jane, also bright and full of humor, was from a prominent Detroit Jewish family. I sometimes spent a night at Jane's house. This was a key activity among girlfriends. You slept in the same room, perhaps tried makeup and did each other's hair, listened to a favorite pop record or Frank Sinatra on *Your Hit Parade*, stayed awake very late, giggling and gossiping in the dark. It was on such overnights that you began naive conversations about sex.

I never stayed at Alice's house; Alice stayed at mine. Alice's house was too little for overnight guests - or it was simply a tacit agreement. I never even met Alice's parents, until years later, when she was home from Bob Jones University for Christmas vacation and asked me to accompany her and her mother and sister to a talk by Dr Bob Jones. Dr Jones, a onetime Shakespearian actor but real holy roller, delivered what was to me a most embarrassing sermon, then asked for anyone feeling 'saved' to come forward and acknowledge Jesus. I sensed, or imagined, my three companions' eyes on me. I looked straight ahead and sat firmly in my seat. No one said anything but, though she and I remained friends for a while, I did not see Alice's family again.

Jane's house was big but on the other side of Detroit, near Highland Park, then the fashionable area for well-off Jews. Jane's father, a lawyer, shocked and enlightened me by remarking, when his son asked him to explain the lawsuit he was working on, that it was about one person trying to get money out of another. This opened a new world of adult cynicism. I knew about cruelty and crime and war; I thought human beings a dreadful species. But I had somehow assumed that people in the professions, at least the people you might know, were dedicated, honest and ethical. I respected Jane's father for his frankness, though it upset me, and wondered why my parents did not have him as a friend, not guessing that, like several Gomper parents, he might be a patient.

Jane's house was also exciting because the hum of the city was so near. At night you heard police sirens, and I would lie awake, wondering about the grim, eventful life beyond Grosse Pointe.

Alice told me later that she, Nina and Jane sometimes got together without me. After an overnight at Nina's house, Nina, a member, had an errand at the Boat Club on Belle Isle. Alice and Jane went with her. When they reached the door of the club, Nina turned and told Jane that she'd have to wait outside, as the club did not admit Jews. Alice was speechless, but Jane simply waited patiently till Nina returned. Whether their tenuous friendship survived this incident, I do not know; we were soon, all of us, in other schools.

It was Alice who joined me, just as a joke, in sending away for a booklet called *The Art of Kissing* advertised on the back of some comic or magazine. Neither of us had ever been kissed. Alice's religion wouldn't have allowed it. I was too young and knew no one, except Jack, from whom I might have wanted a kiss.

The booklet came. We perused it in high excitement. It seems amazing now that twenty pages could be filled with kisses that stop at the neck, but the instructions were padded with purple prose, some of which is with me still. "Kiss the eyelid and feel the rolling orb quiver beneath your lips." Or "Bring your lips down gently as a butterfly on the lips of your loved one." There was the (daring) French kiss. There was kissing the throat and the back of the neck. It wasn't exactly the Kama Sutra, though I suppose we found it titillating, in a ridiculous way. But it did include one curious perversion, inspired no doubt by the frustration of halting at the collar bone. If you couldn't have an orgasm, you could at least have another sort of charge. This was electrical kissing. You somehow wired yourself (and your Loved One) up with batteries. Then you kissed, and a small electric shock passed between your mouths. "My brother," the author wrote confidentially, "got his lips seriously burned." Alice and I had hysterics imagining the wired couple advancing with puckered lips and squealing as the spark of their contact flashed in the air.

My sneak reading of case histories had now advanced to a few of my father's I was able to find. They were not much more exciting than my mother's bed-wetters and phobics. No whips or bondage, just underwear fixation, palpitations, anxiety. Perhaps my father didn't treat extremes, or kept their notes better concealed. I suspected however that the oscular use of electricity *was* perverse and wondered if *The Art of Kissing* was not after all a dangerous book. If you wired up and got addicted, increasing the voltage, you could wind up dead. After our giggles we hid the silly book and then junked it. I should have saved it, a solitary example for some Kraft-Ebbing lexicon of libidinal vagaries. I never met, heard of, or read of, anyone who'd actually had an electrical kiss.

Much more exciting that *The Art of Kissing* was the *Chin P'Ing Mei*, a translation of a 16th century Chinese masterpiece.

Free to ferret among the shelves, I discovered this, 'The Adventurous History of Hsi Men and his Six Wives.' I read both volumes, then I read my favorite erotic passages again and again. "...soon her mouth was making those quivering, snapping motions which one may observe in a dog that is snapping at flies, and her lips without ceasing uttered their tender cry of *'Ta Ta'*." This was not hearts and flowers, but it was heady stuff. It also made me think that strange activity must, after all, be fun.

The plot was pretty exciting too. I began to dress my Storybook Doll collection in scraps of material as the wives of Hsi Men, and renamed the Little Bo Peeps and Hungarian Peasant Girl figures Jade Fountain and Moon Lady and Gold Lotus, the stunning evil heroine who comes to a deserved but horrible end. My sister and I acted out bits of the plot. Not the sex scenes though. For one thing there were no Storybook Dollmen. And "In their unbridled passion they were like two romping phoenixes, or two little fishes tumbling in the water," was not something my stiff little dolls could represent.

My parents, as usual, ignored my literary explorations, as long as no nightmares were produced. Later, I read *Our Sex Life* by Fritz Kahn, MD, and van de Velde's *The Perfect Marriage*. These were How To Do It books, technical and embarrassing. The *Chin P'Ing Mei* remains the sexiest book I have ever read.

Already before Katya came, my parents had me try piano lessons with another refugee. This was such a fiasco even my mother soon abandoned the idea. Anyway, there was my poetic talent. My parents were part of the group and generation that dethroned God in favor of Art. And in my poetry my mother saw budding genius.

My parents had written down things I babbled even in Vienna days, and typed out a few early poems. There was an ode to a milkmaid and a grim little verse about a war-devastated city with "house ribs and brick bones." Even my father, more level-headed than my mother, thought that to produce something like this at age three showed surprising verbal facility.

Unluckily, 'forties America boasted two famous little girl poets, Nathalia Crane and Hilda Conkling. Some benighted acquaintance introduced my mother to their work. After this, there was no holding her. If Hilda Conkling, why not I? I read Hilda Conkling and other poets and I poetized, whether because I was inspired or because I was so much encouraged is now impossible to say. Later, when my English was fluent, it felt like inspiration. Later still, it felt like the only thing I would ever want to do with my life. But what came out was not like Conkling's "I cannot see fairies. I dream them." I didn't have that Conkling touch. Except for a rare line, my own were derivative, self-conscious, pseudo-adult, full of pathetic fallacy and pathetic infelicities:

> The river lies
> A mass of leaves
> Still with the current
> Moving with the stream, etc.

This masterpiece was about the canals on Belle Isle. Someone should have pointed out that currents are the opposite of still. But not my mother. Her English wasn't good enough. And she would have done nothing to dampen me. She, or rather my father, was getting me into print.

My poems appeared in our local society paper, the *Grosse Pointe News*.

This came about through the good offices of a patient, who wrote a column. She was an ex New York showgirl, who'd married a wealthy handsome Grosse Pointer. Her problem was a sort of agoraphobia; she was unable to leave her grounds. As the grounds were large this problem was not acute; but it must, with time, have been evident to anyone who knew her. So my father was not really violating professional secrecy in telling me. I believe he went to see her, rather than she him. Anyway, he gave her my poems, and I was invited to visit her 'cattery.' Mrs X had a passion for Persian cats, which she bred, and had so many a separate little house had been built for them on the estate.

Mrs X greeted us dressed in a pink negligée and mules. She was tall and willowy and very good looking in a languid, sleepy way. She smelled of expensive perfume and cigarettes, her voice was the husky, Marlene Dietrich kind, and her manner at once casual and grand. I was terribly impressed. Glamour, the quality my mother so lacked, always fascinated and thrilled me. As it did my father.

Mrs X made polite conversation, praised my poems, and then drifted out to the cattery with us and opened the door. The cattery was overwhelming in its stench. I could hardly look at the luxuriously hairy, pug-faced, elegant creatures who glided and arched and scrabbled and mewed. I was overcome by that lion-house odour, so strong it took my breath away. Mrs X did not seem to notice, and I managed to make some appreciative remark. The visit was soon over. As more fraternization would have been unprofessional on Daddy's part, I did not go to the cattery again. I thought about it often though, the lovely mysterious Mrs X and her incongruous stinking cattery. And longed to know more about her. Meanwhile, Mrs X kindly published two or three of my affected little poems. Soon after, maybe because of this premature publication, I became totally shy and secretive about my work and ambitions. But I wanted, already then, to be a great poet. It was a good thing I didn't know that those would be the last of my poems to be printed for forty years.

There was one student in my Gomper's class who may have suffered more than I.

George was the tallest, but skinniest, and George had a fetish; his briefcase. No one knew what, besides his schoolbooks, was in it. Anyhow, George guarded this briefcase with his life, and the other boys made a great game of trying to get it away from him. Success produced hysteria and violence, till the briefcase was returned. A good deal of class time was spent on this activity. George would sit, hunched over his desk, grinning nervously - he always grinned - his long legs wrapped round his briefcase, and while Hans Gomper droned and chalked equations on the board, another boy would stretch out a leg and fish for the briefcase till George exploded. So it went on. One day it came to a head. I don't know if it was the briefcase or some last straw insult or just a paper airplane grazing his ear. Whatever it was, George had had enough. He got up, with some dignity, and tossed one of his books through a closed window. A shower of glass rained down on Jane and Henry who were sitting next to the pane. Miraculously, they were not hurt. George grinned harder, with satisfaction. "That did it," he announced loudly, picked up his briefcase, and walked out. George was not seen again. I was to envy him in the half year that followed.

HAPPINESS AT CAMP ENDS WITH ANOTHER FLIGHT IN THE NIGHT

My mother, having lost three babies out of five - it is rumored there was even a sixth, aborted or miscarried just before my parents fled Austria - was determined that the surviving two get maximum protection. The terrible Dr Strapp, the jolly moustachioed paediatrician who pinched cheeks after he inserted needles, adding injury to injury, came every year or two to inject us with DPT - diphtheria, pertussis (whooping cough) and tetanus serum. My little arm usually swelled like a balloon and I spent a couple of days in bed with a high fever. As this happened in summer vacation, shortly before the trip to Vermont, I didn't even get to miss any school.

Moved by the inner demon to see how much pain I could stand, I sometimes lifted my inflamed arm, which every movement hurt, above my head over and over, until I was crying bitterly. My parents put it in a sling and for once shouted at me, to make me stop. Why did I do this? Masochism? No, nothing so simple. Testing myself for possible Gestapos, trying in a sick way to learn courage, the courage I so lacked? The shadow behind the couch has never given an answer. And why the horror of needles? I am no longer afraid of shots, but to this day I can't watch them, even on a movie screen.

I was so frightened of Dr Strapp's shots that once I ran away from home the day he was due. I got as far as the top of our block, Jefferson Avenue, the big busy main street that led to Detroit. My idea was just to stay away till Dr Strapp had gone. But I was scared to wander on. I'd never even walked to the Grosse Pointe city limits alone. And I knew I'd have to face Dr Strapp's needle sooner or later. The one thing on earth my mother would not indulge me in was escape from her health routines. I went back home.

Tetanus was always a danger for riders; on one occasion, the adults had shots too. Even Ellie, who went nowhere near the horses. They all smiled to show me how painless it was. Mine hurt more than ever. I decided there must be an age when injections no longer hurt. They could not possibly keep those smiles if they felt what I did. I longed passionately to grow up.

But after the ordeal came a great reward, the summer at camp.

The eccentric Wunder camp, with its clutch of sometimes still bewildered fellow Europeans, was a disorganized but pleasant place. Even the oddness of my mother's being there too didn't matter. She went again as resident shrink and psychological advisor, Katya as music counsellor.

After the first year or two, I roomed with other, older girls. My mother, Katya, the cocker spaniel, and my father when he was there, had a flat next door, but I didn't see them much. I became an almost normal camper. I couldn't swim yet, but I could ride and I could run. I played Kick the Can and Capture the Flag, I braided lanyards, piped on the recorder, fed rabbits, danced the Virginia Reel, shared other girls' giggles and smutty jokes, learned to play Jacks and Gin Rummy and Fish and Old Maid and steal Wonder Bread at night from the kitchen pantry, to munch in secret or knead into dice for shooting Craps. I was still nervous, still somewhat on trial, but mostly blissful. I was in the mountains, I was Heidi come home. I loved all the camp things, but a part of me was dazed and detached, tuned to the wilderness, drunk on height and air and a space so rich in another life, still so empty of human beings, human cruelty, human grief.

Among the girls I roomed with were Wendy, daughter of a friend who rode with my parents on Belle Isle, and Nina, and a wonderfully agile girl from Boston who could shinny up ropes, walk on her hands and swim like an eel. They were all older and more sophisticated. They already had crushes on boys. Mrs Wunder complained about some still older campers found "struggling in the bushes" but I doubt my room-mates got as far as a French kiss, though as they didn't confide in me I can't be sure. Not to be left out, I developed a mild crush of my own, on a red-headed, freckle-faced boy named Toby. I don't think he knew I was alive. This was before my crush on Jack.

During the day, my room-mates and I mostly went separate ways. They rode at Mr Lawrence's stable, I rode at Captain van Ingen's at the Equinox Hotel. They frolicked in deep water. I struggled with my dog paddle in the baby pool. The Wunders, good Europeans, prescribed after-lunch rest, which we spent playing cards, reading comics, throwing our dice of molded hard bread. And at night, after Lights Out, we whispered and giggled, exchanged ghost stories or dirty jokes and songs.

One favorite dirty story was about the man who buys a rooster, a hen and a donkey. Having been instructed to call them by the prevailing local names, when the donkey bolts he shouts, "Hold my cock and pullet while I go after my ass." This produced hysterics, and has never died; I heard an adult tell it on an Amtrak train forty-five years later. There was also one about the accidentally severed penis that lands in a pickle vendor's cart, and the lady who comes back next day asking for "another one of those wonderful pickles with the bones in them." Only little girls can tell such a story. I didn't remember there were no bones in my parents' medical diagrams. It is the giggly information given in the dark that lodges in your mind.

This being wartime, we also talked about Japanese tortures. The others invented horrors for two counsellors we actually liked, who were going around together. "And the Japs made Tommy pee so it squirted right into Polly's mouth," one girl said, and we rolled around on our beds, stifling shrieks of hilarity. Even I - with horror, delight and admiring envy. These girls had no night fears, no inner demons, no Nazi bogey men. No doubts that America would win the war, that no such evils would ever touch them. They were so secure that even war horrors were material for another joke. If there was a perverse side to such humor, I didn't notice it. But I knew my own, darker vision of the world was closer to reality.

But again, I didn't quite understand the rules, even there.

I sensed that there should be someone at the bottom of our room pecking order and was shamefully glad when, for a while, it wasn't me. But I never grasped the shifts of allegiance and favor. Suddenly, there is a prank from which you are excluded, a secret which you are not told, a great friendship with a pretty junior counsellor who pays no heed to you. Of course, you're younger. But is it only that? And then someone Frenches your bed - turns the bottom sheet up over the blanket, so you're stuck when you try to get in. Laughter. You laugh too. You have to be a good sport. It's a harmless trick. But why was it *you?* And why, after the laughter, are they still whispering?

Twentieth century writing, inspired by my parents' god without comprehending what he said, has mostly opted for the easy escapist wallow in sex, or the ugly wallow in violence. Yet violence often begins with the whispers in the dark; and no sex scene I have read is worth George Eliot's council meeting in *Middlemarch*. But it is hard to write about power for jaded readers with short attention spans. It is much easier to write about sex. Perhaps because I am a natural outsider, I will always be fascinated by the mysteries of power, the speed and irrationality of allegiance shifts, the way they are made and used by the ambitious, the envious, the cruel, the petty jockeying that rules and sacrifices lives.

I was pretty well over my childish crush on Marlene. She was boring, she had babies, she was married to blustering, ineffectual Hans. She was no longer Titania the fairy queen. But I still liked it when she came to kiss us goodnight.

One night my room-mates announced Marlene was about to appear. She came to my bed in the dark, bent over me, was especially affectionate. There was much tittering from the other beds. Suddenly I understood. It wasn't Marlene. It was our sixteen-year-old junior counsellor Annie, who had curly brown hair like Marlene's and palled around with the older girls, especially Nina. Nina, I felt, had probably put her up to this trick. I blurted, "It's Annie," not knowing what else to say. After a while the laughter subsided. I lay awake a long time, baffled and tearful, badly hurt by a joke that I sensed was vicious, without understanding why.

The other black incident of those summers took place during a camp assembly. A bony little boy with jug ears, cropped hair and a nasty grin sat down next to me. In the middle of the meeting, while Hans Gomper was droning on, he suddenly reached under my skirt.

I pushed desperately against his arm, too terrified to scream, unable to face the shame of announcing his assault. It was what he must have counted on. I managed to get his hand away before he actually got inside my pants, and - I hoped and prayed - before anybody saw. But those few moments remain among the most nightmarish of my life.

I told no one, not even my mother. I felt sullied and threatened all the rest of the summer; I lived in fear of another assault. Fortunately, he was younger and in a group we did not often meet. Once, I saw him kicking and flailing and screaming as he was carried off the playing field in Marlene's arms. He was actually quite a little boy. The sight of her soothing him when I wanted to see him dead, putting up with his violence almost with affection, finished *my* affection for Marlene for good.

But mostly I remember the magic that infused everything. The thrilling possibility of meeting a wild animal - deer, porcupine, even bear - at any turn of your path. The great forests that began here and went on almost unbroken to the still greater forests of Canada, the dryad birch trees, the spicy pines, the oaks and elms and maples with their whispering leaves, the secret clearings and lost, overgrown old wagon roads, the orangey-pink salamanders that came out after the rain and would walk, oblivious, on your hand. To misquote Hilda Conkling, I never saw fairies, but I sensed them. I was just wise enough not to share my occult romantic vibrations, my Midsummer Night's Dream pantheism, with most of my companions. What we shared of the supernatural were the usual ghost stories, hardly altered in my daughter's own time at another camp four decades later; the fraternity initiation in the haunted house, the headless corpse in the clearing, the mad camper with a bloody axe wandering through the trees.

The Wunder summer was livened by exciting events. There were excursions, and "war games" where everyone was divided into teams and sent into the woods. You had to take prisoners by pulling off bits of coloured wool tied to your enemies' belts. The opportunities this might give for what Mrs Wunder called "struggling in the bushes" seem to have been overlooked by the staff. I myself escaped enemy action. By the time the strays were rounded up everyone was covered with mosquito bites, and galloping cases of poison ivy followed, casualties of the "war,"

Sometimes we swam in a marble quarry, a mysterious, haunted, haunting place, which terrified me because of its reputedly unfathomed depth. There were visits from famous Vermont writers, Dorothy Canfield Fisher and Sarah N. Cleghorn. [12] There was the yearly play, a Virginia Reel on Saturday night, and best or worst of all, the sunrise hike.

For this hike, we were roused at two a.m., provided with oranges and Wonder Bread, crowded into camp trucks and station wagons, and driven to the foot of Mt Equinox, 3816 feet above sea level. Equinox was the highest peak around and in those happy days had no Skyline Drive, no monastery or hotel on top; a fairly pristine mountain. In scattered groups, we climbed toward the sunrise. The paths were good, but discipline as always was minimal. Nearly everyone started too fast, so many campers, soon puking and faint with exhaustion, staggered back before they were anywhere near the top. I remember the brooding, living silence of the night, the enormous dark presence of the mountain. It was the first stirring of addiction to come. I wanted to go on. But my room-mates, who had

---

[12] *Sarah N. Cleghorn is immortal for a quatrain which appears in many American anthologies:*

>The golf-links lie so near the mill
>That almost every day
>The labouring children can look out
>And see the men at play.

rushed ahead, were shortly down again among the vomiting, so I felt empathetically sick and gave up too. A few campers, including one big-city four-year-old, made it to the summit and sucked their oranges facing the rising sun.

Our new riding teacher, who ran a stable behind the Equinox Hotel, was a retired Dutch cavalry captain, a ramrod-straight old soldier with a good classical education, who thrilled my father by quoting Plato and Xenophon. He was a superb horseman, and had everyone, horses and children, under strict but benevolent control. He insisted on ring work before we set out on the trails at the foot of Equinox, and had the unruly Wunder campers riding like cavalry. His praise was pure gold, and his authority unquestionable. Under his tutelage, I cantered about on giant hunters; his confidence drove out fear, or a greater fear was letting his confidence down. I rode whatever he put me on, even side-saddle on one of his boarders, a huge nasty mare called absurdly "Non-Nicer" who was never ridden any other way. If he'd told me to mount an elephant I would probably have done it. I have marvelled, ever since, at those mad ladies like the Empress of Austria who flew over fences on side-saddled steeds.

The trail rides were wonderful. Afterwards, we would wander back to camp, along the marble sidewalks in the sleepy summer heat, past the hotel with its Uncle Toms serving drinks to white-haired silk and linen-dressed old ladies rocking on the big columned porch. We fortified ourselves for the hot walk with ice-cream cones from the town drugstore, maple walnut, pistachio, chocolate or strawberry, the best ice cream in the world. And sometimes, as a special treat, the Captain would harness two of his big hunters and drive us back in his carriage, and if you were lucky enough to sit beside him, you might get to hold the reins.

Only once, I broke the Captain's trust. I was on my horse Sultan, and one of the first two to mount. The other was an older English evacuee, the best rider and only child allowed on a big fiery horse called Blackout. The Captain told us we could ride ahead alone to the ring. There were a few low jumps in the ring and we couldn't resist trying them quickly, before the cavalcade was in view. But the Captain saw us. He said nothing until we were back and had untacked our horses. Then he called us up in front of the others, and gave us a verbal lashing that cut like a whip. He had trusted us, and we had gone "skylarking." "I'm God around this stable," he roared, and we had better not forget it again. I don't know what the other child thought; I felt as small, guilty and disloyal as if he had been God.

There was no more jumping. I was a pretty good rider by then, and the Captain would have taught me. But my mother thought it too dangerous, and said no. Some years later, she let my sister learn, on a wild erratic mare, and cheered them on at horse shows with scant regard for risk. She learned herself, at the age of sixty. Home for a holiday, I watched her proudly display her jumping. Once, she fell off. She leapt immediately to her feet, raised her arms and shouted "Ho!" We wondered if she was concussed; then I remembered this was what we'd seen a fallen rider do in the Olympics, to show the vast audience of Madison Square Garden that he was not hurt.

Near the end of one camp summer, we were taken to swim in the public pool in town. A few days later, Wendy's boyfriend became very ill. Wendy, strictly against rules, went in to see him. My mother, watching him sip hot chocolate which came out again through his nose, made her own diagnosis, which was soon confirmed.

That night, for the second time in my life, I was roused from bed at midnight and driven secretly to a train. My mother and sister, Katya, the dog, Mrs Dodd, her two children and I went to friends of the Dodds in Connecticut. Then our family, joined by my father, went to a quiet seaside hotel for the rest of out vacation.

We had jumped a polio quarantine, declared the morning after we left. Two other children caught the disease. One was left a wheelchair case, the other recovered. The first patient, Wendy's boyfriend, had bulbar polio and died.

I have often thought of the rights and wrongs of what my mother and Mrs Dodd did that night. Wondered if I would have done the same for my child. If I had, I would have gone straight home and imposed my own quarantine there. I have always been amazed that the kind family in Connecticut, who had children too, were not afraid to receive us. They caught nothing, though Wendy and I had brief flus, which might have been polio in its mild form.

I felt guilty and ashamed because once more I'd been treated as the princess on the pea; once more given the kind of protection accorded the special, the different, the weak. I didn't reflect that other parents, given the chance, might have done what my mother did. I wanted to be strong and brave and one of the regulars. And with writer's egotism I have also thought of the book that might have come from those two quarantine weeks.

The Connecticut family were looking for a boarding school for their daughter. My mother recommended the Wunders' winter Vermont school. With that irony the dark fates enjoy, the girl did go there, and came home with meningitis - an isolated case - of which she died.

ENNE

Mother's Day was an occasion I would have ignored. It seemed to me commercial and silly, even then. But Enne usually presented me with a potted plant to give my mother, and my mother presented me with the same for her. This solemn exchange of flowerpots underlined the ambiguousness of Enne's life.

Her real name was Marie Brennessel; Enne was my baby corruption. She was one of seventeen children on a Burgenland farm, near the Hungarian border. Of seventeen, thirteen survived, and some emigrated before the war. In Nazi times, Enne's mother was sent a medal by Hitler for her prolific production of Aryans. A little later, she was put on the euthanasia list. Fortunately, they did not get round to her before the end of the Third Reich, and the old lady was able to die in peace.

At the age of twelve, Enne, a bright and capable child, was packed off to live with an uncle and go to higher school. The uncle never sent her. He had a bar and Enne worked as barmaid, pouring out mugs of beer at four and five a.m. for the delivery men with their big draught-horse wagons on their dawn rounds. She told me she loved every minute of it. But her mother came to inspect, discovered the truth, and took her home.

Later she lived with an aunt in Vienna and ran a small grocery shop which sold beer and wine and where students came to drink. Again, she was happy, joking with the students, a bold, clever self-confident girl who could hold her own with anyone. But the war came and the students went off to be soldiers. Her little shop closed. After that she began to work as a cook and dietician. She ran the kitchens of various bank cafeterias, till in the great post-war inflation the banks collapsed one by one. Once she also worked making paper flowers. Her crêpe paper roses on wire stems were miraculous, like no artificial flowers I have ever seen.

Enne had never been in service. She was not made for it. She was completely unlike the professionally humble Frau Endlinger, seemingly born for self-abnegation, who presided over my great-aunts' last years, often quoting the grim motto of "Always do more than your duty," a motto, Frau Endlinger said, she had learned at her mother's knee. I don't know how my parents found Enne - perhaps, unemployed and desperate, she decided to answer an ad. At first, she was cook, and still lived with her aunt. But when Schwester Lucy was fired, my father asked her to move in and take on me. Enne was doubtful. She knew, and her aunt had warned her, that she would be giving up independence, for the first time in her working life. But she loved me already; and once she took the job, she was hooked.

It was a devotion I never did anything to deserve.

Like my mother's, most of Enne's stories are lost. When it occurred to me to explore Enne's past, she was not senile; unlike my mother, she stayed sharp and lucid to the end. But she was retired, living in Vienna again, where I hardly saw her, and then she was dead. All I have, besides the uncle's bar and the student shop, is the triumph of her goiter operation. This was done by a famous professor who called her "Mitzi" and showed her off to his pupils, because she was such a success. Famous professors loom very large in the minds of less famous Viennese. (Goiters were so common in Vienna then, my father had a joke about the child on a tram who points someone out to his father: "Look, Papa, there's a man with no goiter." The father says, "Hush, don't embarrass him!")

Enne also talked about the joys of outings in the Wienerwald with friends when she was a girl; it sounded as though they had more fun on a Sunday than we often had in a month. "Everything," said Enne, "was more beautiful in the *Kaiserzeit.*" The uniforms, the pomp, the parades. This sentiment too is very Viennese. And there was a story of a possibly dangerous railway journey all alone in the Great War, when she lost her money or missed her connection and a kind strange soldier helped her.

Enne never married, and I doubt she ever had a lover, even a special male friend. Enne was what they would have called then a decent girl, and too clever and headstrong for most men. When she went to confession at seventeen, "The priest asked me questions about things that I, *unschuldiges Mädchen,* innocent girl, had never even heard of. I never went to confession again."

In the way of children, I paid less attention to Enne than to anyone else close to me because, unlike my parents, she was always around, always available. And always working. Up before anyone to get breakfast, supervising the shopping, supervising and doing cleaning, washing, tidying, ironing, and cooking the marvellous Viennese meals my father adored and judged with gourmet's rigor. If the *Knoedel* were a shade too *gatschat* (gooey) or the *Linzertorte* a shade too dry, Enne would be told. She would know anyway. She was a perfectionist. My father's praise would have meant nothing if his standards had not been as high as hers. *"Die Frau Doktor,"* she would say, in Viennese dialect, *"weiss garnet was Sie friesst."* The Frau Doktor doesn't know what she's eating. Compared to my father, it was true.

WR tried to persuade me to show more interest in Enne's superb cooking. "These things will die out. You should learn to do them." But I was going to be a great poet, and inspired by my mother's contempt for housewifely skills, was hardly about to spend my time rolling out *Strudel* dough to the thinness of the snow-white tablecloth underneath. When I did try to help in the kitchen, Enne gave me short shrift. *"Kind, geh weg. Du kannst das nicht."* Child, go away, you can't do this. She was right. I had neither the patience nor the manual dexterity to master anything of her craft. I did pick up a few of her simpler recipes, but none of the complicated baking which was my father's delight. WR too was right; these things have died out. Puff pastry and *Strudel* dough can be bought frozen, factory made; no one I know, even in Austria, now rolls out that amazing, flawless tablecloth of dough. And hardly anyone would want to. I have Enne's Viennese-American cookbook. Nearly all the dishes are not only complicated but surpassingly rich, a health-conscious diner's nightmare. The Viennese could hardly leave a vegetable without a sauce or a meal without a calorie- and cholesterol-high dessert. My father disliked vegetables, and would say that too many might give him "vegetable poisoning." Meat, rice, *Knoedel*, pastry and whipped cream, those were the things. It is true that I have never tasted better food than Enne's, and that both my parents lived past ninety on this lethal cuisine. For most of their lives, of course, animals were not yet factory-farmed, full of hormones, pesticides, antibiotics, and artificial food made from other animals' guts.

Enne asserted her rights and opinions in no uncertain terms. On her first trip to Gmunden, offered a straw pillow by one of my great-aunts, Enne drew herself up and said she came from a poor family, but never in her life had she slept on straw. Then she threw out the classic accusation, "With you, *Frau Professor,* humanity begins at the Baron." My great-aunt got her a feather pillow and no more was said.

And Enne complained. The complaints were a sort of private Greek chorus that accompanied her long, perfectionist working day. She grumbled to herself about her feet, her bunions, her knees, her *Kreuz* (sacroiliac).

"Die Enni ist ganz hin auf die Fürss," she would say picturesquely in her dialect as she clomped up the stairs. (Enne is all wrecked on her feet.) She complained about *"die Schwarzen,"* the black employees, about the quality of this and that, about her sisters in Massachusetts, about her acquaintances in the Austrian *Verein*, the Austrian Club. But never, though she disciplined us when it was needed, as my parents frequently didn't or were not there to do, did she complain about her charges, my sister and me. She loved us with the unstinting spinster nanny's love. But this love was not cloying or anxious or guilt-producing. It was simply there - and always there.

What Enne complained most about was Katya. She saw Katya as an interloper and something of a sponger. She resented my parents' adulation of her talent and my mother's devotion to Katya herself. She watched with grim face and sour comments Katya staying in bed till noon and my mother dashing upstairs between patients to bring her morning coffee (they knew better than to ask Enne). She could not understand Katya's night-owl hours, Katya's touchiness, Katya's primping, Katya's arty musician friends, more drain, she thought, on my parents' hospitality. Before, on family outings, it had been Enne who was taken along to the movies, the concert or the play. Now, there was also Katya, and Enne, though still asked, would frequently refuse.

It was that and the overwork. Though being overworked was as natural to Enne as breathing. Work was her strength and no one could do it as well as she. In vain my parents remonstrated, trying to get her to let the other help take on more. As Enne grew older, she developed the natural crankiness of a strong-willed person whom life is passing by. Periodically she would threaten to leave, to go to her sisters in Massachusetts. There were quarrels and scenes with my mother. The upshot was always that my sister and I cried and begged her to stay. The family without Enne was inconceivable. Just as it must really have been inconceivable for her to be without us. Enne would stay and things calm down till they boiled up again. These were the only scenes in our smooth bourgeois household until my sister and I reached our teens.

Enne's favorite phrase on such occasions, to describe what she'd had from all this work and from leaving her country to go with an unrelated family to a strange land was *"Nichts, Nichts, und wieder Nichts."* Nothing, nothing and again nothing. My parents paid her well enough but that was never the issue. Enne had nothing to save for, nothing much to spend on. She never went out except to one or two fellow German-speakers, including a fellow housekeeper from our Vienna apartment house who'd married her emigrant Herr Professor after his wife died, or to the Austrian *Verein*. She did not buy knick-knacks - again, totally unlike our Frau Endlinger in Gmunden who coyly confessed that her great secret passion was to have a *Vitrine,* a glass-fronted cupboard where you could put porcelain on display. If Enne had a secret passion, she kept it to herself. She might have made a marvellous, if autocratic restaurateur, but by the time we grew up she was too old and I don't think such ambitions ever entered her head.

What Enne suffered from, what Katya's presence brought home to her, was that her hard work and excellence brought her respect but from my parents no real liking. In their early America days they might have clung to her more as a piece of their old Austria, and they still needed her, still treated her well, but they did not like her much. She was too dominating, outspoken, hard; prickly, like the nettle, *Brennessel*, that was her name. Though she was never like that with Verena and me. Her resentment at my parents' lack of warmth alienated them, of course, yet more.

The vicious circle grew worse when my sister and I left home to study, though by then Katya had left too. One day Enne threatened again to leave and my parents said all right, go. They claimed that with her bossiness and prejudices they could not have kept their other help. I didn't believe it; some stayed for years. It is one thing they did I cannot quite forgive.

Enne retired to Vienna, to her old district, the 18th, where she had kept a shop for the students decades and empires ago. She bought an apartment, a big living room, a tiny bedroom, a kitchen cum hall. The toilet was next door, shared with the neighbours, a family of four who lived in a single room. One cold water tap served the whole floor. This was typical of Vienna in the late 'fifties.

Enne, used to American comforts, had a bathtub and sink installed in her kitchen. The removable bathtub cover did duty as a work surface. It is a common Viennese conversion. The people in the house were scandalized by such luxury. *"Warum muss sich diese Alte so viel waschen?"* they wanted to know. Why does that old one have to wash herself so much? Enne, independent as ever, paid no heed. Weakened with rheumatism and failing sight, she continued her cooking and cleaning, did her mending by the TV, made her coffee in the white china Karlsbad machine because that was the best, and always had with it a cookie or a slice of cake. *"Die Enni trinkt kein lehren Kaffe,"* Enne drinks no empty coffee, she said in her rich

Viennese, referring to herself in the third person as one does to children, as she did with me and my sister to the end of her days. And she aired her bedding on the window-sill of the tiny bedroom, and put her wooden spoons in a jar on the kitchen sill to be kept white by the sun. As always, she would brook no help. *"Ich muss meine Arbeit machen. Das halt mich aufrecht."* I must do my work. That keeps me upright.

She visited my husband and me once in Switzerland and we, or I, visited her several times in Vienna. The house was one of those large, old, lower-middle-class apartment houses with a forbidding front on a bleak street. The double windows had big window bolsters to keep out winter draughts - though Enne of course aired the apartment for at least ten minutes, morning and evening, whatever the cold, as she had our rooms when we were small. The stone-flagged, echoing halls, bitterly cold, smelled of cabbage and carbolic soap and on Fridays of cheap frozen fish. Of poverty. And to me, with some regressive sense, of danger, of fear. Enne's presence over-ruled all that. Inside, you were back in the best part of your childhood, cosy, cheerful, safe.

Enne no longer talked about the good old days of the Empire. She talked about her good old days in Grosse Pointe. She was full of warm and funny memories, stories about the animals, about the gormless help and the crazy patients, like the one who wanted to weigh the fat Austrian cat. We laughed a lot, as we always had. But sometimes she lapsed into bitterness. *"Und was habe ich davon gehabt, alle diese Jahre?"* And what have I had from all those years? *"Nichts, Nichts und wieder Nichts."* She missed my family dreadfully. Still older and pricklier, she quarrelled with what there was of hers, her sisters in the Burgenland, and her one remaining couple of old friends. At the end she was very alone. A neighbour from the end of the hall, a fat woman whose legs were bowed almost circular by arthritis, limped to the shops for her. *"Eine gute Patsch,"* Enne said, a good old shoe. From Enne it was praise.

On my last visit, I brought my baby daughter. They took to each other at once. We left Enne relatively well, still determined to manage alone. A year later, we returned from Turkey, where we had often been hard to reach, to find Enne in a nursing home. An old friend of my parents - the ex-Montessori teacher who'd started me reading and whom I had got Enne together with on my last visit - had found her a place when she became ill. She had a sunny private room, but complained heatedly. The personnel, all 'Slavs,' were sloppy and barely spoke German. This seemed to be true. We had at that time no home of our own, and the friend assured me there was probably no better place for Enne to be. Before we could think of a transfer, she died. Her relatives, I believe, had her buried in the Burgenland, I don't know where. She would not, anyhow, have been sentimental about visits to the grave.

MY MOTHER GOES HORSE CRAZY AND I ACQUIRE A SAVAGE BEAST

I have said there was not much magic in Grosse Pointe. This isn't quite true. To me all suburbia, and all flat country, is stifling. But America then was still close enough to its wilderness past, even if much was already polluted, even when the forest, as in Vermont, was only second growth left by the farmers, the loggers, the charcoal burners when they moved on, that there was still the air of nature only recently tamed and with vivid life of its own. Even in Grosse Pointe.

In fall there was the magic of the coloured leaves, raked into piles for sweet-smelling bonfires. My father showed us how to roast potatoes in the embers, and we ate the charred scraps with as much glee as if they'd been Enne's best *Zwetschken-knoedel*. Then came Hallowe'en, and the carving of Jack o'Lanterns to station by the front door, golden and grinning with their lighted candles inside. We dressed up to go trick-or-treating; even I went shyly out. But I didn't care for candy or pennies. I wanted the enchantment of the pumpkin's flickering laugh, and the *frisson* of imagined ghosts. My father wrote one of his best papers on Hallowe'en, inspiring the poet Conrad Aiken to compose a poem. We didn't then say Trick or Treat, though in High School I did once go window-soaping with members of my class. Unconscious of the irony, we said, in lugubrious voices, Help the Poor.

Now the trees are much bigger and bonfires are forbidden. Some sort of giant vacuum comes along to suck up your leaves at the curb. And because of all the arson in Detroit, there is a teen-age curfew on Hallowe'en night.

In spring there was the flowering Japanese cherry and the forsythias; my father always had early forsythia branches on his desk. But American spring is late and brief, turning almost at once to summer. Winter, though I hated the cold, was the most magical season. You saw red cardinals against the snow, and mysterious tracks in the garden - squirrels, pheasants, rabbits, and often the creatures themselves. The cocker once caught a pheasant, which my parents ate. The lake froze; there were iceboats, and skating, and men fishing through holes. The snow fell in great flakes; you could see the perfect star-lattice shapes, like those you cut out of folded paper, and catch stars, little pin-pricks of cold on your tongue. The snow transformed everything. Traffic was muffled and slowed, the drifts piled in the streets, snowmen with hats and carrot noses and coal buttons stood in gardens. The trees were coated with crystal, the houses elegant and mysterious in their blanket of white. In winter, Grosse Pointe was beautiful.

From my usual sickbed, looking through the window at bare black branches (Stencilled in black, against a calm gray sky, one of my poems began), I was aware of something enchanted and remote. Something I wanted to capture in words and could not, the thing I could almost see in the wintering trees. I had a puzzle book with pictures of bare trees; you had to find an animal or a face in the leafless twigs. What I wanted to say was something harder to find, something beyond my play-reading and paltry fantasies of popularity and horse-show success. A sense of wonder at a presence you cannot name and all too often lose the urge to find before you come near it. I still look at bare branches, at wood grain and wood knots, for creatures, for faces, but what I really wanted and still want - in child's words, with adult hindsight, is something like this: I want to *see* the face of the wind.

As a good Freudian child, I was a compulsive confessor. Except about school, I told my parents everything. I didn't have much to confess. Being so timid and so indulged, I never, unlike my bolder sister, got into trouble. Once I accidentally broke a finger off one of Daddy's Gothic statues. With some irritation, he forgave me. The only other crimes I committed were playing the radio too loud or otherwise violating my parents' sacrosanct after-lunch rest. And listening secretly to horror programs I *knew* would give me nightmares. *The Shadow* (who "knows what evil lurks in the hearts of men"), *Inner Sanctum,* with its introductory eerily squeaking door. *The Hermit's Cave,* latest and spookiest. Heads aloft on pikes, toads brought by a curse raining plip plop on the victim's roof. By today's standards, they were baby stuff. There was also the more upmarket *Suspense,* which produced one classic, *Sorry, Wrong Number,* where a handicapped woman alone in a house tries desperately to phone the police before an intruder reaches her room.

Other children seemed to take all this in their stride. Not have nightmares. Not lie awake shivering and finally call for mothers to sit with them till they fell asleep. In these late night sessions - the only time I had my mother's undivided attention, or she mine - I broached other worries.

Will America really win the war? Is my poetry really good? Will this lack of sleep make me *seriously* ill?

My parents consulted each other about their neurotic offspring. I knew they thought I was masochistic. Also (I was to learn later) compulsive, obsessive, anal-retentive. What I *felt* was night fear and the inner demon, and the weight of a wicked world. My parents were perplexed by what they read as a burden of neurotic guilt on my little shoulders. They looked for solutions in Enne's "compulsive neatness," in the idea that I was simply an intrinsically masochistic character. (Anna Freud had said so once, it was reported, though I don't know when she saw me, let alone observed any masochism.) With normal parental blindness, they did not see that I was the focus of too much attention, interpretation, indulgence; and they would not have believed that I could absorb, by osmosis, the repressed fear, the unfelt survivor's guilt, from our flight.

At least they were very patient with me. I remember my mother, who must have been very tired after a day of her crazies, sitting heavily on my bed, whispering reassurance, while Enne snored in her room across the bathroom and my father snored in his very private quarters, the 'maid's room' half a landing below. When I couldn't sleep, it was my mother I wanted. Unconsciously, I accepted my parents' classification of my beloved Enne. She was not someone who solved problems, who could soothe my concerns about Nazis, intruders, bad news or inner demons. She was someone who did the physical work.

My mother became concerned about masturbation.

Not if we did. If we didn't. She knew I did because I of course confessed; or maybe she asked me. Paradoxically, her approval did not free me from anxiety. I had an awful suspicion that no one else I knew ever did it. That it was one more family eccentricity. That it was un-American. And my mother's infantile German term for it was one that made me cringe so much I could not bear to write it down, even now. Just as the words "penis" and "vagina" still make me wince. They belong to my parents' case histories and the giant lurid medical book I was hardly big enough to hold. All the four-letter words seem nice by comparison.

So, like a child to whom it is forbidden, I kept resolving to stop. And not succeeding. I felt not guilty but ashamed, freakish, as usual. My mother, having had no confessions from Verena, came to me one night and asked earnestly if I could find out about my sister and tell her. She was worried because Verena didn't seem to be doing it yet. There must have been some analytic superstition that kids who did not masturbate would have problems with adult sex. This was going too far. I was not going to quiz my sister about a subject we'd never discussed. And I never, needless to say, told anyone except my mother what I did myself.

At one of the rare parties I went to, a couple of giggling girls asked me if I knew what "M" was. Embarrassedly, I said yes, but I didn't say the word. Later, I discovered that they meant menstruation, otherwise then known as The Curse. I still shudder when I think of the social disaster I narrowly escaped.

Masturbation was one of the few solitary indulgences my mother regarded as healthy. Others, the threat was, led to disease. If you stayed up too late with the radio or a book, you might become seriously ill from lack of sleep. To tell this to an insomniac was highly counterproductive. I began to lie awake at night with worry that I wasn't asleep. My mother had to assure me that I wouldn't after all contract TB, and give me a sleeping pill.

Chills too were dangerous. And going among crowds in summer might get you polio. So I grew up a dithery hypochondriac, torn between my terror of doctors and a compulsion to consult them for every cough or mole.

My mother, whose family was military, professional or simply genteel, retained a stolid naiveté about the ordinary workaday world. She took recommendations right and left, often on a whim, assuming because someone addressed her with deference and conviction, that qualifications existed. Partly it was just her excess energy, her impatience. My mother did not deliberate long. She had to act. Whatever was lacking, a specialist, or self-declared specialist, was brought in at once to set it right. The foible grew with age. In later years, she gambled on the stock market on the advice of her secretary, who was married to a broker; fortunately, she could afford to lose. She sent her chiropodist's boyfriend, a cook who boasted German business connections, to try to sell the villa in Gmunden. She took financial advice also from an old Vienna friend who had inherited a million dollars, as if mere possession of that much money made a financier.

This tendency, coupled with worry about the health of her only two surviving children, led to a mania for medical specialists. I had tests for my metabolism, for anaemia, for my sight. I wore glasses from the age of eleven, even two pairs for a while, a separate one for reading. My oculist was later cashiered for taking kick-backs from the optician, and I went back to a single pair. Dermatologists treated my acned skin, put hot and cold packs on my face, punched out blackheads, prescribed lotions for my itching head which made my hair oilier and my head itch more. Posture experts drew lipstick lines on my spine and ordered me to walk around with a book on my head.

One orthopaedic surgeon even suggested an operation for my slightly drooping arches. Luckily this time my mother was not convinced, or my terror put her off. Another old Vienna friend, also orthopaedist, prescribed exercises. I sat on a chair and picked up pencils with my toes. I was also prescribed saddle shoes with metal arch supports. Bemoaning the other girls' chic penny loafers ("American girls will all ruin their feet," my mother said) I consoled myself in the shoe shop by the long stances in the fascinating x-ray machine.

Besides all this, my mother became fanatical about riding.

During my Gomper years, we all got horses. My father bought a beautiful black gelding from the Belle Isle stable. Ebony Blue had one white-spotted eye, supposedly blind. It did not affect how he moved. The story was that he'd belonged to a Grosse Pointe car industry mogul, who ordered him destroyed after the eye injury. The stable owner couldn't bear to do it, so Ebony was sold, cheaply and in secret, to my father. Ebony Blue was to me a dream name for a dream horse. I wrote slushy poems about him and longed to be big enough to ride him. When I did, he was as good as expected, with gaits like no other horse I've ever ridden.

My mother bought a sorrel ex-polo pony from Captain van Ingen in Vermont. Winnie was fast and nervous and sometimes hard to control. When my mother couldn't cope, she would change horses with my father, who was not so fanatical but fearless and a better rider. I remember him laughing, saying "Dancey, dancey" as Winnie snorted and pranced while my mother looked on in chagrin.

Later they got me the horse I named Sultan, a coarser, inelegant version of Ebony, and for my sister another of the Captain's ex-polo ponies. He was a sad ageing little horse with a big head and a heart-breaking asthmatic cough, which was assumed to make him slow and placid enough for Verena and sometimes Katya to ride in safety.

The horses had to be exercised. My parents rode every Tuesday and Thursday and we all rode every Saturday afternoon and Sunday morning. We rode in the bitter cold wind, when Verena and I would have preferred the Saturday movie, or loved just once to linger over Enne's Sunday breakfast of *Striezl* and cocoa and over the coloured Sunday funnies that came with the *Detroit News*. We rode when it seemed our fingers and toes would never thaw again and we were desperate to get home and out of our boots. My mother had permanent bruises from hers. She didn't care, any more than she cared about hanging her dirty jodhpurs next to her bathrobe, above the mirror in her American-socialite style dressing room, with its big sliding-door closet and dresser-top jumble of French perfumes and scarves and handbags and Nivea jars, all steeping in the smell of sweaty horse. No doubt she would also have made us ride in the 90-100 degree heat of the Detroit summer, if we hadn't been lucky enough to be in Vermont. With the horses. The horses were shipped back and forth by railway, when there was one. Later they were shipped in a racehorse truck. I once figured out that the money spent on this horse transport was enough to cover my own family's then living expenses for a year.

My little sister was a natural rider, brave and adept from the start. Soon she was out of Western saddles with straps, onto English, and off the lead ropes. One day Verena wanted to test her skill by taking the trail alone, just across the canal from us, meeting us at the next bridge. My parents agreed. But when she rejoined us, she was frightened and shaken. Another couple of riders had passed her at a gallop, one on either side, and she had barely been able to control her horse.

My parents were enraged at this lack of riding manners which had put a small child in danger. They knew who the couple were, and my father lectured them. They were not pleased. The next time we met them, the man rose in his stirrups and shouted, "Why don't you take the other path, you dirty foreigner?"

To me the words were like a slap in the face. But my father shouted back, uninhibited by his heavy Austrian accent. "You stop that, Mr Johnson, or I'll break every bone in your body." He could not have broken big burly Mr Johnson's little finger. Probably the phrase jumped into his head, gleaned from a patient or overheard from those crime programs my sister and I listened to in defiance of parental will.

I quaked with terror at what Mr Johnson would do. But he did not take up the challenge; the Johnsons rode on in furious silence. My father had a word with the stable owner. The Johnsons boarded two horses, my parents boarded four and brought guests. There were no sequels. But I still quaked every time I saw the Johnsons and somehow, after that ugly insult, Belle Isle was no longer a subject for poetry. I was relieved when, some time later, we found another boarding stables nearer Grosse Pointe.

At Belle Isle one of the boarders was a tall, handsome white mare. Her owner, an elderly man who always came alone, was devoted to her, and she to him. You had the impression that no one and nothing absorbed him more. He had taught her tricks; to count, to pull a hankie out of his pocket, to nod her head, to kneel on command. Kind and friendly, pleased by my admiration, he told me his secrets. You just needed patience and a lot of carrots, which my doting parents were happy to provide. Counting was the easiest. While repeating your arithmetic question, you picked up the horse's foot and bent it, so he learned to paw on command. Then you gave him a carrot. Soon I had Sultan doing problems in algebra. The trick was to rapidly produce the carrot when he reached the right number, before he could go on. This wasn't exactly Grosse Pointe Hunt Club stuff, but I was terribly proud of Sultan. Except for my dubious poetry, his tricks were my major accomplishment - as they were his.

One day we came to the stable and saw the white mare down with heaves. Someone had borrowed her, ridden her hard, and fed and watered her while she was still in a lather. Heaves was everyone's dread. The medical lore was that you had to keep the horse on its feet, or it was done for. The mare's owner and Art who ran the stable worked desperately to save her. She was given an enema, put in a sling to hoist her up, dosed with whatever the vet could give. After a quick look, I stayed on the other side of the stalls, unable to bear it. Nothing helped. In a few hours she was dead.

I can't remember if I prayed for the white mare; you say Please God because you know no other words. But it was one more example of the absolute unfairness of the world. I was already old enough to see this unfairness in the papers every day. But for a child it is still brought home when someone you know loses what seems central in that particular life. After that the magic went out of our tricks, and Sultan's notions of algebra were allowed to lapse.

Once in a while we had a family outing that did not involve the horses. We went to the museum at Cranbrook and looked at crystals changing colour in changing lights. We went to the zoo at Royal Oak and rode on the miniature train. We went to the Shrine Circus and saw snarling lions put through hoops, and high-wire acrobats dangling by ankles and teeth, and clowns and tight-rope walkers and performing monkeys and dogs and seals, and spangled riders balancing on the fat rumps of steeds whose chins were reined back against their chests so they cantered like clumsy plump ballerinas, like the hippos in Disney's *Fantasia*. We ate pink cotton candy floss and loved it all. The possible cruelty of circuses never entered our heads. I thought animals were taught tricks the way I'd taught my Sultan.

And once we had a truly proletarian outing. My father took Verena and Enne and me to Eastwood Amusement Park.

Eastwood Park remains one of my visions of hell. A bleak windswept plain, bare earth, weird spindly structures, a set for a horror movie. A giant roller coaster, too daring for the likes of me, steel tracks writhing against a winter sky. We went to the hall of mirrors and through a turning barrel in which you had to try to stay upright. All more grotesque or frightening than actually fun. I sensed we were in truly alien territory, but my father was not bothered. He was agile, good at these things, and he may have felt some faint echo of our beloved Vienna Prater. And then, through a parental slip-up - my mother would have been more cautious - we went to the freak show, and saw the Man with a Siamese Twin.

The man, quite ordinary looking, stood in front of the audience, opened his shirt and trousers, and revealed the bottom of a small naked child dangling from his middle. "Dis is my baby brudder," the man announced in a toneless voice, and proceeded to explain how it functioned, the circulation of its blood. After that, we fled, and we never went to Eastwood Park again. The horrible image stayed, and the thought of what this man's life must be, travelling from freak show to freak show, calmly opening his pants to show the dangling half a child.

So much of my memory of this period is focused on the family animals because in my loneliness they were central to my life. As they were to Katya's and my mother's. On their respective death beds, my mother was to ask for the cats, my father, by then a widower, for his lady companion. My father loved the animals too but not as much as he loved women. Or the violin.

Our cocker Ticky and our first Shepherd puppy, Wolf, got on together without problems, until Wolf grew and Ticky went on heat. They were kept apart, but not all the time; and what my parents hoped their size difference would prevent, it didn't. When there were shouts of dismay in the yard, I ran down to see. It was all over, but the two dogs were still joined, back to back. Ticky, being so much smaller, hung ignominiously from below Wolf's tail, her hind legs in the air, trying pitifully to balance on her front paws. This was before all those wolf studies that explained their awkward state was natural bonding. So it may have been, but the six-legged beast looked more miserable than natural. Gibson poked at the dogs ineffectually with a broom and then threw cold water on them. The cold water worked.

That was my first sight of sex. I cannot say it was encouraging. Especially as friends of my parents regaled me later with the urban legend of the clandestine couple who become inseparable in an opera box and have to be carried off on a stretcher, still joined. I have wondered since if this story was invented to scare young girls away from illicit sex. No one ever mentioned married couples who got stuck like dogs.

Ticky, of course, became pregnant. The vet said delivering such big pups would kill her, and did an abortion. Not long after, Ticky grew very sick. For a day she was listless and feverish. Then suddenly she jumped out of her basket and began to run around the room, dropping turds and yelping in a high weak voice, clearly in great distress and pain. Katya, the only adult home, telephoned the vet and we sat together helplessly waiting and crying. I did pray again, not believing but maybe prepared to give the name I said another chance. Ticky went on running and yelping; then she collapsed, twitched and died. As she had been my first sight of sex, she was my first of the process of death. This one was not encouraging at all. Katya called the vet again and said icily, before her voice broke, "It's too late, the dog is dead." As far as I was concerned, not only the vet had muffed it. God had too. I was not going to pray with a shred of conviction again.

We all mourned Ticky, Katya most of all. I think Katya loved Ticky as much as I loved Wolf. But unlike me she was prepared to go through it all once more.

I have a photo of myself from my first album of photos taken mostly by me, with my birthday present red box camera. Hans Gomper was a keen photographer and one of the Gomper perks was photography lessons, including developing your masterpieces in the Gomper darkroom. Most of my other pictures are of our horses, with and without riders, and of Wolf. I have written under the picture of me: *Wolf's Owner and Trainer.*

The picture shows an affected and unhappy child. The caption shows how much the subject adored and identified with Wolf. Like many captions, however, it is not quite true. In fact Wolf was sent away for professional training.

When after our burglary we bought Wolf, we broke all the sensible rules in the *Practical Puppy* and other dog books. He was the last left of the litter. He was hand-shy. He was already four months old, and no one else had wanted him. But he and I fell in love. It was easy. Neither of us had seen much competition.

We did not follow the dog book strictures when it came to putting little Wolf to bed. He was locked in the patients' bathroom with lots of newspaper on the floor. He howled and hurled himself against the door until we couldn't stand it and went down - to find him injured. He spent the rest of the night next to my bed and from then on slept in the hall outside my bedroom, with the door open. We took him to the vet, who pronounced mysteriously that Wolf's limp was not due to his wild crashing against the door but a calcium deficiency. Wolf was given painful calcium shots. I couldn't bear it after I saw the first one, and my mother had to hold him as he tried to bite the vet. Later, he developed what may have been distemper and, as it turned out, may have affected his brain. Again it was my mother who administered medicine and dealt with Wolf when the vet came. Medical procedures were something that, even for Wolf, I couldn't stand being a party to.

With the aid of the dog manuals, I did my best to teach Wolf to heel, sit, come and stay. Wolf was lively and clever but not easy to train; I was impatient and erratic. My parents decided that in any case for a proper guard dog specialized training was in order. While we were in Vermont, Wolf was left with a German lady pro who must have been as fierce as he. He came back more disciplined but more savage. What he had mostly learned, it seemed, was to direct his attacks at the 'gun arm'; one had to hope intruders were right-handed.

Trained or not, Wolf was my passion, my alter ego. Wolf did what I could not. He cowed and frightened his enemies. The trouble was, his enemies were practically everybody. As a mature dog, he took to attacking strangers and growling even at family. The only person he never growled at was Enne, who mostly fed him. On his bed in the hall, he even growled at me when I kissed him good-night. Lavishing kisses on animals was a family habit, and I persisted, though this was reckless to the point of insanity. To kiss a large growling dog on the forehead or muzzle is asking to have half your face torn off. (Katya had a horror story about a friend's pet Doberman; the friend wasn't kissing him, just hanging out laundry.) I can only explain it now by saying that Wolf was my most exclusive relationship and I had to confirm our closeness and my faith that he wouldn't hurt me. My parents didn't see or didn't realize the risk. Later I outgrew the habit of kissing dogs. If you must kiss animals, a quiet horse is cleaner and more suitable. I don't think even my mother kissed the alligators.

There were more warnings. Wolf flew at milkmen and postmen; we had to put a large Danger sign on the gate. He also snapped at my father once when my father came close to me. And when, still optimistic, my father tried gingerly to 'introduce' my friend Alice, Wolf yanked away from him and tore Alice's dress from collar to hem. Alice, brave girl, was not upset. But after that, when visitors came Wolf was locked up.

Had we been sensible, we would have disposed of Wolf already then. We were not sensible, and not only because I loved him to distraction. Even my parents - certainly my mother - may have had some secret liking for owning a savage dog. I suspect numbers of dog owners do. There is something seigniorial about it; the image of the booted aristocrat with his great mastiffs by the fire, the power a powerful creature confers. Among the few stories of her Austrian past my mother loved telling were ones of the family German Shepherds in Gmunden, who must have been rather like Wolf but kept a bit more in line by the old ladies in black silk. How terrified the neighbours had been. How my father had to go out in a rowboat to rescue a little dog their Lux had chased half across the lake. Etc.

All this of course came to a head. One day, home with one of my flus, lazing in bed with my textbooks, drawings, soap operas and tea, I heard a strange noise outside. It was a bizarre, inhuman moan, a sound I hope never to hear again. This moaning came from my father. A minute later, overcome by the family sense of drama and forgetting all Freudian rules, he burst into my room. His right arm was covered with runnels of amazingly bright, scarlet blood. "Look what your dog has done to me," he cried and vanished. It was not his finest moment. But he was probably in shock.

It happened in the garden. My father was there with Wolf and Enne. He picked up a plant stick to prop a drooping rose. My father had not done much in the garden since we'd been fully staffed, and this was the wrong time to begin. Wolf, remembering his training, may have imagined that my father was about to hit Enne with the stick. At any rate, he did what he'd been taught. He went for the weapon arm, and fortunately got it, rather than face or throat or my father's violin-bow hand. Enne, the heroine of the hour, without a moment's thought for her own safety, grabbed Wolf's choke collar and pulled him off so my father could escape.

My father was rushed to hospital to be stitched up and given a transfusion. Wolf, quite calm now, was taken to the vet's. I did not try to see him again. I knew what would have to happen, and the usual lies about a nice new home on the country were mere formality. I knew too it was not his fault. As soon as it was clear my father was not gravely injured, I began to cry for Wolf.

I was taken to my mother's room to sleep, but I couldn't. The kind of grief I felt then has no comfort, and wisely, no one tried very hard to comfort me. That long night is as vivid as yesterday. I cried all night, sitting on the cold toilet seat in my mother's bathroom, shivering as the central heating went down in the small hours and my slippered feet grew icy on the tiles. Between bouts of sobbing, to stop myself thinking about Wolf, I read my mother's latest Book of the Month Club selection. It was Sinclair Lewis's *Main Street*, for me quite an adult book. In spite of my grief I was interested in the social dilemma, which seemed to have echoes of our schizophrenic life in Grosse Pointe, and in spite of my grief I looked for sex bits. By daybreak the worst of my mourning was over. It was over because during that night something in me had hardened, something had died. I would never again love an animal as much as Wolf. I would never again want a dog all my own.

A few days later, when I was still in bed (the trauma had of course lengthened my flu) my mother came in and deposited a little ball of fluff on my quilt. The ball of fluff was a new German Shepherd, six weeks old. I began to cry again. Then I played with the puppy, knowing I would love it, but not the same way.

My mother would not give up German Shepherds simply because one had savaged my father. She had decided, however, to get females instead of males, and get them very young. And there was to be no more professional training. Our dogs from then on were spoiled and not very obedient, but less of a public danger.

We soon got a second, smaller dog to replace Ticky, this also much for Katya's sake. The second was male, and that was the pattern from then on. There was to be no repeat either of the Ticky tragedy. The small dog, Pretzel, was a highly intelligent and delightful Dachshund puppy. I suppose my parents selected this breed partly for its short legs. For a male Dachshund to mate a female Shepherd would have required agility outdoing the Kama Sutra. And for extra safety the female was spayed.

Lupie (I couldn't quite give up the name) grew up to be fairly safe, if a bit unpredictable. Neither her mind nor her sense of smell were very keen. She would welcome some strangers, bark at others, bark at me if I put on a hat. But she never really bit anyone. She was generally sweet-tempered but stupid, and not a patch on Wolf. By everyone's tacit agreement, she became mostly my mother's dog, and shared my mother's bed during the sacrosanct rest hour, taking up most of the space and snoring while my mother lay doubled up in a corner, cramped but apparently content.

We didn't always ride alone. On Saturdays we began to ride with my parents' one Detroit American friend, a Mrs Dodd.

Mrs Dodd knew us through Nina's mother. She was a society woman, from the South, and bigoted, and not as glamorous as Mrs X. I didn't quite see what my parents saw in her. They seemed to laugh a lot together, especially she and my father. Her husband didn't ride. He was a surgeon and very busy. We saw him briefly when we went back to their house for tea after riding. It was the only American house we regularly visited. The Dodds lived in Detroit but on an elegant street, in a big house, bigger than ours, with a big garden, and servants.

Mrs Dodd had five children, the oldest nearly grown up, the youngest a baby. The first four were all good-looking, athletic and confident. The brother and sister nearest my age were superb dancers and swimmers. Wendy Dodd became one of my room-mates at camp. Jim occasionally danced with me at dancing school. Wendy and I perused movie magazines together, and sometimes in early summer they invited us to swim at the Boat Club, where Jane was not allowed to enter. My parents wouldn't join the Boat Club because of its anti-Semitism, but their principles did not forbid them the odd swim. I paddled sadly in the shallow pool while the Dodd kids did swans and jack-knifes off the high board.

My parents seemed pleased to spend time with the Dodds. I never felt truly comfortable with the Dodd kids. They were nice to me, but they were too sporty, capable, casual, All-American to put a dreamy misfit like myself at ease. And Mrs Dodd outraged my prudish sensibilities by matter-of-factly undressing when we shared a cabin at the club. She had a good figure in clothes but her rear was flabby. I was secretly horrified by the sight of this rear. I thought adults shouldn't expose themselves, should maintain their dignity, such as it was. It was bad enough to see my own mother.

I was also nonplussed by the way Wendy horsed around with the black maid. I knew the Dodds were "prejudiced." I had heard my parents talk disapprovingly about it. I had heard Mrs Dodd say, "Lincoln didn't really want to free the *Niggroes*." She pronounced it with a short vowel which seemed to put them still farther down her scale. If the Dodds thought black people inferior, why were they so intimate with them in public, more than I was with Enne, who'd brought me up from a baby? I couldn't understand. And I didn't like the small, pale spoiled toddler. Nor the pet monkey, who scared me. Also, I thought it perverse to have five children. At ten I already favored zero population growth.

The great friendship with the Dodds ended as mysteriously as it began. The rumor I heard, much later, was that Dr Dodd had caught my father kissing Mrs Dodd in her car and given my father a black eye. My mother, said the friend who told me this story, was very indignant - at Dr Dodd, and Dr Dodd later apologized. But the friendship cooled. When I asked my parents, before I was old enough to hear the rumor, they murmured that Mrs Dodd had taken too much to drink. And anyway, by that time, we were no longer riding on Belle Isle.

Katya began to give recitals every year or so, usually at the Detroit Institute of Arts.

These recitals threw the house into turmoil. Katya's practicing, Katya's sleep were not to be disturbed by a single squeak. For once my sister and I were hushed in no uncertain terms. Katya's nerves must not be frayed. My parents called this the artistic temperament. Enne thought it a lot of hysterical fuss. Everyone's nerves, in the end, were almost as frayed as Katya's. When we finally arrived at the auditorium with Katya, now resplendent in her "formal," the tension was so great we felt it as our own.

Katya, who played superbly, as might be expected from a star Edwin Fischer pupil, was wasted on me in my childhood. She specialized in Bach, Mozart and Schubert; by thirteen I'd got as far as Tchaikovsky, and that only because of my crush on the young pianist. I sat fidgeting in those wonderful concerts, studying the audience, looking for interesting faces, whispering with Wendy Dodd in the bits when Katya stopped and people coughed and clapped. "Watch how their heads bob," Wendy said, "when she goes fast." And we tried not to giggle. What I liked best were the receptions afterwards, when you got triangular sandwiches and little crackers with relish or caviar, and Katya was relaxed and smiling, and I felt proud to be part of her circle and quite grown-up.

But something did get through to me in the early days; not when Katya performed but when she practiced. It came in and from snatches; Katya herself once said, "All music is beautiful heard through a closed door." Some of her encore pieces, like Poulenc's *Little White Donkey*, and certain phrases and melodies, half-heard when I was doing homework, reading, or with the dogs in the garden, moved me in a strange way, like the call of mourning doves, bare branches in winter twilight, the old Austrian clock ticking in my mother's room. They made me restless and nostalgic for something at once familiar and unknown, a feeling as keen as love but impossible to name, a bittersweet feeling with endless reverberations that like the bathroom mirror reflected infinity. By the time I listened to music whole and understood that Katya was as fine a pianist as I would ever hear, she had twinges of the back trouble that was soon to end her performing for good.

A few of the famous friends from Katya's Berlin and Paris days actually turned up in Detroit.

One was the pianist Arthur Schnabel, whom I was not allowed to meet. Apparently he had no patience with children, unlike my father's later friend Serkin, who had half a dozen of his own and at post-concert congratulations always gave me a warm if absent-minded hug. I hated those occasions, being strictly a parental appendage and, unmusical as I was, out of place - hated them, till I started coveting young musicians.

What I gleaned from the Schnabel visit was this: asked why he never played on the radio, Schnabel said scathingly that the least he demanded of his audience was that they be fully dressed. I was so cowed by the great musician's statement (my parents gave him the title of Genius) that I vowed never to hear classical music on the toilet and still feel guilty if I even listen to it in the bath.

A quite different guest was the actress Eleonora Mendelssohn, grand-niece of the composer, who came to Detroit to play in *The Madwoman of Chaillot*. She talked to *me* - for a long time and as if I were entirely grown-up. She was intense and beautiful and projected a glamour quite unlike the brittle glamours of Grosse Pointe, a faded but lavish eccentric Old World fascination and elegance I can no longer describe but measure by an effect still strong after more than half a century. She talked a great deal about health and healing and her lack of faith in doctors and conventional medicine. In my house, where medicine was law, this was truly amazing, the first anti-parental heretical opinion an adult had given me in my life. I was too young to evaluate it but I never forgot it and it sowed seeds. I was even more impressed when we went to the play and I saw her brilliance on stage.

It was Eleonora's only visit. Later, she made a bizarre marriage, a gay friend of Tenessee Williams, and years later I saw her name in the papers; her husband had attempted suicide, and she herself had died mysteriously, from an overdose of sleeping pills.

As my handwriting was sloppy, like everything demanding dexterity, I was tutored in penmanship.

My tutor was a Hungarian married to a psychiatrist away at war; this status made her very noble in my eyes. I also admired her hair, which was blonde, very long, and coiled in a braid round her head. She tried, with limited success, to make me produce the neatly curved, flowing letters of Palmer Method writing I had been unable to master at Trombley. Gomper's didn't bother about it but other schools did. She also tutored me in arithmetic, my weakest subject, and introduced me to one of my first adult novels, *Gone With the Wind*. I liked it well enough but it didn't live up to the title. I was still a child; I still preferred books where the wind was a character in itself.

Besides penmanship and ballet I also had private lessons, with shame and secrecy, in swimming. At camp, I'd never got beyond the dog paddle. One of Katya's friends, who taught music at Gomper's nursery school, was also a swimming teacher. She spirited me off from school every two weeks or so to a big pool reeking evilly of chlorine, where I mastered a little sidestroke and breaststroke and a few weak, flailing strokes of crawl. Crawl I hated because putting my face in the water panicked me - water in the nose made me start choking and gave me acute sinus pain.

Along with sinus pain, I agonized about my first sight of dirty graffiti. One day we had to use the men's cabins because the women's were undergoing repairs, and I read with horror on the wall, "Girls, I have six inches of dick to fuck your cunts." This introduced me to new terms, quite different from the technical language of my parents; children then didn't swear so much. It also gave me a queasy feeling about the pool. I wondered if the writer with his six inches of dick might still be lurking somewhere about, and was relieved when I managed to do enough fumbling sidestrokes to get by and those lessons were done.

The last half year at Gomper's is a blur. The nursery school stayed on Pallister, the upper moved, to rented classrooms in a Hebrew school nearby. WR did his best but the material was not inspiring. The brighter lights - except for me, if I counted - Nina, Jack, Alice, Bernard, Henry, were all gone. So were some of my larger tormentors. New tormentors replaced them, though there was now more schizoid withdrawal than violence. One new boy sat in the corner all day, writing obscene poetry. One sad, acned new girl was so near-sighted that when she read from the blackboard she appeared to be wiping it with her nose. "We were very frightening on the train," she wrote in a memorable essay on the one journey she had probably ever taken. They were all kind of frightening in the classroom. Things came to a head. WR, maddened by some remark or act of the obscene poet, threw a dustpan at him and cut his hand. The sobbing boy was comforted by Hans Gomper, who was not happy. I myself, set upon by one of the other boys, finally turned. With the pent-up rage of years, I swung my metal lunch-box at his head. I missed, but he backed off. I was somewhat sorry I missed. After that he left me more alone.

This was Gomper's lowest point, the dark before the dawn. From its shabby rented classrooms and pitiful student body the school arose a few years later, a veritable phoenix, with new buildings, new spacious country grounds, to become respected and famed not only in Detroit but throughout the nation. It specialized in 'gifted' children.

But that was later. Then, neither WR nor I could cope with it any longer. Quite aside from the oddities of the pupils, it wasn't a high school, and I was supposedly at ninth grade level and the only advanced student left. My mother couldn't very well found a high school too. She decided, on the advice of my penmanship tutor, to send me to a private girls' school, Grosse Pointe Country Day.

GREEN MANSIONS IN VERMONT

We never went back to Wunder camp. It had nothing to do with jumping the quarantine. My parents' relationship with the Wunders and Gompers remained good, but the camp itself moved to Massachusetts. Probably their lease was up; and there was a rumor that the town, which had cases too, blamed the camp for the polio epidemic, though it was more likely the campers caught the disease from the town pool. Things were edgy in those days for anyone who spoke German; someone also reported mysterious night signals from the camp. The police investigated, and the suspected spy communication turned out to be merely the flashlight beams of campers going to their dorm.

Wanting to stay in Vermont, for two summers we rented houses on the edge of Manchester. The first was a turn-of-the-century mansion, with a stable and grounds including a big pond for swimming and a glorious long lawn stretching down to the marble sidewalk of Manchester's main street. The other, a white, Colonial-style house nearby, had only a garden, but this included a murky, mysterious pond that I paddled about on dreamily on my rubber raft; and we were able to use the pool and stable of the other house, which remained empty. Later, the mansion was demolished and the superb lawn turned into building lots.

Both houses were much too big for us, and my parents, company-starved in winter, wanted sociability. We all invited friends. I had Alice, my sister had her friend Kitty from next door in Grosse Pointe. Then there were all-summer residents with whom we shared the house, Katya and her cousins, Karl and Meta, and Meta's son Johnny, a few years younger than Verena, and his friend Franz, the grandson of Karl's attendant, old German Margaret. She and Gibson did the cooking and cleaning; Enne, in summer, went to her American sisters.

There was also WR, now my parents' secretary, Shorty, our private groom, and many visitors. Old friends from Vienna, now fellow emigrés, distinguished new emigré friends from New York like the publisher WK and the historian KE, came and went all summer long.

Karl needed an attendant because he was totally paralyzed from the waist down. He had caught bone TB in Germany at the age of twenty-four, just when he was due in the U.S. to work for his uncle's printing business. His spinal nerve snapped in the stretching machine that was supposed to help him get well. In winter, he lived with the now retired uncle; in summer, from then on, with us. I still had my friendship with Alice, and sometimes saw Jane. But it was Karl and WR - the paraplegic of forty, the repressed homosexual in his twenties - who became my best friends.

With WR I discussed novels and poetry, and played badminton and walked and rode; like nearly every able-bodied protegé of my parents, WR had to learn to ride. Our relationship was a warmer continuation of the pupil-teacher one. It was to become more complicated, and more unhealthy.

With Karl I discussed everything. Even sex. Karl's disability made him a natural confidant. He was consistently witty and good-humored; the freak accident which had ended a very physical life did not make him bitter. Karl had been, I heard, rather a playboy, who roared around Europe on a motorbike and spent much time on the pursuit of women, Disabled, he devoted himself to being reflective, intellectual, funny and wise. He still attracted women, and his role of counsellor or guru no doubt had much of sublimation.

It could not have been sublimation better spent. On more than one occasion, Karl was my saviour. It was Karl who stopped my mother from having a whole book of my early poems printed by a Grosse Pointe bookshop, at her expense. ("If you do that, the child may never write another line.") It was Karl who told me that masturbation was just like sneezing, a dictum which held more sense, comfort and absolution than all my poor mother's medical books and homilies. He also told me much of what men feel about women and about sex, and was the first person I heard say that you have to *work* at a relationship. (I didn't believe that last, of course. I thought passion and total honesty were all the thing.) And Karl calmed my fear of going *really* crazy in a way no one else could do.

Later, it was Karl I turned to for advice and consolation when my first boyfriend ditched me, in an especially ugly way, just when I was most vulnerable and most in love. "The hardest thing," Karl said, "is that we all want so much to be happy, and life is fundamentally tragic." It was a truth he had learned to live with, and that the affluent of the twenty-first century pretend very hard does not exist. He also said, "No one will ever hurt you so much again." This too, in a way (touch wood), was true.

Karl gave me darker truths as well. When I was overwhelmed, in my pubertal way, by the world's suffering, "Any horror you can imagine is at this moment being inflicted on some wretched soul." But then, "If a million people suffer, each of them is only suffering for himself, as one. You do not have to try to imagine a million people's suffering." That was somehow very consoling. Though the grim corollary is Ivan Karamazov's example of the child locked in a dark privy; even one, God, is one too many.

It was also Karl who tactfully brought down my high-flying fallaciousness, who pointed out, when I did show him a poem, that "Build me a wall of broken wind" is not a felicitous line.

For Karl himself there was a late happy ending. He made a close and affectionate marriage, and had a successful career as a graphologist, a profession he taught himself. No happy ending was ever more deserved.

Though Jewish like nearly all my parents' friends, Karl was not exempt from the German love for practical jokes, with sometimes a cruel edge. The famous too are not exempt. Mozart wrote a concerto for a horn player and before the performance filled the horn with blue cheese. Adolf Busch once terrified his son-in-law Serkin at a provincial concert by sending him a note purporting to be from the mother of an illegitimate Serkin child. Poor Serkin racked his brains in vain for the relevant encounter. I believe they let him know the truth just before he went onstage.

A milder one was devised by Karl and me for my father. Finding a photo of a gawky flapper someone had left in a book, we concocted a letter to accompany it - from one Huberta Glockenspiel, who claimed to be the secret child of an obscure Sterba relative and a famous Viennese Cardinal. She wrote that she needed money. Karl put an Austrian stamp on the envelope, and my father was completely fooled. He spluttered that this was outrageous and he would not send her a cent.

Then WR and Karl, great friends always, thought up something for Alice and myself. We had been writing to our onetime fellow pupil Bernard, signing ourselves "Spirits of Eros." Suddenly we got a card from the local constable, whose name was (really) Scarey. It asked us to appear in court in a week, charged with "disseminating obscene literature through the mails" - in those days a serious Federal offence.

We were left to quake for several days. I relied somewhat on my parents' ability to fix things, but poor Alice was fearfully upset. For pious Baptist Alice, such a charge would have meant a terrible disgrace and the end of her school career. I don't know if Karl and WR expected the trick to work so well or realized how much it would make us, especially Alice, suffer. It was one of the few occasions when Karl was unwise. Before the court date, of course, we were enlightened. The relief was so enormous we were the regulation American 'good sports' and forgave our tormentors at once.

That summer - the summer of the Hawley House, the white Colonial with the dark pond in whose muddy depths little crayfish swam - Alice and I were in love with the young pianist Simon.

We drove the household wild by playing our records of the Tchaikovsky concerto all summer long. We went on to the Pathétique, the Romeo and Juliet Overture, and sometimes, for light relief, the Nutcracker Suite. For me, it was the beginning of the switch from *Your Hit Parade* to classical music. But Tchaikovsky, then much under-rated by musical sophisticates, was not my parents' pet composer. And the pop spirit had not quite left us. We composed, half joking, pop type lyrics to the great Tchaikovsky themes, declaring our love.

Along with passion went mysticism. Of a sort. Alice's ventures into the supernatural were limited by her stern Baptist beliefs. I was ready for anything, as long as it didn't scare me too much. We paid twilight visits to the cemetery nearby. I thought Vermont cemeteries as beautiful and evocative as any place on earth, with their noble trees, their sloping lawns, their white marble stones engraved with poems and staring Byzantine-eyed death-angel faces framed by bird-size wings. We studied the old gravestones, explored the walks, and left with a sense of exalted peace. My most religious hope, even then, was that the surrounding wilderness would survive. Still, we loved all the artefacts, even the sentimental Victorian statues. "Be then austere my angel and of stone," one of my less absurd poems began. After that, it went downhill.

Our reverence for this sacred place was jolted a bit when we discovered a diving board at one of the cemetery pools. It belonged to the caretaker's son. He liked the cemetery too. Not only could he swim there, but drive around in his father's truck, though at fourteen he was legally too young to drive.

Our Tchaikovskian ecstasies reached their peak when my parents took us to the summer music festival concerts at Tanglewood.

Simon was there, not playing but conducting. Versatile as he was, he'd become one of Serge Koussevitsky's star pupils. We sat on blankets on the grass, munching Gibson's sandwiches, only half-absorbed by the music, waiting for the golden moment after the concert when my parents would bear Simon off with us for a Howard Johnson's (28 flavours) ice cream. That was the true high point of the evening. We wore our nicest dresses, I usually one of B. Altman's Love Letter Cottons, ordered by mail from New York, in a colour luscious as the 28 ice creams, deep plum or emerald green, or we wore our matching "crazy prints," multi-hued zigzags on white cotton with puffed sleeves and draw-string neck and waist, dresses my mother had bought for us both. Alice, who could make her own clothes and was tall and long-legged and strikingly pretty, looked great in everything. On me, the wonderful dresses were droopy and baggy, even with expert alteration.

Simon didn't seem to notice how either of us looked. He usually had a young female fellow pupil in tow. He paid us the polite attention due to offspring and friends of the interesting Sterbas. He did call Alice "Alice in Wonderland" and we shared admiration for Lewis Carroll and quoted bits to each other. He said he would take us both out to lunch sometime in Detroit. This great event never materialized. We went to Tanglewood every week in high hope; we came back dashed, but hoping again. All we wanted, really, was a little token of affection, a compliment, a brotherly hug. I was too young for anything else and Alice was forbidden by her Baptist rules anything *ever* but engagement and marriage.

When Simon came for weekends, it was the same. He talked music with Katya and played for us all. He was friendly and courteous but that was it. Still, our hopeless love, fed by each other's mooning letters in winter when we were apart and I miserable (Alice was at her Baptist boarding school) went on for a couple of years. Until Alice fell for a BMOC (Big Man on Campus) at her college and I too changed objects of passion. By then my parents had their own Vermont property and I fell in love with the caretaker's married son, just as hopelessly but going now for the macho image, from the man with a piano and a baton to a man with a hammer, an axe and a gun.

MY FORAY INTO SOCIETY

Except for those already mentioned, we didn't see the patients. That WR had been a patient himself I didn't know till much later. But when I was twelve or thirteen my mother took on an emergency, a girl a year or so younger. Her parents had separated and she was seemingly bent on starving herself to death. My mother saved her, not just from starvation but from shock treatment and forced intravenous feeding. And as she was such a special and serious case, my mother bent the rules again, this time more. It should be remembered that these were earlier psychoanalytic days; and in the period of Freud himself things were much laxer. There were good precedents, like the autistic child Bettelheim had taken into his home.

Terry was not yet well enough for school. My mother found a tutor so she could have lessons at home. In summer, Terry stayed with her tutor at a Manchester inn, so she could continue her treatment. My mother decided Alice and I, especially older, responsible Alice, would be a good healthy influence for Terry, and we were introduced.

Terry didn't look as if she'd been starving. She was pale and puffy-faced, sullen and overweight. She seemed fiercely attached to Ellen, her tutor. Alone with Alice (Alice told me later) she was very aggressive. I think we were more afraid of her than she of us. But Ellen we liked at once, and after a few encounters, Terry was more forthcoming, and we did become friends. The friendship continued in winter, and when Terry was fit to go back to my own new Grosse Pointe school, Country Day.

Terry's parents were now divorced, remarried and living elsewhere, and she didn't want to live with either couple. She lived with her tutor, or with her grandmother in her grandmother's giant lakeside mansion. Her grandmother, a widow, was normally alone there, except for twelve servants. Mostly, Terry and I saw each other at my place. Once or twice, I went to hers.

It was my only entry into highest Grosse Pointe society. Like F. Scott Fitzgerald, I believed that the very rich were different from us. I did not realize that we ourselves were counted among the rich, if not the very. I expected formality and grandeur.

My first shock at what Terry contemptuously called The Mausoleum was the English chauffeur. (English chauffeurs were of course fashionable, like Philippine maids.) The chauffeur was young. He did not look like a British movie butler, as I expected, but like a movie race track tout. He was quite entertaining, given to wry, sly remarks, and Terry bantered with him in a way I suspected neither my mother nor her grandmother would have approved.

Briefly, I met the grandmother, a very ordinary little old lady with a querulous voice, like the soap-opera mothers-in-law. The house was pretentious and somber, nothing much in the way of what my parents called good taste. But Terry took me to a distant wing and introduced me to its wonders. There was an electric massage machine for reducing, which slapped your rear with a large elastic belt. We had ourselves massaged, amid hysterical giggles. Then there were old pop records, and a record of something called a Trepidation Contest. This had belonged to Terry's parents. It was in true dramatic sport announcement vein. "Contestant X grabs the farting post." Appropriate sounds. "And now Contestant Y." More elaborate farts. At the end of the contest, which was more than long enough, the winner was disqualified because, it seems, he shat. Terry said the record was a sort of party piece. I marvelled at how the very rich spend their time.

Terry began to blossom. She was sharp-tongued but warm, clever and funny. We liked the same musicals - *Brigadoon, Call me Mister, Finian's Rainbow.* We loved David Wayne and Danny Kaye. She too, she said, hated Grosse Pointe. At the height of our friendship, she invited me to spend spring vacation on her grandmother's island in the South.

I was very excited. I'd seen almost nothing of the States, nothing at all south of Chicago. We went down by sleeper. In the morning, picture-book, woolly-white-haired black Southern waiters served us a Southern breakfast, eggs and cornbread and the first kippers I'd ever had. That was lovely. Less lovely were the segregated stations, with their barriers and separate toilets and divided waiting rooms. I knew about segregation. But actually seeing two coloured (as you called them then) women sitting meekly on their side of the barrier was still an ugly shock.

The next lap of our journey was by motor yacht, to the island.

The island seemed a paradise. Great trees dripping Spanish moss, brilliant flowers, eight miles of beach, white, pristine, empty. It had once been a plantation. I was shown a historical document, the list of plantation slaves.

In a tiny English sports-car, Terry drove us to the beach. She was too young for a license, even in Grosse Pointe, but on the island no one cared. We swam and walked and collected perfect sand dollars and coloured shells. After sunbathing, we doused ourselves with strong tea, which Terry said was the best way to tan.

Once we walked too far and got caught by the tide. We had to scramble over sharp driftwood and wade waist-deep in water, as the sea was covering the sand. We only just made it back. Terry said you could never walk off the sand because of poisonous snakes. We had already been regaled with horror stories of cottonmouths and water moccasins. In summer the snakes were so bad you did not dare even to step out on the patio without high boots. The paradise had its limits. My mother, medically hyper-alert as always, had provided me with vials of anti-venom. I don't know who would have given the shots.

Terry's father and stepmother arrived with friends on another yacht. The yacht anchored near the beach and we had a barbecue. The women, husky-voiced, scarlet-mouthed, resplendently tanned (though to me their skin looked leathery and old; I was beginning to sense the advantage of my teens) sat nursing their drinks and kept saying, to my bewilderment, how intriguing everything was. Didn't the sea look *intriguing.* Terry said they got that from her favorite aunt, a beauty and social leader even though she'd married out of society. *Intriguing* was everybody's requisite word.

Also vacationing were the grandmother, and Terry's two younger brothers, who lived with her mother and stepfather near New York. The grandmother spent much of her time in town, playing bridge. She complained about her son's cattle (another hobby of his) cutting up her carefully tended lawn. In the kitchen, she two-stepped around singing the then most annoying popular song, "If I'd known you were coming I'd have baked a cake, baked a cake, baked a cake. How d'ya do, how d'ya do, how d'ya do." Still not cured of my Fitzgerald illusions, I didn't think it the kind of song a fabulously rich old lady would sing. I didn't know what I expected - a quavering aria from the *Queen of Spades* - but somewhere at the back of my mind were the great-aunts and Tante Gotte and Tante Emmi, with their dignity and their black silk. There were more shocks to come.

One day Terry's younger brothers came with us to the beach. We sat around and chatted; they became garrulous and confidential. They told us how they and their friends fooled around with beebee guns, about vandalism, breaking street lamps, about one boy's eye being - accidentally - shot out. They told us about the fastest girl in their school, a fat girl everybody thought was a slut. One day all the boys got together, invited her to someone's home when the parents were out, and held her down while "we all had a good feel." I listened to this tale of gang assault with horror and disgust, but my shyness, my anomalous position, their confidence and - yes, my cowardice - stopped me saying what I should have said. My silence was shameful, and I am ashamed of it now.

Terry's father was a strange mixture. He talked like a stock Grosse Pointer, but he and his second wife read Ivy Compton-Burnett to each other in bed. He was convivial, popular, an enthusiastic drinker, but he wanted to make the lonely island his home. I was too much a cultural snob to see there might be such complexity even in Grosse Pointe.

Terry's father had an idea for making the island self-supporting, even profitable. Water chestnuts, he said. A water chestnut crop for Chinese restaurants. The climate was ideal. He waxed very enthusiastic about water chestnuts. And about hunting. One night at dinner, we were treated to a mass of small birds the men had shot. Squabs or whatever. It seemed to me a dreadful lot of killing for so little meat. Craven as before, I ate and said nothing. Terry's father, beaming at his sons, spoke of the glories of "hunting and fishing and the good clean life that goes with it." Thinking of the assaulted girl, I choked quietly on my birds. My one respite from my own hypocrisy were Terry's aunt's daughter and her friend, girls of nine, the only younger children, after my Gomper's 'Child Care' experience, I ever made friends with in my teenage years. We read and drew and played games together, and one of them confided, "We like you because you're little and you're just like us."

Footnote: The family went on to prove that wealth need not bring happiness. Not long after, Terry's brothers, living the good clean life, had a hunting accident. They were out alone, and one accidentally shot the other, who lost a nearly lethal amount of blood before rescue came. Terry's stepfather choked to death on a piece of steak. Terry's father and stepmother were divorced in turn. He took more and more to drink, and ended by barricading himself on the island, with a young girlfriend from town and a gun to keep trespassers away. In the end, I heard, he killed himself. I don't know if the water chestnuts ever materialized.

Terry herself, my mother's most spectacular success, became a beauty, with one of those exquisite feline faces, high oblique cheekbones, small firm chin, greenish come-hither eyes and a perfect sensuous mouth. Even the ambivalent WR was not immune and paid her more of that kind of attention than he ever did me. We stayed friends, and after I left home for college, she became my parents' boarder. She continued to shock me with glimpses of Grosse Pointe crudity, of the hard-drinking world my parents only saw from behind the couch and I saw never at all. "When you go to college," a leering friend of her father's told her after too many cocktails, "they'll sure break your cherry pie." Occasionally, in this world, something does progress; it is not the sort of remark such men would probably make quite so freely now.

Our cherry pies still intact, we fell in love together, in Vermont (yet again) in my last summer before college and while Terry was still in school, with two half-brothers, the sons of the publisher WK. Terry, younger but more daring, and with the adult one of the two, soon went to Petting Below the Waist. She confided that when they have orgasms men groan like bears. Neither of us had heard a bear groan but I guessed what she meant. It was a bit off-putting, I thought; it would be hard not to laugh.

Our loves led to various traumas. My parents approved, in view of the exalted ancestry of our suitors, even though mine did rather annoy them by once "preparing" their precious piano for compositions à la John Cage. In the end we both got cruelly ditched. My boyfriend was a child like myself. Terry's was all of twenty-eight and had no excuse for leading on someone so vulnerable and so young. Childhood, pace Freud, is not everything. There are later turnings that can send you up or right back down. I remember Terry, only fifteen, going joyously off to New York with a new, daring black lace nightgown, prepared to give her all. It was no longer wanted. My mother's witcheries could not shield her from her pain when the source of it was my mother's most respected set of friends.

After that Terry became wilder. She lost her virginity, recklessly, to a stranger on a train. She went out mostly with older men. I still have her letters from this period, witty, mocking, rebellious. She deserved something more.

Terry went to my college, as a freshman when I was a junior. Unlike me, she wasn't so happy there. We moved in different circles and already in college began to lose touch. She married young, an older Grosse Pointer, had children, divorced, married again. After college I never saw her. Benny, one of our minions, was approached one day in the supermarket, *many years later, by a ravaged middle-aged woman. "Don't you remember me, Benny? I'm Terry." He was stunned. He would never have recognized her. He said, sadly, that she did not seem surprised.*

Digression:
My Tante Lina's Fan

Besides Tante Lina's paintings and her tapestry hanging of George and the Dragon, I have her party fan.

It is made of ivory and pleated cream-coloured silk. He name - Lina - is painted on it in gold, black and red, the letters extended into curly twigs and tendrils, with a coronet above. (Harttmann, Frau Endlinger used to say, was in fact a *good* von.) On back of one of the pleats someone has written in pencil, *"Aberrr wwwoh!"* and signed roundish initials, now hardly legible, perhaps K and R.

I used to think this phrase meant "But where?" as literally it does. I wondered if it referred to some forbidden rendezvous. Now I know it is actually an exclamation, the "wo" short for *wass,* what. It means, in the slang of the period, something like "But really?!" This both limits and extends the possibilities. It is unlikely to have concerned a rendezvous. It could have been by the refused Crown Prince of Romania. Or simply another girl at a ball, reacting to whispered gossip or a faintly scandalous sight. Whoever, whatever it was, Tante Lina never erased it. It has survived, with its mystery, on the foxed splitting silk, for a hundred years.

PIN-LESS AND LETTER-LESS IN GROSSE POINTE

Her attitude to Grosse Pointe society was one of my mother's most ambivalent and puzzling.

On the one hand, she was a self-proclaimed rebel against the high society in which she herself grew up. A few stories I did glean from her childhood show an aggressive, disruptive child. The time she kicked her brother under the table during their catechism lesson, until when her brother didn't respond and the priest's face grew scarlet she realized she was kicking the priest. The time she shot arrows (presumably blunted) at a boy tied to a tree - he was supposed to play St Sebastian or some other martyr - a boy, my mother said proudly, who grew up to be a Cardinal. The tricks she played on her governesses, such as balancing a bucket of water on the door to the governess's room. My mother was also proud of her high governess turnover. Best of all, her hunting story; she prided herself on her shooting. The attic in Gmunden housed dormice, as well as the beautiful stone martens that prey on them. Having just shot a dormouse, young Ditha entered a formal tea party of her mother's, holding the dead animal, her party dress stained with blood. That kind of episode delighted her. Later, as an adolescent, she was studious and intellectual, contemptuous of the social round.

And yet. Though she agreed with my father in deploring Grosse Pointe's 'vulgarity', shallowness, racism, reactionism and heavy drinking, I think she was pleased by my sister's eventual social success, and pleased by social rank in her patients. I can't think it coincidental that the patients she chose for my fraternizing came from Society; and the tones in which she spoke of the prominent rich were hardly disapproving.

Also, though my parents voted Democrat and espoused Roosevelt-style liberalism, my mother's view of taxation was heartfelt Republican. I remember her talking indignantly about the 'top dollars' siphoned off by the Government, unless your accountants could find a way out.

Perhaps my mother's childhood rebellion was partly inspired by her family's obvious preference for boys, and that she was more hurt than she admitted by the family's lack of means to live up to their rank. Whatever the reasons, her tinge of respect for values she and my father affected to despise was one of her less endearing traits. Not least because it fostered some similar ambivalence in me.

But I only became aware of it when I went to high school in Grosse Pointe.

My first days at my new school have that nightmare edge of blackness, like failing sight. Country Day was quite genteel, as befitted a school for the cream of Grosse Pointe. No one spanked me, pulled my hair, put pieces of rainworm down my shirt or locked me in a closet. It appeared that no one would. One or two top girls were directed to be welcomers, to be nice to the new, foreign child, to show me my desk, my locker, show me around. And they *were* nice. But it was soon evident that not only was I the class baby, smaller and two years younger than anyone else, but that with my lanky hair, owlish glasses and orthopaedic shoes, my lack of chic, co-ordination and connections, I was a dud.

The worst misery of those first days was that I was also a dud in the one area where I'd been sure of myself. At Gomper's I was an intellectual star. At Country Day, coming in at mid-year, I took the mid-year exams in Latin, Algebra, French and English and except for English failed every one. The fact that these were exams particular to the school, for which the others had prepared and I not, did not at the time occur to me. I faced the awful prospect of being put down a grade and being with the two girls who had tormented me at Trombley, who already giggled ominously every time my name was said in our joint common room roll call. Clearly, they hadn't forgotten.

My mother as usual fixed things to save me. She decided to employ WR, already working as secretary in my parents' Detroit office, to come every afternoon to tutor me in all the subjects I'd failed.

Then, for a bit, it didn't seem so bad. The girls continued quite polite. I managed to score a basket in my first basketball game, though I'd never played any of the Country Day sports except baseball. My first basket was also my last. During this athletic period a pretty blonde girl, almost as small and young-looking as myself, began to chat with me. She discovered I rode, and asked me if I'd like to come with her to the Hunt Club, where she kept her horse. I was thrilled. I thought I had made a friend.

Robin and another girl called for me that evening. There were no chauffeurs or parents along; Robin herself drove. The friend was a girl from the tenth grade who wore very adult makeup and looked about twenty-five. It turned out that Robin, far from being young, was one of the class's oldest. Like me, she hadn't done too well in exams. The girls' talk was all about dates, parties and boys. I listened dumbly, having no qualification to add a single word.

At the Hunt Club I sat almost alone in what seemed a giant arena and watched Robin and a few others ride to music in a luxurious sawdust indoor ring. Robin's horse was a big stylish chestnut hunter, who looked as though one pull from his mouth would have dislocated my arms. He tossed his head and bared his teeth when Robin untacked him. Robin admitted he was not an easy horse.

I realized I was out of my element. Nevertheless, I asked Robin to ride with us once or twice on Belle Isle. She came, and remarked that my mother's mare had "good confirmation." She found nothing to say about my poor Sultan, with his coarse head and childish tricks, obviously below the dignity of hunters like hers. After that, till near the end of high school, I was left to the company of such fellow misfits as sought me out.

One of the first things I noticed at Country Day was the jewelry. Girls often wore sterling ID bracelets, some with names of boys. Some had boys' signet rings. And all the girls from ninth grade up had tiny mysterious enamelled brooches.

I didn't dare ask at school, so my mother found out and explained. The brooches were sorority pins, and the rings fraternity rings that boys gave to girls they went steady with. It seemed some girls had steady boyfriends already at fourteen or fifteen. And that almost every girl belonged to a sorority.

The Grosse Pointe sororities were quite respectable, involved in charity work, like the Junior League. They were not rumored to hold initiations like those sororities in rougher schools where, a *Time* article said, a girl died from kidney damage after a beating. But there were nasty stories about the brutality of the local fraternity initiations, which could include beating with canoe paddles. We heard about it from the Dodds.

The welcomers had done their duty, and my classmates' initial friendliness soon wore thin. No one was rude to me, but no one seemed eager to have me around. One big, rough girl began a bit of rough teasing. Fortunately, she was one of the first to leave for boarding school, which was yet more fashionable than Country Day, and where many Grosse Pointe girls were sent after high school began. I was still bewildered by everything, not least the math and Latin. I could not have got through my homework without WR.

Despairing, I wondered if sororities were the key to acceptance. But weren't they the sort of club, like the Boat Club, the Hunt Club, etc. which my parents, loyal to their excluded Jewish friends, would on principle never join? My mother did not seem to think so, though I doubt that in those days any Grosse Pointe sorority knowingly admitted a Jew. Anyway, no Jews were supposed to be living in Grosse Pointe. With the blithe ignorance of American mores which years of American patients had not dispelled, my mother also informed me that talent like my supposed literary one might help; someone had told her so. You could, for instance, get published in the school magazine.

I decided to prostitute my art. Anyway, this would be like doggerel. It didn't count. I wrote a soppy story carefully calculated to win the Honourable Mention in the school's literary magazine short story contest. It was based on that favorite school story gimmick, the post-accident facial scar. It was worthy of the soap operas I was outgrowing. WR found it very funny, and suggested such lines as "Bessie threw herself on the bed and sobbed." That was the right tone. I didn't want it to be too good. I didn't want the first prize. I was too shy to face walking up to the stage in front of the whole assembled school to be presented with a slim volume of Kahlil Gibran, the usual award.

I got my Honourable Mention. I decided commercial writing must be a snap, but I would never do it again. I was slightly ashamed of the story. And my prostitution was not rewarded. No sorority, then or ever, asked me to join. But by tenth grade some of those off to board were replaced by new pupils and there was a new rule forbidding sorority pins in class. So my exclusion was at least not instantly visible to all.

Clothes were of course very important in Grosse Pointe.

Country Day girls came to school in skirts and sweaters, white bobby socks and penny loafers. No one wore trousers to school. Sweaters were "sloppy Joes," big baggy Shetlands sometimes borrowed from boyfriends, or cashmere or lambswool twin-sets, usually in pastels. Skirts were straight or pleated, solid colours or Tartan plaid. Sometimes you wore cardigans with the buttons in the back. And a locket or single strand of pearls. There was also the "Dickey," a white collar attached to two brief panels of cloth tied with ribbons at the waist, meant to simulate a blouse worn under your sweater, something like a man's false shirt front.

Changing for athletics in the locker room informed me about underwear. Bras were worn as soon as you had anything to put in them, though "training bras" had not yet been dreamed up by the hard-selling bra industry. Pretty lace camisoles were trendy then, over the bra. With camisoles went white petticoats; otherwise you wore a full slip. As summer vacation was early June to early September, there wasn't much time to wear summer clothes to school; but they would be very feminine cotton dresses or white blouses with skirts again usually pastel.

Hair was mostly shoulder length and slightly curled, generally at home with curlers or bobby pins. One girl, daringly, had a "butch cut" like a boy's crewcut, but there may have been some medical reason. She grew it out soon after. In my last two years at Country Day short, ear-level haircuts, feathery and soft, became the in thing. Bangs were not popular then and long hair was held back with a headband or a silver barette. Hair was normally washed once a week (when did it change to every *day?*) on Thursday or Friday, so you looked good for your weekend date. If you had no date, you'd probably wash it anyway, so as not to reveal that your weekend was empty.

Almost no one had pierced ears or wore ear-rings to class. Bright nail polish, eye make-up or high heels worn to school marked you as vulgar, not properly Grosse Pointe. But red lipstick was okay, from age fourteen. Fourteen, ninth grade age, was a breaking point, for many the beginning of dating as it was of high school, of the real teens. Being an immature, under-sized twelve-year-old among fourteens and fifteens was hard going. My mother, though she treated adolescents, seemed unaware how this age and culture gap would affect my life.

My own clothes were never right. The loafers with gleaming new pennies inserted in the slit below the tongue were forbidden; my doctors had prescribed laced shoes with metal arch supports. My hair was greasy even after washing because of the lotion, also prescribed, to make my head stop itching. My head needed more washing, less brushing and no lotions, but no one then figured that out. And whatever I used to curl my hair into the desired page-boy, it curled either too much are too little or reversed its curl in the first wind. However zealously I studied *Mademoiselle* or *Seventeen* or the girls around me, I couldn't acquire that carefree, casual smoothness. My socks drooped, my hems drooped, my sweaters bagged in the wrong places. If my indulgent mother ordered me a *Seventeen* dress, the colours would be tawdry or garish, quite different from the picture, or the dress turned out to be the kind that only suited someone buxom or six feet tall.

The Grosse Pointe look was so simple. A cashmere twin-set, pearls, a plain gray wool skirt - I could put them on, but I couldn't achieve it. The look was of course also something ineffable, that of a rich confident society in its prime. It amuses me now to see those coveted clothes on old British ladies, the sort who do church flowers and have cucumber sandwiches for tea.

My sister Verena and I realized, long after the event, that our early Country Day days were much alike. Even though she became not only accepted but a leading light, Gibson's "social butterfly," and brought a whole gang of Grosse Pointe society girls to frisk in our Vermont pool. But at first, as she was in a younger, hence ruder class, she was openly bullied and teased. The only girls willing to make friends with us then, we confessed to each other decades later, were the girls afflicted with serious B.O. Mine soon went on to another school. I myself had found her a bit strange and the B.O. bothered me too, so I never asked her home.

My next acquaintance, a pleasant but very adult-looking girl with permed bleached-looking hair and bright red nails and lips, had a very different problem. She was a polio victim and got about on crutches. I thought it mean that no one but me paid much attention to her. It may not have been the crutches; she wasn't the Society type, and from what she said, she was aware of the others' snobbishness. She too did not stay long.

My next friend, the one who lasted and whom I often saw outside school, was a plump girl called Betty who was deeply unhappy at home. Her father was a widower with a live-in housekeeper nothing like Enne. Betty described her as mean and malevolent.

Betty and I discovered a common love for French and classical music; we stayed overnight at each other's houses and discussed books and animals and sex and Betty's problems and how we hated the snobbish school. She came to Vermont and once when she ran away from home she consulted my mother and my mother talked her out of it.

This friendship was tested by something worse than B.O. Betty burned her hand severely with boiling bacon grease left sizzling, she said, by the housekeeper. The treatment of choice was to use the dead skin as dressing. For more than a week, with Betty in her usual seat next to mine, girls wrinkled their noses, asked what smelled like Limburger cheese, was there a dead bird stuck in the ventilator again? Betty would say miserably, "It's me. I'll move to the back of the room." The smell was in fact almost unbearable, but I felt I at least could not desert her. It seemed monstrous to me that her father did not keep her at home, as my parents surely would have, till the hand healed.

Betty and I remained best friends until we graduated. Then we went to our separate colleges and our separate ways. I married young and embarked on a wandering life. Betty married young and promptly had six children. Put in touch again through older mutual friends - her college teachers, my husband's colleagues - we wrote to each other. Her letter was a list of the vital statistics of the six: hair colour, eye colour, weight, height, hobbies, etc. She seemed to have forgotten Mozart, Verlaine, and our dreamy speculations under Vermont trees. I, who believe in Zero Population Growth, could not find the impetus to keep up the correspondence for long.

I began to read adult magazines, *Life* and *Time*. And the *New Yorker*, which I loved. I also read books of short stories. There was a prize-winning story called *Sweet Sixteen*. It was about a boy and girl who meet going skating. They skate together, he takes her home and kisses her goodnight. His lips are as "sweet and baby-soft as a new raspberry." He says he'll call. She waits in vain. There was an eloquent last line, "And I know now that he'll never call. Never." I found this story evocative and magical, in spite of the raspberry kiss.

I began to try to write adult stories, *New Yorker* style. "She sat up primly and began to do her fingernails," my *New Yorker* story began. My mother read it, declared it excellent, and sent it to our immigration sponsor, Laura Z. Hobson, who had remained a friend. I think my mother had some benighted idea it might actually go to the *New Yorker*. She told me Laura Z. Hobson liked it too. Like much of my poetry it was in fact merely a jejune and affected attempt to be what I so longed to be, to be grown up.

On one of our New York trips, I was taken to see the famous lady herself. She was not only a successful novelist but wrote a popular daily column. She was also attractive, gray-haired but youthful, chic, very assured. We talked, I very shyly, about writing and plans for college. She didn't tell me my work showed genius or that you had to suffer to be great. She fixed me with her big luminous eyes and said, "When you get to college you don't want to be a greasy grind." I wondered if she had noticed my oily hair. I said I would try not to be, though I suspected this advice was already too late.

Before Country Day, the experts had begun on my teeth.

The first who tried to deal with my jutting fang was a Dr Muschl, as to be expected a fellow Central European. Dr Muschl subscribed to the Norwegian Method. This was supposed to avoid extractions, of which I was terrified, and which my parents were against. But with two teeth doubled up, one a critical upper eye tooth, the others crowded as well, it seemed problematic where Dr Muschl would find space.

Dr Muschl, a mild nondescript little man, had a framed motto on his wall. It read like this:

> Without teeth
> There can be no chewing.
> Without chewing
> There can be no food.
> Without food
> There can be no health.
> Without health
> WHAT IS LIFE?

I pondered this dental propaganda while Dr Muschl made me bite into pink wax and gooey stuff like plaster of Paris, and took x-rays, and began to insert wires and hammer on metal bands. Surely people managed some food, even toothless. Or got false teeth. And without food you wouldn't just be unhealthy, you'd be dead. The motto was a mystery, like Dr Muschl's Norwegian Method.

The Norwegian Method involved an elaborate appliance you wore only at night. There was a head cap made of blue grosgrain ribbon, and wires and elastics that hooked onto the braces in your mouth and then onto the cap. It was something like being a horse with a tight curb bit. The bands cut into my cheeks and the cap into my forehead, so the only way I could sleep was to pad the whole lot with masses of cotton wool. The family could not help but laugh. "Santa Claus," they said as I got ready for bed. In spite of the padding, I went to school with pink marks on my face and my sometime insomnia, needless to say, got worse.

On one visit to Dr Muschl, I met the first and only flasher of my childhood. As I came out of the office, a homely boy leered at me on the stairs. "Wanna see sumpin?" he asked and began to undo his pants. "No!" I screamed and dashed down and out to my sister and Gibson waiting in the car. I leapt into the car - but it was the wrong one. I have always been bad at telling cars apart. I found myself in a strange car with a strange man. For whatever Freudian reason, the car part of this memory is lost; I suppose I promptly leapt out again. I have Verena's word for the incident. Anyway, from then on, I was escorted up and down those stairs.

The Norwegian Method did not seem to work. We opted for extraction after all - four back molars. I was given laughing gas. After a moment of panic, I went right under, hearing organ music and jolly roaring guffaws, It was a glorious high, one of the best half hours of my childhood. I would gladly have gone through it again. But there was no more laughing gas. There was the next orthodontist, Dr Brown.

Dr Brown was wholly American and up-to-date. Proudly, he showed me his gallery of Before and After. Photos of buck teeth, bulldog chins, receding chins, a series of horrible freakish profiles remodelled by Dr Brown to normalcy. I was assured I too would lose my Dracula fang. Dr Brown festooned all my teeth with braces and little connecting wires. It wasn't actually too painful and at least now I could get some sleep.

There was one snag. The conscientious Dr Brown wanted me to continue seeing him all summer. With our long time in Vermont this was impossible. A dentist was found in Albany, a two hour drive away, to tighten my braces every two weeks. He was the one I liked best. He was young and cheerful and funny and had me laughing while he tightened the wires. It did hurt rather more afterwards. When I came back to Dr Brown he took x-rays and clucked disapprovingly. He said my teeth had been moved so fast the roots were starting to disintegrate; any more time with Dr Jones and I'd risk losing my teeth altogether. So much then for the nice Dr Jones.

Dr Brown went on treating me until I finished school. I had another two years of orthodontia with yet another dentist when I was at college near New York. At the end of it my eyeteeth were where eyeteeth are supposed to be. It needed more frequent appointments than modern orthodontia but caused less pain. What I suffered with my braces and retainers was nothing like what my daughter suffered with little rubber bands, a new high-tech version, I suppose, of the Norwegian Method. At eighteen at last I could smile for photographers, chew gum and eat corn on the cob again, and be kissed without fearing injury to someone's tongue.

I had no winter loves, not after Jack.

I did have a winter fantasy figure, a boy I saw only once, who lived down our street. He went out with one of the most popular Country Day girls, who was in the grade just above mine. One glimpse of his good looks was enough to put him into my lonely fantasies. I pictured it all like the scene in the *Sweet Sixteen* story. We would go skating - well no, because I couldn't skate. It would have to be summer then. We would somehow meet and sit on the grass and he would kiss me. These fantasies were painfully vivid and arousing, though my only contact with this boy was finding his name in the school paper and the society columns, always linked with his girlfriend's. Sandy 'n' Chick were at somebody's birthday party. Sandy 'n' Chick were at a Country Club dance. Sandy was knitting Chick a pair of Argyle socks. Seeing those names made my stomach lurch, like seeing, in the Gomper school car, Jack and Ruby's linked hands. That was all. It was a masochistic salt on the sore of my loneliness. I don't know if my parents or Freud would have understood.

After being *popular*, and as big a part of it, what counted at Country Day was athletic prowess. And as at Gomper's the worst period of my school day was sports, even though I didn't have to dodge cruel balls thrown at me by great louts twice my size. I wasn't supposed to dodge. I was supposed to catch, throw, bat, volley, cradle, stop, dribble, drive and whatever else you do with a bloody ball.

We played field hockey, which I'd never seen before, basketball which I hadn't either, baseball which I was lousy at, and in my second year we were introduced to a new game, Lacrosse, which I believe was invented by the American Indians. You were given something like a butterfly net, which was used for catching and throwing and also for carrying the ball toward the goal. You swayed the net as you ran so the ball wouldn't fall out. This was called cradling.

I was equally bad at all these games. On the hockey field I lurked in the rear as a remote fullback, praying no ball would come anywhere near me. In baseball when teams were chosen I was always last, as any side with me could be sure of a strike-out every time I came to bat and so was likely to lose. My one basket in basketball was a fluke; I could neither dribble nor guard nor even properly catch or throw. Volleyball was sheer nightmare. Lacrosse I had some hope for as it was equally new to everybody. However, I was the only girl who managed to throw a Lacrosse ball, which is small and very hard, so that it came down on my own head.

Some girls not too eager or good at sports redeemed themselves by being cheerleaders at extra-mural games. I didn't go out for this either. The leaping and yelling seemed to me embarrassing and absurd. Dutifully, I did attend some of the games, when our varsity team played Sacred Heart Convent, Detroit Liggett, Grosse Pointe High or Bloomfield Hills. It was de rigueur to attend. Even Mlle Goubet, our very strict, academic and excellent French teacher, who deplored girls being let out of class to play varsity hockey, put in an appearance once or twice. Much as I hated the sports myself, I was impressed by the dedication and skill of our teams, They gave themselves unstintingly. At hockey practice, girls occasionally fainted from over-exertion, and in games they played to their limits. Watching them, red-faced and tousled and near exhaustion, score a final basket or drive a final goal, you had the feeling that nothing in their lives would ever mean more. I never knew any of them well enough, then or later, to find out of this was true.

Coward that I was, I shouted with the rest of the audience. Alagaroo, garoo, garoo, pie-ex, pie-ex, hica pica dominica allaca ballaca ba. Country Day, Country Day, Rah, Rah, Rah. CDS CDS CDS CDS CDS etc. (train whistle sound) - Watch our steam! And so on. To make it worse, we sometimes had 'pep rallies' before the game, to practice the cheers and drum up "school spirit," another of those qualities I thoroughly lacked. At one of the rallies, our tiny wizened headmistress surprised the whole school by appearing with scrawny arms exposed in a sleeveless vest and feathers on her gray head, beating a tom-tom. I was secretly appalled. It still seemed to me that some kind of distance, of dignity, should go with authority. Betty agreed; she disliked Miss B. anyway. The other girls were thrilled to bits.

In keeping with all this, the big school banquet of the year was the Athletic Association Dinner held in the gym. There was chicken à la king and girls were awarded their varsity letters for games, even for cheerleading. The only girl who never got a single letter to put on her sweatshirt was me. I picked at my chicken and hoped no one would notice that mine was the only name not called.

I did have one distinction. I came in bottom of the whole school in the motor fitness tests. Though I was light and good at a few things like hanging by my hands, I was defeated by the horrid contraption called the horse - ironically, since I loved horses. We had to leapfrog over this object onto a mat. My legs simply refused to clear it. After about three humiliating tries, as at baseball I was struck out. The results of these tests were posted on the hall bulletin board for all to see. My classmates, kindly, did not subject me to more than a passing remark.

At the AA dinners, everyone became animated and emotional. Dreadful school songs were sung, to the headmistress, the headmaster (head of both CDS and DUS, its brother boys'), to the school itself. Like the cheers, they have lodged in my unwilling mind. I can still sing them when sufficiently drunk - my only performance piece, but it brings down the house. "As we stand here we lift our voices singing, to one who is held dear in e-hevry heart. She keeps her standards held high above us, and makes her I-deals seem of us a part." (to the Headmistress). "Mr Blenksop, oh here's to you, you're a friend strong and true. We'll have a gay time, a happy play time, 'cause we all love to be with you." (to the Headmaster). Etc. That second one, surely, is no longer used.

At my third dinner, two girls opposite me earnestly discussed their dates for later that night. A tapping of glasses heralded an important announcement. Mr Blenksop was to retire. The Blenksop song was ardently sung. The two girls, who'd probably hardly seen Mr Blenksop who was mostly at the brother school, stopped chattering and burst into tears. A minute later, they dried their eyes and went on with their conversation as if it had never stopped. It struck me that no one at Gomper's had shown this talent, and that perhaps it was peculiar to Society and only flourished in places like Grosse Pointe. Not hypocrisy, really. Sincere emotion ("Sincere" was a much used compliment). But on tap.

After the dinner, I went down to wait for my ride home while other girls, noisy and excited, rushed off to their parties and their boys. Whoever was coming for me was late. A lone blonde from the senior class, whose date was late also, waited with me behind the front doors, fretting and impatient; we were the last left. "Oh come on date," she kept saying. I wondered what his name was. When a car hooted for her at last, she dashed out into the spring rain, giving me a nice, genuinely friendly goodbye smile. Soon my car came too. I went back to our Viennese living room, where my father, having seen off his last patient, would be listening to Mozart or Beethoven while my mother fussed over the animals and Enne snored upstairs.

Having got to see a couple of the other girls' rooms, I announced I wanted mine redecorated.

My mother as always agreed. I chose white paper with tiny pink rosebuds, blue curtains, a kidney-shaped dressing table draped in the blue with a white ruffle. On the dressing table were the regulation glass tray holding glass animals, and my Storybook Dolls.

Like my clothes, it was all wrong. The blue material looked coarse. The pink rosebuds were nerve-wracking. I felt it would be too extravagant to have it done again, so the room stayed like that till after I left for college, when the walls went back to a solid colour. My mother's blue hooked rug remained throughout, the fruit of I don't know how many analytic hours.

At Gomper's I had been bullied and often miserable but not such an outsider. We were nearly all odd; that's why we were there. At CDS I was in a completely alien world. I wanted to reject it as it did me. I didn't have the guts for open rejection. When the other girls wore black arm bands to school because a Democrat had been elected, I did not crow it was my parents' candidate who'd won. I discovered I was a moral coward as well as a physical one. But once in a while I screwed up the courage to make a contradictory statement about Current Events or American History, where dyed-in-the-wool Republicanism prevailed. The Current Events teacher was one of our two youngest, Jean Harris, a pretty woman with fashionable expensive clothes, whose cool manner and forbidding Grosse Pointe chic especially intimidated me. She later became very famous for shooting the Scarsdale diet man, her erstwhile lover.

My outbursts were rare and took all my nerve. My heart would bang against my ribs, my ears ring, my tongue seem stuck to the roof of my mouth. But if I managed to squeak out my little piece of dissent, I was happy for days, and that much stronger.

Even in English, my best and favorite subject, I was at first out of step. Our English teachers were a mixed lot. There was flute-voiced, very New England Miss Frame who reputedly carried a story of tragic love - a jilting or a war death or an accident on the wedding day. Miss Frame was aloof and not an easy marker. She once reduced one of my most 'popular' classmates to tears. I could not help some *Schadenfreude*; at least it wasn't me sobbing in public, and at least it was possible for even such girls as this to break down. No one thought worse of the girl. They thought worse of Miss Frame.

Miss Frame - strangely, I thought - made us write an essay or story centered on a pillow. Later, riding with my parents on the outskirts of Grosse Pointe, I met Miss Frame walking alone on a bitter winter Sunday. It was a bizarre encounter. In Grosse Pointe almost no one walked; 'fast walking' as exercise was far in the future. And certainly not in this desolate flatland with its few groves of trees, now all built over with grids of ranch houses, factories and shopping malls. Except for the odd Sunday hunter after pheasants, Miss Frame was the only pedestrian we ever saw. I stammered some shy, embarrassed greeting. Miss Frame smiled. "Isn't the snow beautiful," she said. "It's just like a big white pillow." And walked on. I wondered if pillows *were* her obsession, if they'd figured in her secret tragedy. I was of course never to know. Soon after that she left the school and was replaced by Mrs Stonebrook.

The girl Miss Frame had reduced to tears became Mrs Stonebrook's favorite, writing florid romantic poetry under Mrs Stonebrook's tutelage, and waxing ecstatic, as did others, over Keats and Shelley read in spring outside under the trees. "I fall upon the thorns of life. I buhleed," Mrs Stonebrook intoned and the girls sighed. Betty and I thought her gushy and affected; we kept it to ourselves but at least did not pretend to join the general adulation.

My last and best English teacher was Mrs Penney, an English war bride. She introduced me to Huxley, Ibsen, Shaw and, through a scruffy little leaflet, to the British Humane Fur Crusade and anti-Gin Trap campaign. I was deeply inspired by all four. I had not known there were groups actually campaigning against such cruelties, groups that I myself might one day join. Mrs Penney spotted a kindred spirit and we became, in a discreet way, friends. The others liked her less. She was too critical, too sharp, too hard a marker, she was resented for her outburst that "Mrs Stonebrook has been spoon-feeding you." I heard later that not long after we graduated she was divorced from her Grosse Pointe husband and went back home.

I never told anyone at school what I wrote. After my Honourable Mention, I left the school magazine alone. I showed my poetry, if at all, only to Karl, WR and my parents.

My poems were inspired by the usual pubertal things, landscape, loneliness, love and death, the cruelty in the world. They started with what I hoped was a flourish but usually got lost before the end. It never occurred to me to spend time trying to work out better endings. Poetry, like love itself, had to come like a bolt from the sky. When I got stuck, I put my notebook aside and waited for the next bolt to fall. The bolt was usually yet another beginning. But I had plenty of time, I thought, to perfect my chosen art.

Because their world was so confident, so self-contained and secure, I was fascinated by the pretty, popular, athletic girls at CDS. I watched their effortless running, their perfect muscular legs, the boys' fraternity rings flashing on their strong hockey-stick wielding hands. The way they wore their Sloppy Joe sweaters with that fold near the hip, casual but just right, the way they put on lipstick, the way their silver barettes held back their glossy hair. It was less intense, more diffuse than my obsession with the Trombley girl in pink angora and as then there was nothing lesbian about it. I loved to look at beauty and I didn't get to see any beautiful boys. I didn't get to see any boys at all. And I was intrigued by the secrets of the girls' success, by the private lives I was never to know, by the locker-room conversations in lowered voices, that one couple had broken up, another begun going steady, that some boy had been drunk, that some 'fast' girl was dating an older boy.

There seemed to be no real shadows on their existence, though I knew this couldn't be true. There were divorced parents like Terry's, a brother drowned in a sailing accident, a case of polio. But on the whole, in those early TV days, young Society seemed oddly sheltered. I remember one student talking with pitying amazement about a man she had seen "with newspapers under his coat to keep warm. I didn't know anyone could be *that* cold." Whatever lay beneath, the sunniness rarely failed, at least not in school. Nor the *good sportsmanship,* the *sense of humor,* the air of *sincerity*, the ability to greet like best friends people you probably didn't give a shit about. Those qualities you were eulogized for in your school yearbook. The Country Day girls did not come from a world where you might have to flee your home in the middle of the night. They still don't, though now they live with burglar alarms, hot lines to police and fire departments, searchlights trained on the lawn, and the ghetto starts at Little Venice, right on the border of Grosse Pointe.

I became a compulsive reader of the society columns. Besides sheer masochism, it was my only way of learning what went on, what was in, how far I was out.

It began in my first CDS year, when I opened the Detroit paper to find a whole page devoted to photos of a luncheon at the Women's City Club, hosted by one of my classmates for my class. I scanned the photos frantically to see if any face was missing. None was, except mine.

No one at school mentioned the lunch in front of me, just as they didn't explain their sororities. But sometimes they talked in low voices about things I couldn't follow at all. At Country Day the key word was *popular.* And judging by those columns, I had the unpopularity prize.

Later, it wasn't quite so bad. By my senior year, my class was down to only thirteen, as so many of the poshest had been sent to boarding school. There were three or four of us who didn't date, and another who was very tall was reported at parties with a boy I knew was a head shorter. In the very physical world of Grosse Pointe, I wondered if this counted.

Dating, from what I could overhear, was mostly going steady. You went steady with one boy for a while, then you had a falling out and went with another. One couple were steadies for six years. One pretty girl went out with twins from Grosse Pointe High. Couples going steady presumably necked or petted, above or below the waist. Below the waist was very daring. I didn't know how far they went or if any girls actually lost their virginity. My information came only from magazines, None of the dating girls were ever friends enough with me to give any secrets away.

The boy-less girls were all in Senior French, which made a sort of bond. We went once to the French teacher's apartment for dinner, and to French movies when any were shown. We speculated about whether our strict but humorous 'Mademoiselle,' now quite old, was a virgin. She was very proper but she was *French*. We decided she must have been pretty and hoped, because we liked her, that she'd had at least one love affair.

We also sometimes went to the local cinema on Friday night and at school sometimes out for lunch together, to the nearest hot-dog and hamburger joint. There you ate Swankie Frankies (hot-dogs wrapped in bacon and stuffed with cheese) and listened to a song called *Near You* with a lilting piano theme, and I felt bittersweet sixteenish yearnings though I wasn't yet sixteen. It was as near as I ever got to being a real American teen.

Digression:
Initials on a Lost Window

The Gmunden villa, when I lived there on and off in the sixties and seventies, still had most of its old furniture and effects, the great gilded Baroque mirror, the Bosnian rugs and octagonal Bosnian coffee tables, the jewel-coloured, long-stemmed crystal glasses, the white and blue Harttmann china with an H and a beribboned coronet. Etc.etc,. A very twentieth century American friend who visited us referred to it all as Imperial Garbage. The villa also had its original double windows, one set opening out, one set in, the outer ones removed in summer to be replaced by heavy green shutters, a back-breaking and hazardous task accomplished by the old Croatian gardener until he retired. After that we left the shutters off, although Frau Endlinger, who had always sneaked up to close the shutters on bright days, claimed that sunshine would fade the Bosnian rugs.

One of these old windows had the initials of one of my great-aunts, engraved in a wobbly childish hand, with the little v for von between the capitals. Some craving for a small, secret, permanent mark. It needs perseverance to engrave on glass. Perseverance and a diamond. Perhaps she borrowed one of her mother's, doubling the crime. I wonder if she was punished for it. Or maybe, as it was the maids who cleaned and probably also opened and closed the windows, no one in authority ever saw. It may have been my discovery. The window of course is gone now, replaced with modern double glazing after the villa had to be sold and was turned into flats for Gmunden's nouveaux-riches.

SUMMERS IN PARADISE

In Vienna and Grosse Pointe, to my family I was the Princess on the Pea. *Die Prinzessin auf der Erbse* my father always said when I cut every shred of fat off my meat, fished every shred of milk-skin out of my coffee, couldn't sleep because of wrinkles in a sheet, pulled at tight hairs in my pigtails until my mother's neat braiding - one of the few things she herself did to get me ready for school - looked like the *Struwelpeter*. Fear about big things does not stop you fussing about little. That this delicate child might one day sleep like a log in Kurdish tents and wolf down cheese cured in hairy goatskin would have amazed my parents. Though not delighted them. My parents believed in comfort, in the good bourgeois life. They saw no point in roughing it. They had had enough discomfort, they would say, in their youth.

At Sugar Bush, our summer house, I became simply a princess. At Sugar Bush there were no peas.

Sugar Bush, a rambling one-storey chalet-cum-ranch-style building in a clearing some six hundred feet above the Bennington valley, was antiqued brown clapboard with gables painted in robin's egg blue. It was not an architectural gem, but pleasantly unobtrusive; and it had everything. A superb mountain view, its own reservoir, a big swimming pool fed by the reservoir, its own generator, a sugar house for conversion to stables, fields and meadows for riding rings and my mother's gallops, a marble bathroom with sunken tub, a split-level dining room with exposed rafters and built-in couches and book-cases and a great fireplace with a copper mantle, a paved court with flower beds looking up to the wild hill behind, and 366 acres all its own. This land, mostly second-growth forest - the early loggers and charcoal burners had felled the original trees years before - was then deemed so worthless that the real estate tax was twenty-eight dollars a year. Last but not least was a caretaker, a picture-book Vermonter who spoke pure West Country old English and lived conveniently at a dairy farm not far down the hill.

The house was completely furnished, including dishes, kitchen equipment, and a built-in hotel-size fridge with wooden doors. There was even linen, towels, and books. The fridge went on working for decades, and some of the furniture turned out to be early American antique.

Best of all, Sugar Bush was completely surrounded by mountain wilderness. On our first night there WR went to his room and found a porcupine trying to climb on his bed. There were not only porcupines, chipmunks, skunks and deer but occasional wildcats and bear. Even sometimes - though we never saw one - a rare blue moose wandering down from Canada, from the great forests of the north.

The catch was that Sugar Bush could only be occupied a few months of the year. It was built of one thin layer of wood, with no insulation. Heating was just adequate for short fall visits - the original owners had come then, to hunt. The water supply, piped from the reservoir a third of a mile uphill, was only usable when the temperature was above freezing. Sugar Bush, then, was two miles from its nearest neighbour and three from its own mailbox, about eight miles from the nearest store. In winter the dead-end dirt road that led there was barely driveable. Sugar Bush, cheap at the price, was a glorious white elephant.

We bought Sugar Bush after two summers of looking around in Manchester. Our demands befitted princesses on peas. We wanted land, views, stabling, swimming, wheelchair access for Karl, and space enough for guests, chamber music, and the odd analytic hour with summering patients.

We looked at some beautiful Colonial houses, rooms too small and impossible for wheelchairs. We looked at building land with sparkling streams - not enough view. We ended up with this millionaire's hunting lodge, the only standing building in the Unorganized Township of Glastonbury. Sugar Bush had been built by a broker named Hazard who, the story went, started it after he'd made a killing, then lost again and could barely finish it. Various family tragedies followed and the Hazards sold. When we bought the house it belonged to a New York radio announcer and his wife. He was mostly in the city and she mostly alone at Sugar Bush with two poodles and eager to get out. My parents didn't mind the lack of winter amenities. They only wanted a summer place. And the dangers of such isolation - break-ins, arson, vandalism - seemed then in Vermont as remote as the house itself. Also, for Karl, with the addition of a porch and ramps, the house was ideal.

I feel guilty telling this. But once in a while, if you're very lucky, money can buy paradise. And one of the best things about paradise in childhood is that it can leave you fairly incorruptible. Afterward, I was never impressed by anything else that money could buy. Sugar Bush made me immune. When you have bathed in marble it may, paradoxically, be easier for you than some others to do without a bathtub at all.

The time between school and Sugar Bush was bliss. Once the injections were over there was no cloud on the horizon. In those days I loved Grosse Pointe, the whirring sprinklers in the garden, my sun-filled room, the last-minute shopping, the hot nights with insects thudding against the screens when we stayed up late to get things ready. I had a fit of tidiness - I who almost never made my bed and left clothes on the floor for Enne to pick up. I took all the books off my big bookshelf, dusted them and put them all back. This was my only contribution to our Grosse Pointe housekeeping.

My mother, a star packer, packed for everyone. It was the one domestic skill I did learn from her and later it stood me in good stead. She was as excited as her children. To gallop across the Vermont meadows was her greatest delight. Like me, she lived through the winter for the summer. I had no idea what in her life she might be missing; she certainly did not seem unhappy like me. I do know I never felt closer to her than in those just pre-Sugar Bush days.

At last came the longed-for morning. It was a major exodus, the excited dogs on their leashes, the complaining cats in their baskets, the big cars loaded to the gills with trunks and bags, equipment, books, tins of food. My father guarded his precious violin.

WR usually drove with us, in his own car, and once my adored Simon, in whose car I rode for a while. This however was near disaster. Simon was not the best of drivers. He was stopped and threatened by a burly man he had ineptly overtaken. Soft answers to wrath do sometimes stop you getting beaten up; alas, they diminished him in my Heathcliff-and-Rhett Butler-clouded eyes. Soon after that, waiting for the others, Simon stopped on a railway crossing and only screams from the rest of the convoy alerted him that a train was approaching. I was not entirely unhappy to get back into the family cars.

The first day, we always drove through the Detroit-Windsor tunnel and on across Canada, through an endless flat landscape, big fields, lines of trees, little towns with brick houses, anonymous prairie towns and farms that seemed to me places where all Heidis would wither and die. I sometimes tried to imagine myself doomed to live in such places, and imagine the people who did. These settlements on the Ontario plain were to me mysterious and chilling - like downtown Detroit. It was a sort of masochistic frisson to think of yourself trapped in a town called Morpeth or Cayuga and happiness to leave them behind.

To relieve the landscape monotony, Verena and I played I Spy games, or sang *Ten Green Bottles, Tavern in the Town, Clementine, You Can't Get to Heaven,* the old songs from camp. At last we passed Buffalo, and stopped for the night at a very old-fashioned hotel in the Finger Lake region of New York State. There was a big green lawn and a colonnaded porch with rocking old ladies, like the Manchester hotels. There were crisp white towels that said HOTEL CANANDAIGUA. WELLINGTON FIFIELD, Proprietor. I loved this name. I wanted to meet Wellington Fifield. I would have liked to absorb every detail of this halfway house to heaven. Only one night the pipes banged and the Cocker howled for no visible reason, just when I'd been reading H.P. Lovecraft, discovered at a drug-store on the route. Briefly, I was back in nightmare - but by day all was bliss again.

We would leave Canandaigua early in the morning. The landscape grew more wooded and hilly. We passed through - to me, dismal - Albany and Troy, where I noticed only urban squalor, and then we were over the Vermont state border and the proper mountains began. At last, beyond Bennington, we turned off the tarmac and onto the dirt road that led to the Unorganized Township of Glastonbury.

Paradise is not in fact at all boring to live in. It may however be boring to describe. So I will keep it minimal. My Sugar Bush days were composed of everything I loved. Riding, swimming (by now I could swim), walking, berry-picking, playing badminton (shuttlecocks did not frighten me like balls), reading, sunbathing, listening to music, talking to people with whom I was happy and from whom I could learn. We went to the Tanglewood concerts, later to Marlboro, and occasionally to a movie or summer theatre play in Manchester or Dorset. Once a summer or so, we hiked on the Long Trail, staying overnight in a mountain-peak hut. WR and Katya's cousin, Karl's sister Meta, whom all the young agreed were the most "fun", presided over our excursions.

I had three months of Sugar Bush every year. I never tired of it. I never wanted to be outside our domain. Every absence, except a hike to a solitary lake or summit or an outing providing a glimpse of my latest unrequited love, was time begrudged. Even trips to the *Vogue and Vanity,* a wonderful dress shop in Bennington run by fellow Central Europeans and catering to the Bennington College girls. My mother and Katya bought most of their clothes there; under Katya's tutelage, my mother became almost well-dressed. And with Lanz, Greta Plattry, Claire McCardell, the slightly peasanty clothes that suited me and at bargain prices so I didn't feel guilty, so eventually did I. But after trying on three dresses, I was anxious to be off home.

In one of the Huxley novels I read in those days one character asks another for his idea of perfect happiness. All of mine are based on my Sugar Bush summers. To lie on a diving board in the sun, feeling the rough wood against your legs and the cool rising from the water, and read a Victorian ghost story. To swim nude at night, then put on a thick warm robe and run in to a fire and laughing people and hot spiced wine. To sit on a porch at evening, watching the wooded mountains across the valley turn slowly from deep green to blue and the first bats fly out from under the eaves (and Karl wheel himself out with the screen doors banging behind him, Karl lighting his pipe, and hear my father begin a Bach solo sonata, metronome clicking, in the other wing). To reach the top of a longed-for peak. To shut your eyes and roll down a steep stretch of lawn and then lie still while the dizziness goes and open your eyes again to a sky full of cold clear stars. To ride alone in the early morning, cantering up a long low hill, and find the valley hidden under thick white cloud, only the summits visible, abnormally huge and near, seeming to float like ships on water, and say to yourself, with the passionate exclusiveness of adolescence, there is not, there never can be, a more beautiful view in the world.

Enough, or too much. We left our 366 acres mostly to themselves. We did blaze and clear a few trails for walking and riding, mostly joining up old trails and wagon tracks. The woods were full of instant archaeological remains, traces of the settlers, the fifty Glastonbury families who had so recently gone, mostly to find work in the valley below. Cellar holes and charcoal pits, rusting wheels or stoves, remnants of bridges and fords, gnarled fruit trees gone wild, boundary walls of roughly piled stone. They were as evocative in their way as Indian arrowheads or Byzantine ruins, and to me a cause for jubilation. Sometimes the forest takes over again. Sometimes, somewhere, nature wins. It was not of course to win for long. The Unorganized Township of Glastonbury is still unorganized. But there are new houses down the road and the loggers are back; even my parents foolishly sold timber to clear-cutters near the end of their Sugar Bush years. The trails we naively made, helping to kill the thing we loved, are now used by motorbikes, and by snowmobiles lethal to hibernating animals who wake and die. A big superfluous piece of expressway has been carved through the woods not more than a mile from Sugar Bush. The remoteness and privacy and silence is gone.

Not even in Sugar Bush was my happiness unalloyed. The inner demon saw to that. Perhaps it was guilt and a sense of hubris; I was too fortunate, I had too much. The looming Heidi misery of return to the flatlands and school, the dread of winter, which mushroomed after the half-way mark of our summer, was not pain enough. In Detroit there was schoolwork and the pangs of school to distract me from my inner demon. In Vermont there was no task or pain. I never knew what might set off my secret obsessions and despairs - a passage in a paper or book, a photo of some atrocity, the sight of a wounded animal or something disgusting that lodged, perversely, in my mind.

With adolescence, there came also hours of what I called the glass wall; a feeling of being detached from everything by an invisible barrier, like a sudden closed window between oneself and the world. This, like an occasional strong déjà vu, happened both winter and summer. There were times when I became a bit afraid of going mad. My parents reassured me. They knew what psychosis was like and didn't think I was really a candidate. They ventured the rather lame idea that the glass walls had something to do with the trials of my orthodontia, one theory I could not buy. All I knew was that even at Sugar Bush I had days when my distressing obsessions were so pervasive I wonder how I kept going, how I covered my despair.

Along with adolescence too came more minor family altercations. Usually they concerned my lateness; I was always late. Or the rights of Vermont wildlife, which Verena and I upheld. If porcupines gnawed the porch steps or the garden hose, that was no reason to shoot porcupines, Whenever we could we chased the trespassers away before the adults saw them.

When any wildlife was done away with, it put me in a frenzied rage. I upbraided or shunned the culprit, and once I remember rather pointlessly cutting my arm with broken glass when my mother and Meta dispatched a nest of harmless snakes. Aggression turned inward, Papa Freud would say. I still resent the snake massacre. Spiders terrified me, but I was not in the least afraid of snakes. I often picked up garter snakes, until one shat on me, and when something that looked like a baby copperhead appeared in our marble bath, I gritted my teeth, grasped it firmly behind the head and carried it out to safety.

My mother, with the hunting instincts of her class, was not to be cheated of her prey. One summer, when I was no longer there, she went out in her nightgown and clubbed a trespassing porcupine to death with a baseball bat. The staff, who watched this, never tired of describing the scene.

There is an Oriental saying that for happiness and success you should attach yourself to a lucky man. After his childhood and until near his death, no one was luckier than my father. Again and again he landed on his feet and now he had his cake and its eating. He had vacillated between medicine and music and opted for medicine with some regret, partly because of his bursitis and, he told me later, partly because of my mother's ambition and urging. (Actually part of his medical school days were spent in a castle in Italy, working as a tutor and masseur to a frail child Countess. He still managed to pass all his exams.)

Now, besides chamber music with Katya, he had lessons with top professionals, Adolf Busch, Alexander Schneider. He played the Bach double concerto in a Detroit concert with the violinist who later became concertmaster of the Seattle symphony. One summer he played in the Marlboro Festival orchestra. And in the Busch Trio recording of the Beethoven 'Ghost' Trio he turned the pages, being, he said, the ghost.

Also, at Sugar Bush my father saw a lot of his lions. Two favorites, the renowned German publisher WK and the famous (in those circles) historian KE, friend of Hermann Broch, Thomas Mann, Einstein etc. came for long stretches every summer.

KE was the classic absent-minded professor, the sort who might drop his watch in the water while looking at his egg. He drove back to Princeton one day with the trunk full of books but not quite closed, leaving a whole library on the East Road to Bennington. Fortunately, one of our clan was driving in to shop not far behind him, and he was alerted and the precious books retrieved.

KE was a savant truly devoted to humanism, to the enlightened liberal traditions of Western Europe, to a now old-fashioned belief in an unbreakable tie between high culture and morality. His (my father said, great) book was called *Man the Measure*, a title that today would bring screams of protest from the politically correct. KE's heart was very much in the right place and I loved him. Squat, awkward, ugly, intense, absorbed and kind, a big straggle-haired head full of big thoughts and childishly appealing; I did not see how anyone could not love KE. He treated me with great sweetness and seriousness, talking to me as if I were totally adult. Inspired, I said things I did not say even to Karl. Once, drying a plate in the kitchen, I stared at the plate and said my greatest wish was to see something, even that plate, "just as it *is*. If you could do that you would have the secret of the universe." Unfortunately, I can't remember what he answered. I can't in fact remember anything he said. It was probably the measure of *me*, of my blind adolescent egotism.

I wanted to believe KE's hopeful humanistic views, some antidote to my own pessimism, and it shattered me to see him defeated. This happened later when I was in college. My cleverest Sarah Lawrence classmate ran rings around him in an argument about the relative virtues of advanced and primitive civilization. (Is tribal art inferior to Shakespeare? She said it wasn't. KE said it was.) She won, and told me contemptuously afterwards that she'd once argued the opposite and won that time too, against someone else. I couldn't bear to see KE reduced to almost spluttering protest. I felt she had been cruel; but I could not say she had argued unfairly.

Again in my college days, on a visit to KE in Princeton I was to see worse, one of those Thomas Mann short story incidents that do of course happen in real life. KE's one, childless marriage had ended in divorce, but he had a motherly housekeeper, who seemed ideal, intelligent, devoted and nice. For dinner, we had lobster, and the housekeeper produced, for KE, a large lobster-decorated bib. KE, shouting and waving his hands like a child, said he refused to wear it. She insisted. She kept insisting. In the end, she tied the bib on, and he succumbed. I looked down at my lobster in agony, not knowing what to do. I had never seen this kind of domestic power struggle before; I grieved for KE but could not think how to help. When the lobster was finished, we all pretended the incident had not happened. Some years on, not long before he died, KE married the housekeeper. Everybody said he had done the decent thing.

We were all happy at Sugar Bush, but my mother, like me, blossomed the most. She was full of praise about her domain. As if its real glories were not enough, she invented one or two more. "The Glastonbury," she informed visitors seriously, "is the oldest mountain in Vermont."

The visitors were many. We always had a full house; my parents, so isolated in Grosse Pointe, were generous and hospitable to their chosen friends, and to Verena's and mine. My mother even made a stab at housekeeping; that is, she wrote out shopping lists, and did much of the shopping herself. She sat at the head of the table and doled out food with as much satisfaction as if she had cooked it. It was somewhat like Marie Antoinette playing shepherdess but it was endearing. And in the evenings she was much more sociable then ever in Grosse Pointe. She joined in games of Chinese Checkers, which she played with aggressive zest, or had us all in stitches as she read aloud social notes from the *Bennington Banner,* as in Austria she had read from the *Gmundner Nachrichten.*

Sometimes when already in bed I would hear the adults - especially when the real night owls, Katya and WK were there - laughing so uproariously that I was jealous. What is it, I would want to know, when my mother came in (the room she shared with Katya was reached through my sister's and mine. My father and his violin slept on the other side of the house.) My mother, still laughing, would not reply; or if she did I would not understand.

Katya had a special friendship with the publisher WK. I do not know if there was an affair. I used to wonder how it worked if there was; she so tiny, barely four feet eleven, and WK over six. I never saw them entering or leaving each other's rooms. Anyway, WK's wife was usually with him. As a special dispensation, being a top lion's consort, she was brought breakfast in bed. Meanwhile, on our morning ride, we would often meet WK and Katya out walking. They went along the road, only as far as the bridge over the little stream where we played Poohsticks. Katya would still be in her quilted robe - she usually dressed only just before lunch - and WK with his usual cigarette dangling from his mouth. Cigarettes never left him, even when he swam, the dignified old-style breaststroke of that European generation. Neither Katya nor WK were exactly walkers. It seemed to my feebly lurid adolescent imagination to have some significance.

WK's success with women was legendary, but there were shadows to the legend. Even my mother confessed she was attracted - "but he is supposed to be sadistic." She did not elucidate. This made WK sinister and interesting, though I could not comprehend what all these older women saw in someone with large white limbs bereft of muscle, and a waistless middle, even if the women were getting flabby themselves. My own desire now focused on wiry macho leanness, like that of the caretaker's son. Passion aroused by mere distinction, the passion for and of the aged, was inconceivable. They should know when to stop. And when my father, who quoted WK almost as he quoted Freud, told laughingly of WK saying when he was asked to save water during a Sugar Bush drought, *"Zum waschen brauch ich es nicht und zum trinken schon überhaupt nicht"*

(I don't need it for washing and for drinking not at all) as he usually kept to wine, I was shocked. Like all middle-class Americans I had read the comic-strip and other ads about the social and sexual exclusion of those with bad breath, dandruff flakes on their shoulders, or - horrors - the merest whiff of B.O., those who needed the salvation of Colgate toothpaste, Drene shampoo, Mum and whatever. Like the other schoolgirls, I kept fantastically clean. I was surprised WK did not smell.

And besides lacking waist, WK seemed to me a bit of a poseur, though I was sometimes impressed in spite of myself. WK had wit and a great deal of presence. But when he asked me once about my ambitions, "Do you think there is a conflict between being a writer and being the best woman for a man?" I found the question crass and offensive. Men happened or they didn't. Great writers would not dream of subordinating their art to a relationship. It never occurred to me that WK had probably been subjected to effusions about my gifts from my mother and, finding me alone on the porch was just making polite conversation with what he probably thought a spoiled pretentious child.

The books we found at Sugar Bush were not my parents' reading. My father read Dostoyevsky, Goethe, Thomas Mann, Kafka, Hermann Broch, etc., authors favored by Freud or published by WK. My mother mostly read the novels sent by the Book of the Month Club, some of which I read too, looking for sexy bits. Katya added books in French, like Colette's. The Sugar Bush books mostly bored me but there were a few interesting oddities. Elias Canetti's *The Tower of Babel,* and a fat green book called *The Fountainhead* by Ayn Rand.

The Fountainhead, recently reprinted, is a silly piece of romantic megalomania, of aesthetic crypto-Fascism. Its lonely misunderstood hero battles against the engulfing horrors of mass culture, refusing to compromise his genius. So far so good, but our hero is a bit extreme. "Don't they realize," he says of a struggling young sculptor whom he commissions to do a nude statue of his (the architect's) girlfriend, "that there's more suffering in Mallory when he can't work than in a field of men run over by a tank?" Even at thirteen I knew that most of the book was absurd. But it was intoxicating stuff. Especially the sex bits. *The Fountainhead* filled my head with more ideas about artistic integrity (leaving aside the nonsense of Ayn Rand, it is sad that with our marketplace morals artistic integrity now barely rates a mention). And it filled my head with dangerous masochistic ideas about sex. Freudian parents can preach what they like; it's the clandestine information that colours your fantasies.

Sex in *The Fountainhead* was a feminist's nightmare, a satirist's dream. Heroine, aloof, beautiful, still a virgin at twenty-five, meets hero who unable to exercise his genius is working in a marble quarry. She's on horseback; he on foot. He annoys her; she lashes him with her riding whip. He breaks into her house and rapes her. She falls violently in love, meets him again, gets more sex. But they cannot yet live happily ever after. She, in some fit of masochistic self-immolation, marries first an inferior rival architect, then our hero's antithesis, a self-made tabloid mogul millionaire. (He is actually akin to our hero in spirit. It's just that the cynicism inspired by his grim boyhood has put him on the other side of the fence. But hero and anti-hero respect each other, like Kipling's East and West.) Hero Howard is totally understanding about his girlfriend's looney infidelities, though they continued to baffle me. "You've chosen the hardest way of fighting for your freedom in the world." This hard fighting for freedom includes the three of them cruising around on the mogul's yacht. In the end, the tabloid goes bust, and Hero Howard blows up one of his own buildings, its architectural purity having been violated by the owners. Howard is judged not guilty, and the mogul gives him remnants of his fortune to build a skyscraper "to that spirit which is yours and should have been mine." The girlfriend, divorced again, marries our hero. Happy end.

In those days I read a lot on the toilet. Books were classified as toilet or non-toilet reading. You would not read great poetry on the john. You would read *The Fountainhead*. I read it on the toilet in the marble bathroom, and read the sex bits over and over again. Virginal rape fantasies don't mean you really want to be raped. But they don't help your image of sex. Sometimes I looked up from my green book to the tiles with pink roses and pink frames and French mottoes that graced the bathroom wall. These also had come with the house. *"L'amour vit d'éspérance, l'amitié vit de souvenirs." "On ne peut ni trop tôt, ni trop tard, gouter les plaisirs de la vie." "Aimer est un faiblesse. Être aimé est une force."* These supposedly Gallic sentiments were a bit of light relief. And by the time I was old enough to consider its topics seriously *The Fountainhead*, thank heaven, was simply outgrown.

The sunken tub in the marble bathroom, pale gray and grainy, was almost deep enough to float in and took a huge amount of water to fill. My sister and I normally bathed together, sometimes with our friends; hot water was not unlimited and the tub not worth filling for one. These communal baths were of course strictly female. My father had his own bathroom and my parents - wisely, I think - did not believe in hetero family nudity.

Katya never participated. She was fanatically modest and private and would keep the bathroom firmly locked for the sacred half hour or hour before lunch when she prepared herself to meet the world. I think she found us disgusting. With American casualness we peed, defecated, washed in each other's presence. Our baths were uninhibited but totally innocent. My mother often joined Verena and me. She already had very pendulous breasts and a sagging belly but she was quite unselfconscious. The communal baths had a lasting effect. As I'd vowed never to prostitute my art, I vowed never to let my body get like my mother's. My mother, unaware, puffed happily in the warm pure Vermont water and asked us to pass the soap.

I always needed to be at least mildly in love.

In Vermont, the landscape I worshipped needed a figure, something to focus all that adolescent libido. Pantheism was not quite enough. After Gomper's, my summer loves lasted from summer to summer till I went to college. Winters were dead; I lived wholly on fantasy.

My love for Simon died one day as abruptly as it began. We were sitting on the diving board talking, both in bathing suits. I wondered if at last Simon would make a gesture, say an affectionate word... and then Verena, frisking in the pool, came out from underwater and yelled cheerfully, "Simon, you look like a hairy ape." I was furious; but love was dead.

My infatuation with the caretaker's son began at his wedding, and like my love for Simon, with a piece of music. This time it was Schubert's Serenade, played on the village church organ. I saw the young man being married, a fair young man in a dark suit, now pledged to a pretty brunette in a white dress, I heard the music, and that was it. It wasn't as much of a thunderbolt as that first surge of emotion during the Tchaikovsky Concerto. But then the new young man in my life was a less dramatic figure. He remained as unconscious of my affection as Simon had been. I just found excuses to hang around when he and his father did repairs or cut the grass; and I was thrilled when we all scrubbed the pool together, pools then not yet being filled with fungicide. Harold was in his twenties, even older than Simon, and didn't really register that I was alive.

The high point of this infatuation was a hike up the Glastonbury, the wild mountain behind our house. Alice, WR and Verena came along, and Harold was our guide. He carried a gun on this expedition because "I never go out in the woods without a gun." This hint of danger made it more exciting yet. After the old logging tracks petered out, there was no path. We toiled uphill over loose earth and big stones and fallen trees, through underbrush and bracken, till the slope flattened out. Then we sat down and ate our sandwiches. The ground was spongy, with small white flowers. We were surrounded by trees; there was no view, and wouldn't be until we reached the firetower two peaks on. Harold must have thought we were crazy to do this hike, but remained affable, if somewhat taciturn.

I never saw so much of Harold in any one day again. The next year, or the next, I was in love with another pianist, one of Katya's pupils, an ex-marine from Nebraska, who looked very macho indeed but was gay. Just as well; by that time I was prettier and getting near an age where some of my moon-calf glances might have met a response.

Harold's father Rob was a true old Vermonter, descended from early settlers. He was a burly, easy-going man with a strong humorous face. Verena and I liked Rob on sight. He liked us, I think, but had a few doubts about our parents. For a start, they didn't really drink; he missed the Hazards' boozy hunting weekends. Expresso coffee in tiny cups from an Italian machine, chamber music in the evening, the sacrosanct rest hour when he was cautioned not to run the mowing machine, must have baffled him.

Rob spoke what later my husband identified as pure West Country English. He said ayuh (aye) instead of yes, how be you instead of how are you, and many years on, when he first saw my baby daughter, "'Er's a smiler, 'er is." My parents realized he was a rare specimen of genuine early Vermont and my mother did try, as often in America, to drop her lofty Austrian upper-crust tones and speak to Rob in as New World a way as she could manage. It sounded out of character. However, Rob took it all in good part, though caretaking was not his chosen line. He had a dozen dairy cows and they were his passion. "If I could afford it," he confessed once, "I'd toss this old hammer and saw in the creek." It was never to happen. Rob continued as our caretaker until he became too ill. He died around seventy, of motor-neurone disease.

Rob's wife, an ex-school teacher who did not share her husband's easy ways and must have felt she'd come down in the world, did laundry and cleaning for us for years longer, till she moved down into town. Once, she showed us where the square dance platform had been, when the

Unorganized Township had enough families to get together a Saturday dance. The platform had long vanished, as has the last Glastonbury barn, a pile of sagging boards when we first arrived.

Rob's once large extended family had their own graveyard, a tiny mysterious place at the end of an obscure lane, where two magnificent conifers, trees that must have been there when the first settlers came, brood over the fading, sinking stones. I do not know if he was buried there, or if anyone has been for years, or if the graveyard in turn has followed the dwelling and dancing places into oblivion.

For us as children, one of the high points of the Sugar Bush day was a before-breakfast ride in the back of Rob's truck when he took our garbage to our private dump at one end of the property. We stood holding on to the cab roof, the morning sun and wind fresh on our faces, while Rob sang and joked in the cab. It was pure exhilaration.

No one - certainly no one in my parents' entourage - thought in those days of separating garbage or making a compost heap. At least packing was still mostly paper and biodegradable. In our last Sugar Bush years, decades on, my mother who loved American gadgets bought a garbage crusher and gleefully fed it with whatever it would devour, unmoved by my tirades about ecology.

The garbage heap however went through recycling of a sort. It was an important source of supply for the dogs of the "Dog-man", Clyde Elwell, an old eccentric who lived in a tiny cabin off that dirt road. He owned about forty dogs, and a Model T car in a highly dangerous condition, in which he occasionally thundered down to Shaftsbury to get supplies. The car was reputed to have very bad brakes, but you could hear Clyde coming and get out of his way. There were threats from the sheriff to have Clyde's dogs shot because of the rabies risk, but we never saw this happen. There always seemed to be about the same number. They would rush out yapping and growling when someone passed but no one was bitten.

When he became too old for the long lonely winters at the foot of Glastonbury Clyde moved down to Shaftsbury and tried keeping the dogs in a house. This was too much for his neighbours. I do not know if the dogs were destroyed; but soon after his move, Clyde fell ill and died. We went to investigate his derelict cabin, intrigued by the stories of reasons for his solitude; he had been crossed in love, he had been shell-shocked or gassed in the First World War. And, the stories went, he would have been a mathematical genius if he had not gone crazy. What we found left in

Clyde's cabin were notebooks, pages and pages of pencilled equations, nothing we could understand. Feeling spooky and guilty, we tiptoed out again, leaving the cabin with its books, as Clyde had no known relatives, to woodworm and porcupines. If Clyde's equations held the secret of the universe, no one will ever know.

One other cabin lay farther along that derelict road, apparently occupied only on weekends, when you might see a shabby parked car. The cabin had a sign with a mysterious name: Camp Stiffit. There were rumors about the purpose of this lonely shack, and it soon disappeared - perhaps demolished, we were told, by disapproving vigilantes.

The other eccentrics not far away, on the Bennington road, were a Lord and Lady.

They had restored an 18th century tavern, in which they lived. Lady Gosford was American, Lord Gosford a proper walrus-moustached Colonel Blimp Englishman, the kind Americans thought typical. We never met the Gosfords socially - my parents remained as distant from neighbours and community as in Grosse Pointe - though one of my mother's favorite gallops was on a path through the Gosford meadows. Lord Gosford came up our way from time to time, on foot with a berry bucket. He always scurried furtively to the side as our horses passed. Once, when their house was opened for some charity, we met his Lordship in the library and remarked we'd seen him picking berries. Lord Gosford, in that vintage bray exclusive to the English upper class, said mildly, "My wife likes building things. I like picking berries." He then explained that he was afraid of horses, which was why he gave ours such a wide berth.

Two other berry pickers we sometimes met were an idiot boy and his mother, who lived in a little converted schoolhouse near Rob's place. Later, the mother died, and the boy was apparently packed off to some state institution. It haunted me, the thought of the boy who had been free and seemingly content, plunged into the nightmare of a strange asylum.

Such meetings, a very occasional square dance or fair, odd bits of gossip from Rob and his wife, were all our contacts with life around us. Only, unlike Grosse Pointe, "around us" was sparse and far and we never felt isolated because the house was filled with friends.

But sometimes, I had qualms. Among the blackberry bushes that lined our roads were a few currants and raspberries, I always found berry-picking wonderfully therapeutic, maybe because it is a return to the stage from which our biological selves have not yet evolved, much as we may like to think so. And Gibson made wonderful pies. Ignorant of horticulture, we did not realize that some of the berries were domestics gone wild. One day Meta and I were filling our cups with currants, when a woman with a child came up the road and stopped to pick at an adjacent bush. Meta objected, in her still very German-accented English, "Excuse me, but you are picking our berries." The woman answered quietly, "I planted these bushes, thirty years ago." Scarlet with shame, I told her to please pick all she wanted, and Meta and I went home.

Katya had finally left Detroit to take a university teaching job in Chicago. This began a series of Sugar Bush visits from her star pupils. They were talented, entertaining and gay.

As a Freudian child I knew homosexuality existed. But I thought gay men were usually actors or ballet dancers, that they minced when they walked, fluttered their hands, and spoke in high voices. And that anyone could be what Americans call AC-DC didn't enter my head.

Mack, whom I had a crush on, was a big all-American ex-marine from Nebraska with a granite jaw, a deep husky voice, and sleepy sensual eyes. In our evening music sessions he sometimes improvised or played jazz. He taught us new card games, and told jokes I didn't always follow but which amused the adults no end. "You know who writes my stuff? My mother," he would say when we finished laughing. He and Katya, whom he called K.A., laughed together a great deal.

At breakfast Mack appeared late, in a striped bathrobe which revealed his hairy chest, and sang "Everybody knows I'm just a gigolo," over his coffee and cigarettes. All this was quite exciting to a green child of fifteen. But the crush was not as ardent as previous ones, and I didn't feel quite comfortable putting him into my first-kiss fantasies. He didn't have all the requisites. I liked fine hands (Simon) and fine features (Harold). Anyway, I didn't really expect more than a pat on the shoulder or a compliment on a new dress. In our Freudian household, there was actually much secrecy and discretion. I did not learn until years after that of all my infatuations this was the most displaced.

My Sugar Bush days, like camp ones, began with a ride.

With our trails and the then unpaved, empty roads we had a variety of wonderful rides. My sister and I loved the adventure of riding alone, and best of all the trail that began at the Glastonbury cemetery.

The cemetery was on a slope above the road that led to Rob's house and down to Arlington. It had fine 18th century marble tombstones with eerie carved death-angel faces and pious names like Fear Andrew and Freelove Stone. Also pious verses:

> Here lies the body of Freelove Stone
> Mouldering back to dust
> Yet it shall arise and leave the ground
> When the Archangel gives the sound.

Beyond the cemetery, before you reached the wilder forest above the Roaring Branch stream, was a mysterious wood of beautiful regular conifers and soft green glades, as tended and landscaped-looking as a park. Sometimes we raced our horses up the track, chattering and clowning. Verena was still a wonderful mimic, though this talent was later dampened by my mother pushing her into private acting lessons. Sometimes we rode slowly and silently, hoping to see a great red stag, as I did one morning when all by myself. Or merely to sense that uncanny presence, the spirit of the wilderness.

Cantering through the park I saw myself as a princess awaiting not only my prince of the moment but this supernatural Spirit whom I loved as I loved nothing human. The exaltation and mystery of these rides overwhelmed me. I wrote terrible poetry. "She on the black horse, though she belongs to none, shall wear on her wrist forever his thornèd mark." (This was after Sultan, taking a corner fast, brushed me against brambles.) I was very taken with the thornèd, with its accent grave.

Never mind poetry. I have only to shut my eyes to see and feel and smell that magic forest, to hear its winds and birds and secret footsteps and overarching, singing silence. The silence is killed by the new Expressway. You can meet more wild creatures; even bear, their old territory divided or lost, have been seen blundering out in broad daylight a stone's throw from our pool. But the great god Pan has fled. The park has vanished too. The last time I walked there I looked for it in vain. The round conifers were tall, sickly and spindly, the little trail a new logging road, the green glades gone.

When my parents, dissatisfied with the livery stable they tried after Belle Isle, decided to buy some land on the outskirts of Grosse Pointe, build their own stable and get their own groom, my mother pulled off another coup. She hired a groom who had worked at the Hunt Club, a small, very fat man called Shorty. He was housed in a room adjoining the new stable, and in summer had a similar room at the stable at Sugar Bush.

Shorty was a real Mr Five by Five; his circumference equalled his height. His evil-looking old face with its big beery nose, jutting chin and sunken mouth was made more evil by one wild eye; he'd been kicked in the head by a horse at least once in his checkered career. His fat little legs were bowed, and he waddled rather than walked. He chewed tobacco incessantly and spat his plugs accurately into spittoons or tins.

My mother's relationship with Shorty was Victoria and John Brown in burlesque. Shorty was an excellent groom; but in Sugar Bush he ruled not only the stable but the roost. Woe betide you if you brought a horse in hot or late, especially before Shorty's half day off. The whole week was scheduled with Shorty in mind. And as concerned horses his word was law. Shorty bought and sold for us and my mother meekly acquiesced.

Some of the buys were dubious. I was presented with a big vicious American Saddle-breed gelding inappropriately named Stardust, who had a mouth like iron and sometimes tried to roll. My father had to ride him most of the time, as I didn't have the strength. And when I wanted a filly to break in, inspired by *My Friend Flicka,* Shorty got one - but she wasn't at all like the filly in the movie or Mary O'Hara's book. She never grew beyond thirteen hands, and when she was ready to break in I was away at college and Shorty trained her. She was rough-gaited, stubborn, unpredictable and given to throwing her head. She was sold after she broke my father's front teeth.

Shorty did produce one gem, a little gray mare who must have been almost pure Arab, fiery but good-natured and a wonderful ride. We never knew where he bought his horses. He would simply produce them one day with his nasty grin, usually saying "Youse asked for it, now youse got it." Whether anyone had asked or no.

Shorty gave us other things we didn't ask for. Western tooled leather belts, buckskin gloves, and for me, Sweetheart Soap and Noxcema for my acned skin. And riding lessons. My parents had a ring built next to the Sugar Bush pool and Shorty would stand in the middle cracking a whip and make us walk, trot, canter, change leads. We never learned anything. The lessons were clearly for the benefit of Shorty, who enjoyed barking orders and whip-cracking.

My mother insisted we take the lessons. She accepted everything Shorty said or did. She laughed uproarious false laughter at his 'witty' sayings. Shorty had sayings for all occasions. "There's nobody home but the clock and that's running." "There's nobody home but the stove and that's gone out." "Where have you been, Shorty?" "Out to take the goldfish for a walk." "You're always behind, jest like the cow's tail." And if you began a sentence with "Well -" "Well?" Shorty would snap, "That's a hole in the country."

My mother also followed Shorty's medical lore. Soaps and creams, teabags on the eyes for eyestrain, and she allowed him to treat her mildly arthritic elbows and wrists with his favorite horse liniment. She would come up from the stable, looking a bit subdued and reeking so of Absorbine Junior that we could not bear to go near her. Later, Shorty's insistence on doctoring cost my sister her own lovely spotted filly, Domino, who died of colic when we were in Europe. Shorty refused to let anyone call the vet until it was too late.

We had to indulge Shorty's whims. If Shorty felt neglected, he threatened to leave. And my mother would say if Shorty left it meant selling the horses. She seemed so convinced no Shorty replacement could be found that Verena and I half believed her. Periodically, indulged or not, Shorty made his threat, usually when drunk; besides his outings, he was always kept well supplied with beer. He would waddle up to the house reeking not of Absorbine but alcohol, hook his thumbs in his belt, grin and grunt, "I'm gonna love youse and leave youse." Verena and I would be summoned, and sometimes even cut up onions so we could appear in tears. After sufficient pleading Shorty gave in and stayed. These scenes were a bit humiliating but bearable. The truly dreadful ordeal was Shorty taking us out. Had this happened more than once or twice a summer, even our mother could not have made us go.

The excursions included Gibson, as Shorty couldn't drive. We had one trip to Saratoga, and one to a County Fair, for horse races. That we enjoyed; except for Shorty's leers and jokes and a nasty little habit he had, not only with Verena and me but our friends if along. He would reach over in the car and tweak the hair on your bare arms. "Cut it out, Shorty," we'd cry, cringing away. We did not dare to pull rank. Anyway, no one had taught us how rank should be pulled. Our mother's policy seemed to be humoring Shorty almost to the last.

The more usual excursion was to Manchester to eat supper at the Paradise, a typical cheap small-town restaurant with booths and juke-box and a menu of chops, steak and fries. Shorty treated Gibson and us, ordering giant steaks, which I hated, "Youse asked for it, now youse got it," he would say, watching intently with his cockeyed pupils and nasty grin as we choked down as much of the tough steak as we could and prayed no one would think we were Shorty's relations.

The waitress at the Paradise was a plump, soft-spoken matronly brunette named Myrtle. Shorty claimed she was his girl, though neither of them gave any sign of it in the restaurant. But Shorty would sometimes come to his breakfast in the kitchen yawning and announce to Gibson in a voice loud enough for all to hear, "Been up late last night. Myrt was over." "Oh yeah?" Gibson would say, and give his polite Uncle Tom giggle. Shorty for his part held Gibson in jovial contempt. "Gibson's got two speeds - slow and slower." He did not however voice racist sentiments, at least to us. In Sugar Bush, Gibson provided his only access to Myrtle and the outside world.

Shorty hated Sugar Bush. "These god-forsaken jungles," was how he referred to our bit of Vermont. My mother urged us to relieve his boredom by sometimes going down in the afternoon to visit him. This had its share of grim entertainment. Sprawled on his bed in his little room next to the tack room, with his tobacco and his spittoon, Shorty would tell us bits of his life story, while we languished in the smell of saddle soap, oats, beer, dog and Absorbine Junior. It is because of these commanded visits that I know almost more about Shorty's history than my beloved Enne's. Enne was always working. Shorty had lots of time.

Shorty had been born to a Scots-Irish family in St Claire Flats, Michigan. At twelve, after a whipping, he ran away from home. All his life after that he had worked around "them ponies." From one end of the country to the other - on race tracks, in livery stables, even in laboratories. He filled us with horror by telling us of horses hung upside down and bled alive to make tetanus vaccine, and some of the tricks of the racing trade, like pin-firing, inserting hot needles into a tendon so the horse would run even if lame.

On Shorty's dresser was a picture of a blond woman with a child. Shorty said she was his daughter, and the child his grandchild. He did not say who the mother had been, nor if he ever saw these relations.

And Shorty would entertain us with his dogs. Shorty always kept his own dogs, first two sweet-tempered bulldogs we sometimes took for a short walk. They breathed so painfully we soon took them back. They were a fine example of the cruelty breeders inflict on other species; with genetic engineering, it will have no bounds.

The bulldogs vanished in one of Shorty's mysterious deals and were replaced by two young boxers. They too were friendly - when Shorty was around. When he wasn't you couldn't get into the stable. They hurled themselves at the door, snarling and slavering, ready to tear you to pieces.

Shorty had trained them that way, more effectively than the expensive German lady had trained Wolf. He would brandish a towel and shout, "Peppy, take him! Shake him out!" and Peppy would seize the towel, worry it and shake it with such violence it was obvious "he" didn't have a chance.

In the end, for all his threats, Shorty didn't leave. One summer, he complained of stomach trouble, and rapidly grew alarmingly thin. When his clothes were hanging on him like empty oat sacks he was at last persuaded to see a doctor. He went straight into hospital where he was found to have inoperable cancer. He was soon too weak to get up and my parents paid for him to go into a nursing home in town.

Some brave person, I can't remember who, dealt with the boxers. Louis, a relative of Rob's came to tend the horses. Verena and I did a lot of grooming ourselves. When I asked Louis for advice on using the hoof-pick, Louis laughed. "First time *I* ever saw the inside of a horse's hoof." Our ignorance notwithstanding, the horses, without Shorty, were less shiny but certainly no less happy. And there was never any problem finding someone to take the well-paid, easy job of being my parents' groom.

Shorty lay in the nursing home dying day by day. The staff seemed sensible and kind. No one suggested intravenous feeding or anything to prolong the agony. My future husband, who was coming to Sugar Bush by then, drove me out once a week or so for visits. He was always mindful of underdogs and nasty Shorty, dying alone, had suddenly become one. My parents went once or twice and felt it was enough, Verena couldn't bear it. Shorty was not exactly a man who inspired affection or loyalty.

Shorty seemed glad to see us. He talked weakly about "getting back to them ponies." We didn't contradict him. He swatted listlessly at flies, and sometimes suddenly rose up, clutching his side, and said, half-joking, "Oh Lord, don't come and get me now." He did not complain. He never mentioned the "daughter" in the photo or anyone else he might want to reach. At the end he was comatose, his face collapsed into a skin-covered skull, his toothless mouth a black hole through which gasping, grating breath wheezed in and out. I looked in awe and terror; Shorty was my first human death and his open mouth seemed a small black door to the dark of eternity.

There was clearly no point in visiting him again. A few days later Shorty was dead. No names of anyone to notify were found among his few papers. My parents arranged to have him buried in Glastonbury Cemetery, near Fear Andrew, Freelove Stone and Richard Matteson Found Dead by the Side of the Road and later, Lord and Lady Gosford and later still, my parents themselves. The unidentified photo was disposed of with the rest of his meager effects. My mother came back from arranging the burial indignant at the price of coffins. A decent simple one, not lined in ghastly colours, was at least in Bennington impossible to obtain.

WR had grown to be a fixture in our lives.

Now no longer employed at Gompers, he was not only my parents' secretary but also tutored children who were my mother's patients. He learned to ride and rode with us, he frequently ate with us, and was loudest of us all in his praise of Enne's superb Viennese meals. He ate voraciously but remained just this side of skeletal. More and more, he spent Saturday night on the spare bed in the library. And after I failed my first Country Day exams he became my tutor as well, for two years.

Writing of WR, I find it hard not to fall into Jamesian cliché, the American innocent among the cultivated, successful, sophisticated Europeans. But with hindsight the relationship is too complex to untangle and the Jamesian innocence disappears. WR was flattering and endlessly enthusiastic but there was a nervous, dangerous edge to his admiration. He was too impressed but also too intimate. He became too much a part of the family, with too many functions. My parents, like most socially isolated rich, cultivated protégés and dropped them - though they could last for years and some lasted for good. WR was too unstable to cope with my parents' ménage and tenuous affections; there was a latent tension that was bound to snap.

My parents, forgetting Freud, chose to shut their eyes to the danger signs. WR was a dream come true; a young, attractive, highly educated, highly intelligent American who worked for them efficiently and soaked up their wit and wisdom like a sponge. For me too WR was something of a godsend. My favorite teacher, now one of my few friends.

For my twelfth birthday, WR gave me a little bronze statue of Don Quixote, with a poem that ended:
   "See windmills as windmills; you will find them then
   More fair than dreams, and matter for your pen."

It was better than any of mine, and the kind of thing we all treasured about WR. That was the high point of our friendship. But once WR had to tutor me in Latin and Math, subjects I hated, things began to go sour.

When he'd been a counsellor at camp, I'd had a brief, very long distance crush on WR. It involved a fantasy in which I, grown up, wore a blue dress and danced with him.; then he drew me out on the terrace (they always drew you out on the terrace in those old Hollywood romances) and gave me one of those mouth-crushing '40s Hollywood kisses. That was all. I didn't know what the kiss would feel like. I didn't know how to dream on. By the time WR was my tutor I was in love with Simon the pianist. Great friends though we were, seeing WR so much made the memory of that fantasy an irritant. For the very young, the next love always leaves the last a little in contempt. My inner demon made it worse.

Other things were irritants. Some of WR's mannerisms, some of his deference, the way he sometimes acted around my parents, at once formal and coy. I realize now I was probably also responding to his own hidden frustrations and rage. WR brought out in me things I could not understand, as on my first sight of him that instant, fleeting sense that he was doomed. Besides, though scrupulously clean, WR, like the first CDS girls to befriend Verena and me, suffered from B.O. It happened when he was nervous; such B.O., my father explained once, is a defense mechanism. It says: Keep away. We all smell worse when afraid. But poor WR had this defense mechanism to perfection.

Still, it may have been mainly the Latin and Math. My dislike of them shifted into rebelliousness. I don't know how it got as bad as it did, but I know I was impudent, that I must have teased and insulted my tutor, trying to see how far I could go, perhaps using him as a scapegoat for my general unhappiness. By our second or third Sugar Bush summer, we were becoming enemies. The tension went on in Vermont. There was some altercation when we were on horseback. My mother, riding beside us, remonstrated - with me. That made me angrier. In the end WR threatened to spank me when we got back, if I went on. I refused to be cowed. I did go on, and he carried out his threat.

Physical punishment in our household was unknown. There might be a slap if you were being simply impossible; this happened once or twice in our whole childhood and was so light it made you laugh. I had never been seriously hit by an adult before. The pain wasn't that great, but the humiliation was overwhelming. I don't know if my mother said anything to WR when I told her about the spanking. She certainly said nothing in front of me, and so I was determined on revenge.

Revenge, as always, was my sharp tongue. There was another scene at lunchtime a day later. I don't know what words were exchanged. I only recall saying to WR, who pinched me in retaliation for some remark, "If you do that again, I'll throw this glass of iced tea in your face." Once more, he did. And I did. With a great feeling of triumph. No longer, as at

Gompers, was I going to be so cowed by the fear of physical pain.

WR sat for a second, tea dripping down his face. Then, in a cold white fury I had never seen in anyone before, he jabbed his thumb nail repeatedly into my bare leg. It was so violent and unexpected it took me a moment to react. Then I threw my glass across the room and ran out screaming. Karl, Meta, my mother, the other adults at the table - my father was still in Grosse Pointe - did not move or say a word.

I went to my mother's big mirror and looked at my leg. Just below my shorts, incised as if with a knife, was a cluster of little half moons, oozing blood. My mother came in then. I showed her my wounds, and hysterical now, shrieked something about getting that goddam sponger out of the house. My mother tried ineffectually to calm me. I realized that she and the rest, for whatever reason, cowardice, dependency - WR was a Sugar Bush mainstay and Karl needed his help - or guilt at having created the whole situation, were not going to cope with WR's violence. Maybe they could not cope with violence at all. The bourgeois shell had been cracked, and they were pretending nothing had happened.

In my rage and despair, I went down to the stable to the one person hard enough to get me vengeance. I showed Shorty my livid wounds. Shorty would fix the bastard. "I'll put burrs under his saddle," Shorty said. I stopped sobbing, gleeful at the prospect of WR, anyway not the best of riders, flying off and maybe breaking an arm or a leg.

But even Shorty was a damp squib. I waited in vain for the burrs. All Shorty did, in our so-called riding lessons, was yell and crack his whip a lot at WR. The trouble was, this was also rough on WR's mount, my poor Sultan - I had graduated to more difficult horses. "Come on, you black beast - I'll make you run!" I remember WR shouting furiously at Sultan while Shorty shouted at him. Sultan, fortunately, was not impressed.

The rest of the summer, WR and I did not exchange a word. I showed Betty my scars and enlisted her help. We Frenched WR's bed and put crumbs in it. We left Charles Atlas body-building ads in his room, showing we thought him a skinny weakling. I told all my other visitors what he had done. WR suffered my puny revenge in silence. I still hoped Shorty would come up with the burrs. A cousin of Meta's, a good friend of WR's, tried to reconcile us. I indignantly told her to leave it alone.

Mercifully, that next school year I was free of Latin and better in math and needed no tutoring. WR went on as secretary and in the end we did speak again. I don't really remember the process of reconciliation any more than the process of enmity. I don't think he ever apologized. But when

I graduated from high school WR and I were once more friends.

The worst thing about the incident was the way I felt betrayed by my adults and the way it diminished WR himself. He had not only been violent but done it in what seemed to me a perverse and *unmanly* way. I did not know anything about his sexual ambivalence. I only felt no real *man* (we all grew up with those glowing macho images) would ever do what WR had done. And I remained stunned by the fact that my over-protective mother had not - when I needed it, no matter how impudent I'd been - protected me. If this still rankles after so long, it is perhaps a sign of good luck; it was the only domestic violence in all my years of growing up.

Tableau. WR, Alice and I, on an evening walk, stop at the dirt road T-junction near Sugar Bush. We sit and listen to the birds' high sweet evensong. I am soon to leave for college (I still plan to be a great poet but don't say so). WR is planning his first trip to Europe. Alice is at Bob Jones University and headed, full of zeal, for the missionary life. We are all in that intense, speculative mood; three people, three roads - we wonder where they will really lead. It is a moment I often look back to. In twenty years, Alice will be a minister's wife and mother of four, missionizing in Vienna (her husband's health has not permitted more remote places and the China he once hoped for is barred). I too will have a husband, and one daughter, but be footloose and far away, have published no poems but my first prose, and my road will have led me to higher mountains than any I had dreamed. WR will have drowned himself in the Detroit River, leaving a wife he brought back from Europe and a son he was never to see.

Digression:
My Great-Aunts' Lives

If my great-aunts' lives, what little I know of them, keep intruding into mine, it is because I feel both such distance and such kinship, I feel pity and irritation and love. Their quiet, formal, constrained existence, the men they may have longed for but could never marry, the salons they could not frequent, the paintings they could not show, their Lady-of-Shallot years in the old villa above the lake, haunt me like haunting memories of my own past.

As children, they were tomboys (Tante Grete wrote about it). They climbed walls and trees. They were sometimes impudent as well as pious; they were confident and bold. For their time, they grew up quite independent women; they studied and worked. Was it only want of money that left them to bloom and fade, to face old age with no one but each other, their only nephew a prisoner in Russia, their only niece a refugee in an America they could not comprehend? Or was there some Freudian tie to their handsome, distinguished officer father; or some Chekhovian taint, a lack of the courage and imagination that might have set them free? In their hearts did they ever rebel - Tante Grete who wrote of lost love, Tante Lina whose paintings were too strong to be confined to the family drawing room? No one will ever know. Outwardly, from what I have learned, they remained chaste, formal, pious, patriotic and somewhat bigoted, subservient to convention, father and God.

Still, for the place and the century, they were lucky. As far as I know, they experienced no violence. They were never imprisoned or dispossessed, they were never hungry. Celina and Grete lived to see their beloved Berti, captured by the Russians when he was working for Siemens in Teheran during the second great war and missing for fifteen years, come back hale and hearty when the Austrian peace treaty was finally signed. (Berti himself lived to ninety-six.) And they kept most of their villa and steep tangled forest, their walnut tree on the water's edge, their rickety boathouse and little pebbly beach, their next-door inn and acres of orchard and meadow, to the end of the last one's days.

Further Digression:
My Other Grandmother

I keep saying "my great-aunts" as if they were the only ones, as if my father's side of the family did not exist. I don't know if there were other great-aunts or uncles. My father himself never mentioned them. Did his mother have sisters and brothers and if so, were they barred from her life because she had come up in the world, marrying a professor? My father's mother's people, like most of the poor and obscure, have left nothing to ponder, nothing to be remembered by. My paternal grandmother herself devoted her life to her husband and sons, sewing to stretch the family budget, doing her constant best to smooth things over, to protect her sons from their father's rages, as much as she dared. She probably had no time for anything else. There are no anecdotes, stories or songs. My father said only that her love and protection were what made his childhood possible to bear. From my grandmother, I have one heirloom; a small pair of Biedermaier earrings, a minute seed pearl in a gold flower on black enamel, surrounded by a hair's breadth wreath of darkened gold.

RUMBAS AND REVELATIONS

A book unlike any other turned up in our house. Perhaps my parents got it because it was anti-Catholic and paid a few compliments to Freud. It paid no compliments to anyone else.

The book was *Generation of Vipers,* Philip Wylie's raging diatribe about America. It is a forgotten book. If its author, who also wrote novels, and stories about fishing for the *Saturday Evening Post,* is remembered, it is for his attack on the Great American Mother, on "Momism" which became a popular term. He also had a go at Businessmen, Statesmen, Professors, Congressmen, Military Men, the Church, the Cinderella myth, American myths in general. It is a very strident book. Much of it would now be labelled sexist, reactionary, or merely dated. We think we have exploded a lot of those myths. In fact, we haven't. The myths have shifted somewhat but much of Wylie hasn't dated at all. And for me, age twelve, this book was a revelation, the first piece of real social criticism I'd ever read. The things that disturbed me not just because I was a misfit - the rigid social conventions, the bigotry, the hypocrisy, the indifference to injustice and poverty, the view of life as a long popularity contest - were what Wylie castigated with brilliant savagery. Having read Wylie, I would never be lonely the same way again.

I burned to share my revelation. But my mother was not one for such discussion. She claimed to have spent many days of her youth sitting by the Traunsee reading Kant, but I don't remember that we ever conversed on an *issue*, let alone philosophy. My father agreed with a lot of what Wylie said, especially about the church. Yes, society was rotten. But it didn't bother him that much. He had his oasis, his Sugar Bush, his Freudian texts, his violin, his witty, ironic detachment. Freud too had despaired of civilization. My father could leave the sick world well enough alone. He had plenty to do with his sick patients. It didn't occur to me until later to question this, the oasis itself and the ethics of adjusting people to a society that is also unhealthy, the question all therapies tend to beg. My father anyhow would not indulge these discussions for too long. He had to get back to his Bach solo sonatas.

Later, I also read Wylie's novel *Finnley Wren.* It had much the same iconoclastic attitudes. It also had - for those days - quite a lot of sex, without the silliness of *The Fountainhead*. What I remember best is that the hero, when little, is whipped for repeating a story from an agnostic adult friend; if Christ had been a contemporary American, instead of crosses on our steeples we'd have electric chairs.

My next revelation was under the tutelage of my English teacher Mrs Penney, the English war bride.
I decided to do a term paper on Ibsen. I read all the Ibsen plays I could find, and Shaw's *Quintessence of Ibsenism*. This was very different from the brash, bombastic, very American Wylie, but the moral message was similar. There was the same exposure of hypocrisy, false virtue, false civic duty, the same insistence on the value of human as opposed to material good. A play like *The Enemy of the People* does not date. Its plot is repeated, over and over, in real life. Wylie, Ibsen and Shaw shaped my thinking. There was still a way to go before I found similar bases for my sense that animals needed protection as much as humans, and nature needed protection from humans themselves - and before I found kindred spirits among my contemporaries, and the guts to raise, more often, a little voice for what I believed.

My parents, still not convinced of my musical ineptitude, decided I should try the flute.
At camp, I'd managed a few simple tunes on the recorder, and I was inspired by the faun's dance in the Nutcracker Suite. Given a flute, I liked the silvery look of it, the feel of the keys. But blowing into the damned thing was something else again. So was counting, sight-reading, and practicing scales. After a short time I was demoted back to the recorder. I hardly practiced; after a year of lessons I was able to play one sarabande (gigues were too quick for me) and stumble over the woodwind bit of *Sheep May Safely Graze*. My parents had hoped for family chamber music, but I was so far below standard that only Lupie, the German Shepherd, accompanied me, howling while I blew.
My flute and recorder teacher was a gaunt harassed young man with a Gothic face, all hollows and bone. He came all the way across Detroit to give me my lessons on Saturday morning. He had no car; he came on the bus, walking down from Jefferson in rain and snow. He looked as if he needed the money. I would watch from the window for the lanky figure in its shabby tweed coat, hoping he'd be late and I could put in a few minutes of practice. He hardly ever was.

Mr Clifton was pleasant and polite and really, now I think of it, patient as a saint. But I, the Princess on the Pea and full of my mother's germ lore, hated putting my mouth on an instrument another mouth had touched. When he demonstrated something and handed me the wet recorder, I found excuses not to play. At least till it was dry. (I didn't want to insult him by wiping it.) It became a kind of game, to keep Mr Clifton conversing, to see how much of the hour I could waste. One of those unconsciously cruel games little rich girls play. Mr Clifton, a very mild man, sighed and put up with me. Only sometimes he wistfully referred to another private pupil, a very talented and diligent boy, who sounded to me like a creep. I was just polite enough not to say so.

Mr Clifton was married, and during the time he was my teacher his wife had a baby, which died after twelve days. It was amazing, said Mr Clifton, how attached you become to a baby, even after such a short time. How hard it was. He said this with quiet dignity. Dutifully I said I was sorry, Privately, disliking babies, I wondered how you became attached to them at all. The human race, from all I was learning, didn't seem worth adding to. What counted was creating something immortal, like great poetry. Mr Clifton's grief, like the wet recorder, was something I did not want touching me.

Before long the lessons were abandoned. In a curious way, I missed Mr C. He was intelligent, articulate and kind. Perhaps I also missed my subliminal teasing, his deference, my nasty power over his time. For this, and for my indifference to his grief, I ask his pardon. He was a talented man, not only a musician but a wonderful cabinet maker. The cabinet he made for my father's sheets of sonatas, a tall tier of narrow drawers, polished and perfect, was one of the few American additions to the old Vienna of our living room. It was something much better than my affected childhood poems, and it housed my father's music until his death.

In my Senior year came the event I dreaded most, even more than the Senior Prom, for which I would be dateless. This was the Senior Speech.

The Senior Speech was a requirement for graduating. You couldn't get out of it. If you were sick on the day, the nightmare event would only be postponed.

Most girls made a comic speech. I decided to be serious. Since I had to get up and make a fool of myself in front of the whole damned school, I would do it in a good cause. I would make a moral reason for my unpopularity. I would talk about Prejudice.

This idea was buttressed by *Time* magazine, then the darling of the right wing, which ran a subdued anti-racist article with a questionnaire to test your racial tolerance. Do you think of George Washington Carver as a great Negro or just a great man? Of Albert Einstein as a great Jew? were typical questions. Most of my speech consisted of this questionnaire, which made stuttering or going blank a bit less likely.

The day arrived. My heart hammering, my ears buzzing, I got up in front of all assembled upper CDS, a great sea of what to me were mostly enemy faces, mercifully blurred by my myopia. (Not wearing glasses on important occasions was to lead me later into tricky situations, into dates with mysterious men nearly thrice my age. Myopia made them handsome, benevolent and young.) On this occasion it helped. I didn't faint, cry or break down. I opened my mouth and the words came out. I got through all the stuff about George Washington Carver and Albert Einstein. "Prejudice destroys liberty. It destroys democracy," I finished grandiloquently. There was a moment's silence. Then, to my amazement, a big round of applause.

Not only that but I got a high mark. And congratulations. Only one girl, a relatively new senior with a Polish name, rare in Grosse Pointe, had the reaction I expected and half wanted, seeking my martyr's crown. "She's got a nerve," this girl was reported to say to another, "making a speech like that in a school like this." I hadn't been outrageous enough; it *was* hedging your bets a bit to have *Time* on your side. And if I did dent anyone's bigotry I was never to know. But my father said later this dreaded speech marked a kind of watershed. From then on I had fits of public self-assertion; surviving the nightmare made some of my agonized shyness fall away.

In our senior year, we had to apply to colleges. Country Day being the posh school that it was, everyone went on to higher institutions, the brighter and more ambitious to the women's Big Seven, Wellesley, Vassar, etc., the others to the two-year junior colleges academic elitists considered simply finishing schools.

My parents left the choice of college strictly to me. My criteria were severe. 1. No sororities (in many colleges you lived in a sorority house if you joined, so this club dominated your college life. Only those Laura Hobson called greasy grinds, and other misfits, lived in the dorms.) 2. No compulsory team sports or gymnastics EVER at any stage. 3. Location in a place I wanted to live. So far there were two: Vermont and New York.

The two colleges that met my criteria were Bennington in Vermont and Sarah Lawrence near New York City. They were the most progressive and radical of the women's colleges. Very free about choice of subjects, evenings out, etc. They were regarded as rather daring and scatty by other colleges. Sarah Lawrence had individual tutorials and term papers but no exams. All that suited me fine. I decided I would prefer Sarah Lawrence, partly because of proximity to New York, which seemed more exciting than winter Bennington. And Sarah Lawrence had some brilliant professors. So academic considerations were not left out.

Sarah Lawrence sent prospective students a long questionnaire, asking what you'd been reading, whom you admired in public life, how you pictured yourself as a woman of thirty-five, etc. Thirty-five seemed light years away. I was just sixteen; I couldn't even picture myself at twenty-one. But I waffled through it all and got in. Sarah Lawrence was then the most expensive college in the States. My doting parents didn't mind, especially as the publisher WK knew some of the professors and approved.[13]

At some point during my college preparations, my mother called me in to give me a serious and solemn warning. "Monika, when you go to college, have all the affairs you want. But don't get married young." This was no doubt inspired by her own failed first marriage, but she didn't tell me about it then. In the event, it was fortunate that I disregarded this well-meant parental advice.

Having no talent, and no practice since dancing school, I still couldn't dance. I confessed to my mother that I was worried about the Senior Prom, though it was highly unlikely anyone would ask me (I was not going to go with a patient again). My mother, the undauntable fixer, arranged for Terry and me to have private lessons at Arthur ("taught me dancing in a hurry," as the song says) Murray's in downtown Detroit. This was kept secret from everyone at school. I was sure they would scoff. "She never has a date. What's she having those lessons for?"

Our teacher was Mr Egerton, a blond young man with a large bland face. Mr Egerton was large altogether. Though I was a bit taller than in my last dancing school days, I still didn't come up much over my teacher's belt.

---

[13] *Dux, my husband-to-be had an affair with an older Bennington graduate just before we met. We decided the difference between the two schools was that at night in the dorms, by candle-light, Sarah Lawrence girls read Dylan Thomas and ate kosher dill pickles while Bennington girls read T.S.Eliot and ate avocado pears.*

He put Terry and me through our paces in turn, especially the samba and rumba. The sessions were dreadfully embarrassing, not least when we all three stood in front of the giant studio mirror and Egerton solemnly opened his jacket to show us his swiveling hips, which we were to imitate. A-one, a-two, a-three. Poker-faced, gray flannel jacket held wide, Egerton waggled and we (I scarlet with shame) obediently did too. "No, like this," said Egerton, and seized our hips to show us.

One day on the way to Arthur Murray's we stopped at Terry's Greek hairdresser to have haircuts. Up to then Katya, who was good at it, had trimmed my hair at home. Now short hair was in, and I hoped for a change to my juvenile, droopy image (*"Douze-ans,"* Twelve-year-old was my nickname at school even when I reached sixteen). Between hairdresser and dance studio, we were caught in the rain. When, wet and giggling, we reached Murray's elevator, my newly cut hair had gone curly, and in the elevator mirror a strange pretty girl looked back at me. By the time we finished with Egerton's swivels my hair was a straight yellow cap and the pretty girl gone; but I hoped one day she might be back.

I got no date for the Senior Prom, and I never went to a college dance. In the event, I didn't want to. I still do something rather like Egerton's hip exercises now prescribed for my arthritic, mountain-worn knees.

Near the end of my senior year, I was more at ease at Country Day. The class, down to thirteen girls, had discovered I had some humor, and that even the popular girls had something in common with me - at least a fear of spiders, a liking for certain movies, songs and stars. Though I didn't tell them I found freckled Van Johnson not nearly as cute as the Turkish actor Turhan Bey, who always got the slave parts and hardly ever the girl in Ali Baba type films. Nor that those somber heroes, Heathcliff and Mr Rochester, seemed to me the most exciting of men. But at least I could now look forward to the final parties without total dread.

One pre-graduation party, to which all the CDS girls and our brother school senior boys were invited, was held at a classmate's cottage on Lake Michigan. It was the only time I ever saw the countryside north of Detroit. We roasted frankfurters, some of the party swam, and the girls who knew them horsed around and chatted with the boys. The four or five who didn't date, Betty and I of course among them, went for a long walk along the beach, partly in the lake, ankle deep, looking down at the bright sparkling water. Unaware of what sun reflected from water can do, I had not thought about using sun cream. When I reached home, my face was beet red. Then it broke out in a mass of water blisters. It was the worst sunburn of my life, and it was the day before graduation.

The next evening I prepared for this milestone ceremony. My face covered with cream and powder like a Shrine Circus clown (it didn't help much) I dressed in my regulation white dress and white shoes. The dress had been ordered from an ad in *Seventeen* and as usual on me it looked nothing like the ad. Like the pink formal, instead of looking original, it simply looked wrong. To make up for that a bit, I sported a big corsage Mack had kindly sent me. At least I could wear flowers from an ex-marine. I heard later that my embarrassed coyness about this corsage was regarded as unseemly boasting. Wrong-footed to the end.

Waiting to go onstage, we wrote sentimental stuff in each other's yearbooks. One girl cried what seemed really heartfelt tears. I thought, she's right. *She* may really never be happier than she is now. For me there were no tears. There was an enormous sense of release. I still had the last ordeal; blisters oozing, powder flaking, I staggered up to get my diploma, to a polite patter of applause.

Afterwards came the big party. Everyone except Betty and me had been asked by a boy or been fixed up with one. There wasn't much point in staying. After half an hour or so, some kind souls going to some other party gave me a ride home, WR arrived simultaneously in his car. On some impulse, we took each other's hands, and walked up to the door together. I didn't care who saw us. I didn't care who in Grosse Pointe saw me do anything ever again. (This was not as defiant as it seemed; the grapevine had told me some Country Day girls had seen WR out for lunch with us and found him very handsome.) I was going to be grown up now, I was going away, I was free. I felt an exaltation that almost lifted me off my feet. I thought, in exactly these words - whatever happens now, whatever I do, wherever I go, this at least is over.

FOOTNOTE: At the end of my childhood, the story of WR and those of my grandmother and great-aunts mysteriously join.

On his trip to Europe, WR went after Paris to Austria, having promised my mother to see how her relatives were. My mother regularly sent them CARE packages and money and had been back herself and found things all right.

WR did not find things all right. He meant to spend three days in the villa. He spent three years. He wrote my parents endless letters telling them how the nun charged with looking after the three remaining sisters was neglectful, even cruel, and scheming to get the faltering, now weak-minded old ladies to sign over the house to her order. The letters were full of cryptic allusions. "It is like Thomas Mann's story of Tobias Mindernickel." Etc. He felt it his duty to stay and get the wicked schemer out.

At first my parents did not believe him. They thought he was going paranoid, afflicted perhaps by his apostasy from his own very religious Catholic youth. They continued, however, to send food and money, letting WR have charge of it all; and gradually they were convinced. WR succeeded in ousting the enemy, and some of his rambling accusations were later corroborated by neighbours. The whole truth of course will never be known. Meanwhile my grandmother died; she was very old but WR held the nun's neglect at least partly responsible for her death.

New help was installed; a young DP (Displaced Person, in the language of the day) from Yugoslavia, and her mother. We visited that summer. The two maids seemed hard-working, competent and kind. Tante Celina was fairly senile but both she and Tante Grete appeared content. WR, back in my parents' graces, was highly praised. But we all wondered, now life at the villa was back in order, when he was coming home.

Only once, at dinner in the villa, WR showed a glimpse of that brutality that left me scarred for years. Talking about his visit to France, he laughingly mentioned the pretty prostitutes of Paris. "There was one who came up to me and kept saying, 'Pas trop chère, pas trop chère'." He told this story even though Tante Grete was begging him to stop. "Not because of me," she said in her excellent French, trembling with distress. "Because of the children." She could hardly know, and would have been shocked to discover, that the Freudian 'enfants' in question were already steeped in sexual lore and the risqué jokes my father collected from his patients. It was an ugly incident and even made me wonder if the ousted nun had been so wicked and WR, vis à vis the old ladies, was entirely good.

We went home, but WR gave no sign of following. Instead, that winter he dropped another bombshell. He wrote that he was going to marry the daughter DP. "I would not be happy with an intellectual wife," his letter to Karl said. "Such a one and I would soon be throwing plates at each other." WR, repressed homosexual and always on the edge of breakdown, was not likely to be happy with any woman. But my parents, my mother especially, were mostly scandalized by the fact that an educated, cultured protégé was marrying, as they thought, so far below. "She cannot even read and write," my mother told friends with her usual hyperbole. We were all carried away by this until I remembered that the girl, whom my sister and I had befriended, moved by her tragic past, had in fact exchanged letters with us.

Still, when we went back to Gmunden everyone put a good face on it. Verena and I, for our part, were mainly baffled by the fact that Karola was not at all pretty. Gmunden was baffled too. Some of the daughters of local society had been quite eager to see more of WR. He was young, attractive, Catholic, university educated, cultured, polite and a passport to America. He could not be accused of any of the American vulgarities that especially the ex-Nazis loved to deplore. In those bleak post-war days, a very choice catch.

WR wanted to bring his bride, and their pet dog, home to the States. There were lots of visa complications. The question of the dog delayed things even more. At last they could leave; but there was some hiatus in installing someone to look after the old ladies; Karola's mother was by then too ill to work. WR had Tante Celina, bewildered, frail and ailing, sent back to her nunnery in St Pölten..

This part of the story is a cipher. From what little I have learned, there is no proof that WR's action was totally irresponsible, though probably ill-judged. I suppose my mother felt that WR, having taken the whole thing on in the first place and lived so long in the villa, should have stayed until a new nurse had moved in and both old ladies could safely be left. Shortly after reaching St Pölten, Celina died. My mother blamed WR for her death and refused ever to see him again.

WR, having rather burned his bridges as a teacher, tutor and semi-therapist, decided he and his wife would run the business inherited from his father. The business failed. Karola by then was expecting a baby. WR, jobless and without money, drove his car onto the Belle Isle bridge and jumped. No one saw him; his body washed up somewhere else four days later.

Hearing of this, my first reaction was that typical pointless reaction to suicide, though we hadn't seen each other since Gmunden; Why didn't you wait? Why didn't you ask for my help? I wrote Alice, the third at our crossroads in Vermont, and by then a missionary wife and mother. She wrote back that she couldn't help thinking that if WR had accepted the Jesus he turned away from he might have been saved.

Later in my life I saw more of Tante Grete, in her very last years Some of her story went into my novel All Souls and I will not repeat it here. My *memory of Tante Celina, very forgetful when I saw her that last summer, is the sweet smile under the starched white wimple. She still made little jokes.* "Celina war immer ein Spitzbub"(*Celina was always a little rascal), Grete said affectionately. But names and relations evaded Celina. "But who are you actually?" she would say with tender anxiety, passing me on the stairs. Your grand-niece Monika, I would say. The Princess on the Pea, I should have added. Sometimes, it was hard to know.*

ADDITIONAL FOOTNOTE: *My mother followed her aunts into senility, mercifully at a very advanced age. But some of that glowing core, that fierce, proud individuality, remained. She spoke perfect and rational schoolgirl French to her Lebanese cardiologist. When she was still coming to meals, she regaled us all with a cheerful verse,* "Im Totenreich sind Alle gleich." *In the kingdom of the dead, all are equal. Said before every lunch, like a kind of grace. This was curious from one who had never believed in equality among the living. And her last coherent sentence, when the visiting nurse was getting her out of bed, was addressed to me, in Viennese slang.* "Hast Du gedacht das ich schon krepieren werde?" *Did you think I was already going to croak?* "No darling, not yet," *I said, torn between tears and laughter. I could not think of a worthier answer. As always, she had the final word.*